"This exciting collection of essays demonstrates the great vitality of a hermeneutically conscious, critical, and self-critical Catholic theology and its rich resources for inspiring renewal and transformation in both church and society."

—Werner G. Jeanrond
University of Oxford

"'Third naïveté' is the red thread woven throughout this strong collection of contributions to the next step in theological hermeneutics. Informed by an intense dialogue with continental philosophy and critical theory, the authors make a strong appeal for a new kind of critical consciousness needed to recontextualize the best of our theological tradition for today. *Beyond Dogmatism and Innocence* calls for combining the creative interpretative power of imagination of Paul Ricoeur's second naïveté with a less naïve awareness of the 'disturbances and dislocations that saturate contemporary culture.' A must-read for all involved in the renewal of theology and Church."

—Dr. Lieven Boeve
University of Leuven
Belgium

Beyond Dogmatism and Innocence

Hermeneutics, Critique, and Catholic Theology

Edited by
Anthony J. Godzieba
and Bradford E. Hinze

A Michael Glazier Book

LITURGICAL PRESS
Collegeville, Minnesota

www.litpress.org

A Michael Glazier Book published by Liturgical Press

Design by Jodi Hendrickson. Image courtesy of Thinkstock.

© 2017 by Order of Saint Benedict, Collegeville, Minnesota. All rights reserved. No part of this book may be reproduced in any form, by print, microfilm, microfiche, mechanical recording, photocopying, translation, or by any other means, known or yet unknown, for any purpose except brief quotations in reviews, without the previous written permission of Liturgical Press, Saint John's Abbey, PO Box 7500, Collegeville, Minnesota 56321-7500. Printed in the United States of America.

Library of Congress Cataloging-in-Publication Data

Names: Godzieba, Anthony J., 1951– editor.
Title: Beyond dogmatism and innocence : hermeneutics, critique, and Catholic theology / edited by Anthony J. Godzieba and Bradford E. Hinze.
Description: Collegeville, Minnesota : Liturgical Press, 2017. | "A Michael Glazier book."
Identifiers: LCCN 2016048934 (print) | LCCN 2017003804 (ebook) | ISBN 9780814684153 | ISBN 9780814684405 (ebook)
Subjects: LCSH: Catholic Church—Doctrines—History—20th century. | Catholic Church—Doctrines—History—21st century. | Bible—Hermeneutics.
Classification: LCC BX1747 .B48 2017 (print) | LCC BX1747 (ebook) | DDC 230/.2—dc23
LC record available at https://lccn.loc.gov/2016048934

Contents

Acknowledgements   vii

Introduction   ix
    Anthony J. Godzieba and Bradford E. Hinze

Part 1: State of the Questions

Chapter 1: Biblical Hermeneutics Since Vatican II   3
    Sandra M. Schneiders

Chapter 2: Between Mountain Peaks and a Crumpled Handkerchief: Hermeneutics and Critical Theory   18
    Francis Schüssler Fiorenza

Chapter 3: Emerging Forms of Intercultural Hermeneutics   40
    Robert J. Schreiter

Chapter 4: The Aesthetics of Tradition and Styles of Theology   56
    John E. Thiel

Part 2: Disputed Questions

Chapter 5: From Dialectic to Disjunction: A Paradigm Shift of Catholic Interpretations of Secularism   87
    Dominic Doyle

Chapter 6: A Theological Reading of Scripture? Critical Problematic and Prophetic Vision in the Aftermath and Crossroads of Disciplinary Transformation   102
    Fernando F. Segovia

Chapter 7: Negative Dialectics and Doxological Hope: Elements of a Critical Catholic Theology   138
    Andrew Prevot

Chapter 8: A Synodal Church: On Being a Hermeneutical Community   160
    Ormond Rush

Part 3: Rewriting the Questions

Chapter 9: Revealing Subversions: Theology as Critical Theory 179
 Judith Gruber

Chapter 10: Postcolonial Hermeneutics
 and a Catholic (Post)Modernity 203
 Susan Abraham

Chapter 11: ". . . And Followed Him on the Way" (Mark 10:52):
 Unity, Diversity, Discipleship 228
 Anthony J. Godzieba

Chapter 12: Lamenting at the Limits of Dialogue
 in Ecclesiology and Hermeneutics 255
 Bradford E. Hinze

List of Contributors 279

Acknowledgements

The editors wish to express their sincerest thanks to all the contributors who generously and graciously agreed to work on this volume. We also wish to thank Carlton Chase, doctoral student in theology at Fordham University, for his editorial assistance. Moreover, we wish to thank the staff at Liturgical Press, especially Lauren L. Murphy, the managing editor, and Hans Christoffersen, the publisher, for supporting this project from the outset.

Introduction

Anthony J. Godzieba and Bradford E. Hinze

Behind every important development in Catholic doctrine and practice since the beginning of the modern period have been debates about the interpretation of Christianity's classic texts and traditions and their ideological and practical implications. Over the past century there have been breakthroughs in retrieving the origins of beliefs and practices, recovering the rich, myriad, and multifaceted literary forms, and recognizing the ways these venerable traditions have been received, applied, and negotiated in the lives of diverse audiences with their contrasting worldviews. This volume sets out to analyze the most recent developments in this ongoing history of critical theological interpretation.

The chapters here originated in a three-year seminar (2013–15), held as part of the Catholic Theological Society of America's annual convention, which examined central issues of hermeneutics and ideology critique in Roman Catholic theology. The original essays have been revised for this volume.

Our authors have all been influenced by certain central figures in continental philosophy who have shaped the discussion and debates about hermeneutics and critical theory in Catholic thought during the second half of the twentieth century and on into the twenty-first. Four major figures whose work shaped the development of philosophical hermeneutics are Martin Heidegger, Hans-Georg Gadamer, Paul Ricoeur, and Hans Robert Jauss, all of whom have influenced more than two generations of scholars. One group of critical theorists who have been recognized for their interrogation of the arguments and assumptions of philosophical hermeneutics are identified with the contributions of the Frankfurt School of Critical Theory, most notably Theodor Adorno, Max Horkheimer, Walter Benjamin, and

Jürgen Habermas. Another group, associated with French phenomenology and post-structuralism, includes such diverse figures as Emmanuel Levinas, Jacques Derrida, Michel Foucault, Gilles Deleuze, and Jean-Luc Marion. These lists could be extended, but for our purposes we want to acknowledge that the authors in this volume have all been influenced by some of these figures as they have negotiated debates about the meaning of the hermeneutic circle, the impact of pre-understanding and prejudice in interpretation, the categories of understanding, explanation, and application, and the roles of power, ideology, and distorted discourse in understanding and communicating the faith.

The contributors to this volume are not solely or primarily philosophers, but are theologians—in this case, Catholic theologians—who have wrestled with this heritage of continental philosophy but have explored its ramifications in one way or another in areas of theology. As a result, the contributions in this volume are certainly not to be evaluated solely or primarily in view of their particular use of this philosophical heritage, but rather in view of how they have contributed to the advance of "faith seeking understanding" in the light of these continental formulations. Overall, the authors suggest an approach that might be termed the practice of a "third naïveté," one that blends deeply contextual interpretations with a critical theological analysis of the roles of history, culture, power, and grace in church and society. Our title, *Beyond Dogmatism and Innocence*, suggests a way of interpreting these overlapping aspects in a productive way. We will come back to both of these phrases in a moment.

Readers may be asking important questions at this point: Why did theologians turn to these continental philosophers as resources in the first place? What specific theological areas required new resources? For an answer, we need to look briefly at the modern context of Catholic theology, most especially the shift from a logic-driven, propositional, and juridical theological method to diverse methods more attuned to historical consciousness, rhetorical persuasion, narrative, and aesthetics.

During the nineteenth century, theological questions concerning the interpretation of Scripture and tradition were posed in polemical terms against Enlightenment thinkers (especially their arguments on behalf of "natural religion") and against Protestant theology (especially its emphasis on *sola Scripture* and its later turn to subjectivity and to experience as a locus of religious truth), and in political terms regarding issues of the church's contested relationship to the state. How did this polemical frame of mind that marked the thought of "the long Catholic nineteenth century" express itself? It did so in the guise of the neoscholastic theological method that governed Catholic interpretation of Scripture, tradition, and doctrine for almost a century. The approach of the neoscholastic theological manuals was syllogistic in style and deductive in argumentative form. It was a rigid, objectivist methodology employed as a defensive apologetic that for the most part refused the nineteenth-century retrieval of historical consciousness and the hard work of interpretation.[1]

Already during the early decades of the nineteenth century, however, a shift was occurring.[2] Theologians began to take historical consciousness seriously when questions regarding the historical development of Catholic doctrines began to be raised. The fundamental question was momentous: how can one bring together the absoluteness of divine truth as revealed in various doctrines and the clearly observable historical development that these doctrines had undergone? How can one have identity and difference, continuity and change? The roots of the theological turn to history reach back to the pioneering work of Johann Sesbastian Drey, Johann Adam Möhler, Franz Anton Staudenmaier, and Johann Baptist Hirscher (often identified as members of the Catholic Tübingen School) and John Henry Newman.[3] The first theological topics to feel the force of this turn were

---

[1] For more detailed discussions of the fate of neoscholasticm within Catholic theology, see Mark Schoof, *A Survey of Catholic Theology 1800–1970*, trans. N. D. Smith (1970; reprint, with new epilogue: Eugene, OR: Wipf and Stock, 2007); Fergus Kerr, *Twentieth-Century Catholic Theologians: From Neoscholasticism to Nuptial Mysticism* (Malden, MA: Blackwell, 2007). A sketch of neoscholastic theological method and its extrinsicist character is provided by Francis Schüssler Fiorenza, "Systematic Theology: Task and Methods," in *Systematic Theology: Roman Catholic Perspectives*, ed. Francis Schüssler Fiorenza and John P. Galvin, 2nd ed. (Minneapolis: Fortress Press, 2011), 1–78, at 20–26.

[2] See Bernhard Welte, "Zum Strukturwandel der katholischen Theologie im 19. Jahrhundert," in *Auf der Spur des Ewigen* (Freiburg: Herder, 1965), 380–409.

[3] See Bradford E. Hinze, "Roman Catholic Theology: Tübingen," in *The Blackwell Companion to Nineteenth-Century Theology*, ed. David Fergusson (Hoboken, NJ: Wiley

revelation, scriptural interpretation, and the character of tradition, and much of the controversy was clustered around the topic of doctrinal development.[4] In the first half of the twentieth century, historical and hermeneutical debates expanded to other areas such as Christology, ecclesial reform, and the reform of the liturgy. Needless to say, by the opening of the Second Vatican Council in 1965, neoscholasticism's ahistorical dogmatism was revealed as having failed to account for the rich historical sources and diverse cultural issues that informed the church's texts, traditions, and developing beliefs, leading to its collapse as the default Catholic theological method (as well as the collapse of its classical metaphysical framework).[5] Later in the century a much wider range of "disputed questions" joined these other topics on the table for debate: the social and political issues raised by political and liberation theologies; the shift to a world church and the concomitant emerging engagement with non-European cultures; the decentering of Eurocentric theology itself; interreligious dialogue; the impact of secular worldviews and cultural pluralism on the church's mission of evangelization. In the wake of these issues, Catholic theologians turned to the resources afforded by continental philosophy, especially hermeneutics with its insights into history and tradition, and critical theory with its insights into ideology and emancipation, in order to discern how Christian discipleship can maintain any sort of identity and connection with its origins in the midst of incessant historical and cultural changes, indeed what the theologian David Ford has called the "multiple overwhelmings" of the contemporary world: the massive cultural, scientific, technological, economic, political, social, intellectual, and religious transformations that have fragmented much of contemporary experience and identity.[6]

Blackwell, 2010), 187–213; Nicholas Lash, *Newman on Development: A Search for an Explanation in History* (London: Sheed and Ward, 1975).

[4] This is Mark Schoof's suggestion; see his *A Survey of Catholic Theology*, 157–227.

[5] See Walter Kasper, *Theology and Church*, trans. Margaret Kohl (New York: Crossroad, 1989), 1–5, where he calls attention to "the breakdown of metaphysics in their classic form" as having had "the most momentous consequences" for contemporary theology (3). In light of the continental philosophers mentioned at the outset, it should be clear that the critique of metaphysics, with its effects on contemporary theology, is a crucial topic. While not our focus in this volume, readers should be aware that it stands in the background of a number of the essays here.

[6] David Ford, *Theology: A Very Short Introduction* (Oxford/New York: Oxford University Press, 1999), 8.

And so the answer to the question "why did theologians start using hermeneutics and critical theory?" is both simple and complex: because (to use David Tracy's phrase) the plurality and ambiguity inherent in history and culture—in which Christian life is embedded—forced the issue.[7] Neoscholastic method allowed very limited room for the rhetorical work of metaphor and narrative, the creative imagination, and constructive criticism. By the opening sessions of Vatican II, confidence in this method's power came to be replaced by a more historically attuned and rhetorically capacious approach to interpretation in theology. More recently, especially in light of the traumatic events taking place both around the world and in the Catholic Church, more penetrating questions have been raised about the earlier "innocence" assumed in the interpretive work of theologians.[8] The kernel-and-husk metaphor that described earlier theological uses of hermeneutical reasoning—suggesting that the successful reinterpretation of a Christian truth (the essence or "kernel") for a new generation or a new culture meant simply the replacement of the outdated cultural expressions (the form or "husk") with more relevant ones—was shown to be naïve on its face. "Essences" are never graspable *per se* but always historically and culturally situated; "essence" and "form" are mutually conditioning. The complex layerings and interweavings of Catholic faith claims with the fraught cultural contexts in which they are practiced and pondered have impelled contemporary Catholic theologians to be more hermeneutically and critically attuned. Especially since Vatican II, it has been obvious that if Catholic theology is to fulfill both its immediate task to "give an accounting [*apologia*] for the hope" that presently motivates believers (1 Pet 3:15) and its long-term mandate to be "faith seeking understanding" (Anselm, *Proslogion*, preface), it needs to be—and indeed has become in many cases—an ensemble of theologies that are richly interdisciplinary. The chapters in this volume give ample evidence of that theological intentionality and that richness.

---

[7] David Tracy, *Plurality and Ambiguity: Hermeneutics, Religion, Hope* (San Francisco: Harper & Row, 1987).

[8] See, e.g., the famous imagery used by Pope John XXIII in his opening address to the Second Vatican Council: "The substance of the ancient doctrine of the deposit of faith is one thing, and the formulation in which it is clothed is another" (*Gaudet Mater Ecclesiae* §15, trans. Joseph A. Komonchak, https://jakomonchak.files.wordpress.com/2012/john-xxiii-opening-speech.pdf, 4n4; in this note, Komonchak translates the original Italian which differs slightly from the Latin version in the main text).

Part 1 presents essays discussing the "State of the Questions" regarding hermeneutics, critical theory, and theology over the past fifty years.

- *Sandra Schneiders* (chapter 1) discusses the factors that have shaped biblical hermeneutics immediately before and after the council, such as the 1943 encyclical *Divino Afflante Spiritu*, the theological *ressourcement* (return to the sources), and Catholic biblical scholarship's rapid resituation in the larger secular academy. Today, Catholic biblical scholarship is polarized between a "magisterial fundamentalism" and a fascination with methodological experimentation. She argues that the fields of biblical scholarship and theology need each other both to neutralize the extremes and to maximize their contribution to the academy and the Church.

- *Francis Schüssler Fiorenza* (chapter 2) compares the earlier phase of the discussion between Gadamer and Habermas regarding hermeneutics and critical theory (characterized as searching for the "mountain peaks" or single unifying points of meaning) to the more recent approaches pursued by Charles Taylor and William E. Connolly (using Michel Serres's metaphor of a "crumpled handkerchief" with multiple folds) to emphasize the fundamental non-linearity of interpretation. He shows how these discussions pertain to the interpretation of Vatican II, the inadequacy of a translation model of hermeneutics, and the more radical challenges raised by postcolonialism and critical theory.

- *Robert Schreiter* (chapter 3) discusses the theological import of intercultural hermeneutics, which is provoked by border-crossings between distinct cultures. He explores intercultural theological hermeneutics that is attentive to inculturation, interreligious dialogue, and comparative theology. He concludes by arguing for a hermeneutics of globality, justified not only by reflections on Trinity, Incarnation, and Holy Spirit, but also by revisiting the relation of nature and grace.

- *John Thiel* (chapter 4) surpasses the post–Vatican II conservative-liberal divide by appealing to the interpretive category of aesthetics. He distinguishes two sensibilities toward the beauty of the Catholic tradition, which give rise to differing understandings of

Introduction xv

the theological task. First, a classical aesthetics of tradition privileges the sense of sight; second, a developmental aesthetics of tradition values the sense of hearing. He emphasizes the need for each style to recognize the Catholic beauty which the other style finds compelling, thus appreciating "the rich unity of the Church that only appears in the wholeness of the traditions," beauty that each Catholic sensibility grasps in its own limited way.

The essays in Part 2 deal with "Disputed Questions" facing theology today.

- *Dominic Doyle* (chapter 5) traces a significant hermeneutical shift in Catholic interpretations of secularism from a portrayal of dialectical opposition (exemplified by Bernard Lonergan) to the diagnosis of internal disjunctions (exemplified by Charles Taylor and Michael Buckley). Doyle responds by arguing that "dialectic" can be retrieved to avoid oppositional triumphalism and to include the insights of this new "disjunctive" hermeneutic, as illustrated by a reconsideration of the theological virtues as not only transformative of secular culture but also a corrective within the church.

- *Fernando Segovia* (chapter 6) argues that biblical studies should provide an eschatological vision for a world in which liberation, justice, peace, and dignity are desperately and relentlessly sought. He assesses three chronological phases in biblical studies: the first associated with historical criticism (from the nineteenth century through the early 1970s); the second identified with literary criticism and sociocultural criticism (emerging around the middle 1970s); and the third marked by the introduction of ideology critique (late 1970s to the present). He analyzes each phase for their interpretive visions, theological visions, and attitudes toward theological readings. In dialogue with the critical work of his colleagues Wayne Meeks and Carolyn Osiek, Segovia supports and extends their call for biblical studies to address the critical questions of our time and be a public and engaged force in the world.

- *Andrew Prevot* (chapter 7) considers whether the "Catholic fondness for hermeneutics" has functioned as a shield "against the full force of ideology critique." He proceeds in three moves. First, he shows that Catholic theology does not need to rely on external modalities of critique since it has its own internal resources for negative dialectic and critical theory, as found in prophetic, apocalyptic, ascetical, and mystical elements of Catholic theology. Second, he argues that Catholic theologians "safeguard the radical unity of negative dialectics and doxological hope which much critical theory compromises." Third, he proposes an approach combining negative dialectics and doxological hope that "challenges the self-appropriating subject of hermeneutical philosophy and theology" and safeguards the integrity of theology by means of both "a more pervasive critical negativity and theocentrism."

- *Ormond Rush* (chapter 8) considers how the *sensus fidei* (*Lumen Gentium* 12) provides a hermeneutical category for individual believers and the church as a whole. In diverse cultures and contexts, believers "make sense" of their faith under the guidance of the Holy Spirit. It is fundamentally through their exercise of this capacity that the Spirit mediates the church's ongoing dialogue with God throughout history, provoking new horizons of understanding God's otherness. Rush explores the epistemological authority of these local applications of the Gospel, the role of local theologians in bringing such intuitions to systematic expression, and the obligation of local bishops both to attend to their people's lived faith and to bring their local perceptions to bear on the teaching of the universal church.

The essays in Part 3 are not interested simply in proposing future questions for theological hermeneutics and ideology critique, but in actively "Rewriting the Questions" in light of rapidly changing cultural contexts.

- In three steps, *Judith Gruber* (chapter 9) advances the argument that "theology lives up to its own normative foundation only if it is done as radical critique." First, the impetus for critique is found in the contested relationship between knowledge and power. Second, critical theory "uncovers Christianity's complicity with hegemonic power" and at the same time provides a resource for surfacing "counter-hegemonic strategies" at the heart of the Christian tradition. Third, once theology operates as radical critique, its task is to subvert oppressive, hegemonic narratives "so that that the church can be a faithful representation of God's salutary self-revelation in the historical event of the life, death, and resurrection of Jesus the Christ."

- *Susan Abraham* (chapter 10) examines the social theorist Walter Mignolo's "decolonial hermeneutics" and compares it with postcolonial theory. She argues that Mignolo, in attempting to do "better theory," instead essentializes cultural borders. In postcolonial theory, especially in the work of Indian scholar Gayatri Chakravorty Spivak, cultural borders are more fluid and porous. Spivak's strategies emphasize Derridaean *différance* rather than differences in culture or identity. This subtle point of difference between Mignolo's and Spivak's work is the occasion for a feminist sacramental Catholic theology. Abraham defends a more deconstructive approach and sketches a postcolonial theological hermeneutics. Liberation, she concludes, "has to be political—that is, it has to result in the liberation of gendered bodies and their sacramental potential."

- *Anthony Godzieba* (chapter 11) extends Gadamer's trinity of understanding, interpretation, and application into a "performance hermeneutic" in order to account more adequately for the simultaneous unity and diversity in Christian life and in the church. He advocates a model of musical performance-over-and-in-time rather than textual interpretation. This provides a richer way of grasping the truth of the kingdom of God in practice, and also a way to push back against contemporary culture's social acceleration, which drains experience of its temporal depth and dilutes the necessary eschatological heart of salvation.

- *Bradford Hinze* (chapter 12) explores the promises of dialogue as advanced in modern Catholic ecclesiology and continental philosophical hermeneutics. He describes the Catholic repudiation of a paternalistic and polemical approach to the church's communication in favor of a dialogical approach, which is portrayed as operative at multiple levels in the life of the church. This is followed by an analysis of the dialogical character of hermeneutics as advanced by Schleiermacher, Gadamer, and Jauss in terms of a dialogue with authors, texts, and readers. He concludes by exploring how the classic biblical motif of lamentations functions in various literary settings to identify the limitations of dialogue, while providing a venue and process for the purification and differentiation of the aims and objectives of dialogue in hermeneutics, in the church, and in civil society.

• • •

When taken together, the positions in this volume represent what we would characterize as a "third naïveté" in the history of Catholic theology. By using this term, we are borrowing and extending Paul Ricoeur's famous hermeneutical insight first presented in 1960 in his work *The Symbolism of Evil*.[9]

Ricoeur concluded that work with a chapter titled "The Symbol Gives Rise to Thought," asserting that "beyond the desert of criticism, we wish to be called again."[10] He summarized the gains and hopes offered by his approach to symbols and mythic narratives as a grand detour through discourse developed by philosophical hermeneutics leading to "a creative interpretation of meaning," and argued that these gains require "patience and rigor" in employing the critical functions associated with hermeneutics and ideology critique.[11] In what became a signature distinction, Ricoeur proposed that we cannot go back to a "primitive naïveté"—that is, the "immediacy of belief" that can read meaning directly from religious symbols—since the modern person has already gone through the journey of critical thought. Instead, what we can aim for is "a second naïveté in and through criticism. In short, it is by *interpreting* that we can *hear* again."[12] In the attitude of second naïveté, we again become aware of "the vital relation of the interpreter to the thing about which the text speaks directly

---

[9] Paul Ricoeur, *Finitude et culpabilité*, vol. 2: *La symbolique du mal* (Paris: Aubier, 1960); ET: *The Symbolism of Evil*, trans. Emerson Buchanan (New York: Harper & Row, 1967). Note that 1960 is also the date of the first appearance of Hans-Georg Gadamer's *Truth and Method* (*Wahrheit und Methode: Grundzüge einer philosophischen Hermeneutik* [Tübingen: Mohr, 1960]).

[10] Ricoeur, *Symbolism of Evil*, 349.

[11] Ibid., 348.

[12] Ibid., 351.

or indirectly,"[13] and thus reclaim an encounter with religious truth that at the same time is more aware of the inescapable historical and discursive mediations in which these truths are interwoven.

In the period after Vatican II, Ricoeur's formulation proved helpful to many Catholic theologians. It offered a way of practicing theological interpretation and critique that was challenging and productive: that is, a way of being *simul criticus et fideles*, doing theology that was able to engage various forms of contemporary critical thinking without evacuating the truths expressed in Catholic faith claims.

What we wish to suggest, however, is that times have changed. The "weight of reality" (Ignacio Ellacuría) and the flow of history over the past fifty years—with its possibilities for human flourishing as well as its terrifying and dehumanizing aspects—have made it necessary that theology be done from the point of view of a *third naïveté*, one that is intensely aware of the disturbances, differentiations, and dislocations that saturate contemporary culture. Can one still believe when shifting power valences create dilemmas that are never completely resolvable? Can one still hope when power and ideology challenge our discernment of the presence of God's grace in the world? Our authors give strongly affirmative responses and point out the hard work that needs to be done. Hermeneutics and critical theory remain necessary and fundamental for Catholic theology. At stake is nothing less than how the good news of God's salvation can be grasped and lived today. We have intended that this volume provide a trustworthy map and compass for negotiating these compelling debates and challenging options.

---

[13] Ibid., citing a passage from Rudolf Bultmann, "Das Problem der Hermeneutik," in *Glauben und Verstehen: Gesammelte Aufsätze*, vol. 2 (Tübingen: Mohr Siebeck, 1952), 211–35; ET: "The Problem of Hermeneutics," in *New Testament and Mythology, and Other Basic Writings*, ed. and trans. Schubert M. Ogden (Philadelphia: Fortress, 1984), 69–93.

PART 1

State of the Questions

CHAPTER 1

Biblical Hermeneutics Since Vatican II

Sandra M. Schneiders

After several frustrating attempts to fulfill my assignment for this volume, I decided that trying to summarize the status of biblical hermeneutics since the Second Vatican Council was like trying to build a three-masted tall ship under full sail in a Classic Coke bottle. So I have abandoned any attempt to treat the matter historically, or according to personalities, or by classification of theories. Instead, I am going to try something much more modest, namely, to place a few sets of pegs in the wall on which discussion materials can be hung, in order to supply some common vocabulary and a repertoire of concepts that will facilitate further thought and discussion.

Three Factors That Shaped Biblical Hermeneutics Since Vatican II

Three factors have decisively shaped post-conciliar biblical hermeneutics. One occurred before the Council, one spanned the Council from preparation to aftermath, and one developed in the wake of the Council. It is hard to overstate the importance of the first, namely, the publication in 1943 of Pope Pius XII's encyclical *Divino Afflante Spiritu*.[1] The encyclical was certainly not revolutionary in content,

---

[1] Pope Pius XII, Encyclical *Divino Afflante Spiritu* (September 30, 1943), http://w2.vatican.va/content/pius-xii/en/encyclicals/documents/hf_p-xii_enc_30091943_divino-afflante-spiritu.html.

at least by today's standards, and reinforced virtually all the restrictions and caveats of Pope Leo XIII's 1893 encyclical, *Providentissimus Deus*,[2] especially the assertion of the supreme control by doctrine as promulgated by the *magisterium* over scholarly biblical interpretation. But *Divino Afflante Spiritu* opened a new era in Catholic biblical scholarship by recognizing the importance of using certain contemporary methods, especially form criticism, in the interpretation of Scripture. This was one of those recognitions of fact, like that of heliocentrism, that can never be effectively reversed and that is bound to expand in significance. *Divino Afflante Spiritu* thus began the still uncompleted liberation of Catholic biblical scholarship from the dogmatic shackles clamped upon it at the Council of Trent and reinforced by subsequent Vatican documents and actions until Pius XII's encyclical. There is still a tendency among the guardians of orthodoxy in the Vatican to start with magisterial formulations and judge biblical work in terms of its conformity to and defense of such propositions and to equate "traditions" in the sense of long-held opinion or practice with "Tradition" in a credibly theological sense. A major example of this was the refusal of the Congregation for the Doctrine of the Faith in its 1976 declaration *Inter Insigniores*, which attempted to "close" the discussion of the possible ordination of women, to recognize the carefully grounded and qualified finding of the Pontifical Biblical Commission that the New Testament evidence by itself did not preclude the ordination of women.[3] But at least in principle, the virtual total imprisonment of biblical scholarship in anti-modernist obscurantism was undermined by *Divino Afflante Spiritu*.

Catholic scholars have gone well beyond anything Pius XII authorized or probably would have approved, and post-conciliar documents

---

[2] Pope Leo XIII, Encyclical *Providentissimus Deus* (November 18, 1893), http://w2.vatican.va/content/leo-xiii/en/encyclicals/documents/hf_l-xiii_enc_18111893_providentissimus-deus.html. For a good brief treatment of these two most important Vatican documents on Scripture in the modern period within their respective historical contexts, see Raymond E. Brown and Thomas Aquinas Collins, "Church Pronouncements," in *The New Jerome Biblical Commentary*, ed. Raymond E. Brown, Joseph A. Fitzmyer, and Roland E. Murphy (Englewood Cliffs, NJ: Prentice Hall, 1968), 1166–74.

[3] Congregation for the Doctrine of the Faith, Declaration *Inter Insignores* (October 15, 1976), http://www.vatican.va/roman-curia/congregations/cfaith/documents/re_con_cfaith_doc_19761015_inter-insignores_en.html.

such as the Pontifical Biblical Commission's "The Interpretation of the Bible in the Church" (1993) have recognized, albeit timidly, the need for contemporary Catholic biblical scholarship not only to make use of modern critical methods but to engage the agenda of modernity itself.[4] This agenda was pushed forward most recently by the Pontifical Theological Commission's document, *"Sensus Fidei* in the Life of the Church" (2014) by the recognition that faith is, first of all, a response to revelation rather than to theological formulations.[5] Pope Francis has underlined this important principle by his repeated exhortations to pastors at all levels of the Church to preach the Gospel, not the Catechism.

The second factor shaping post-conciliar biblical hermeneutics was the emergence, mainly in francophone Europe during the decades preceding Vatican II, of what was first pejoratively called *la Nouvelle Théologie*. The leitmotif of this intellectual movement, which actually undergirded and found expression in so much of the Council's work, was *ressourcement*, or the rooting of the conciliar renewal in a "return to the sources." These life-giving sources were Scripture, the patristic tradition, which was itself pervasively and profoundly biblical, and the liturgy, which was originally totally shaped by Scripture. *Nouvelle Théologie* was not an espousal of archaism or primitivism, much less of anachronistic approaches to biblical interpretation. It was an affirmation of the non-negotiable centrality of the Bible as Scripture in the faith and life of the Church. It was a promotion of the proverbial "living faith of the dead against the dead faith of the living."

One of the major effects of this biblical renewal in all areas of the Council's work was the reclaiming by the baptized of their identity and dignity as "the people of God" and their mission as the Body of Christ in the world. A major need of this rejuvenated people was nourishment by the living Word of God in Scripture. It is interesting that a presiding metaphor in *Dei Verbum*, the Dogmatic Constitution on Divine Revelation, which was one of the most contested in the Council's experience and was only passed at the end of the very last

---

[4] Pontifical Biblical Commission, "The Interpretation of the Bible in the Church" (April 23, 1994), http://catholic-resources.org/ChurchDocs/PBC_Interp.htm.

[5] International Theological Commission, *"Sensus Fidei* in the Life of the Church" (2014), http://www.vatican.va/roman_curia/congregations/cfaith/cti_documents/rc_cti_20140610_sensus-fidei_en.html.

session, was that of the "table of the Word," deliberately paralleled to the table of the Eucharist.[6]

The Council Fathers, with the exception of the tiny minority who held out to the very end for a two-source theology of Revelation that would have effectively left Scripture subject to the magisterium (the final vote to pass the Dogmatic Constitution was 2,344 to 6), recognized and were determined to end the four-hundred-year biblical fast that had been imposed on God's people in the wake of the Council of Trent. This holy people, spiritually emaciated by scriptural starvation, was finally to be fed and their thirst slaked. By means of new translations, the Word was to be taken out of the deep freezer of an incomprehensible ancient language in which it had been assiduously preserved from "contamination" by "private interpretation," sumptuously prepared by knowledgeable preachers and musicians rather than served up in the pious mush of irrelevant "ferverinos," and joyously consumed by a famished community, not once in awhile on special occasions, but daily if possible, always on the Lord's Day, and especially on the Great Feasts and in the context of the celebration of all the Sacraments. The baptized were to become deeply familiar with the whole of Scripture, not just Matthew 16:18.

The enthusiasm of the post-conciliar church for Scripture was a major impetus for the development of Catholic biblical studies in the immediate aftermath of the Council. The Council had called the church's pastors to a responsibility for which they were largely unprepared by pre-conciliar seminary education, namely, to preach the Gospel well, in the vernacular, daily, and to incorporate it into the life of the church at every level and in every venue. Lay people themselves were clamoring for biblical education. Rather than a dry trek through an inventory of proof texts, biblical education of seminarians and newly minted lay ministers now involved serious, adult study of the Bible as Scripture, and that required professors of Scripture who were capable of providing such education. Demand was creating the supply

---

[6] See, esp., Second Vatican Council, Dogmatic Constitution on Divine Revelation (*Dei Verbum*), ch. 6, sec. 21, http://www.vatican.va/archive/hist_councils/ii_vatican_council/documents/vat-ii_const_19651118_dei-verbum_en.html. This chapter is especially important in its insistence on the centrality of Scripture in every aspect of the life of the Church. For the story of *Dei Verbum*'s trajectory in the Council, see John W. O'Malley, *What Happened at Vatican II* (Cambridge, MA: Belknap Press, 2008), 276–89.

and Catholic biblical scholarship leaped ahead, not without missteps and occasional crashes, but ahead nonetheless. And, of course, once a critical mass of the people of God began to learn what Scripture really had to say about church, the spiritual life, mature morality in the exercise of a free conscience, God, Jesus, and the call to discipleship and ministry, there was no way that the attempt to squeeze them back into their pre-conciliar pews was going to be, finally, successful. Nor were scholars who were learning to interpret the text according to the canons of the modern academy going to re-assume their dogmatically controlled catechetical identities and functions.

By the time the retrenchment began under the papacy of John Paul II, with its "creeping infallibility," suppression of "dissent" and expansion of loyalty oaths, re-imposition of the pre-conciliar clericalist and misogynist ethos in seminaries, and punitive treatment of theologians who attempted to engage pastorally with the real issues of the people of God rather than simply enforce discipline, it was really too late to re-embargo the Word of God. The thirty-year trek in the theological desert that ended with the election of Pope Francis certainly dampened the biblical renaissance that had begun in the period before the council, that blossomed during the Council, and that had flourished for a decade or so after it. But it did not succeed in reinstating among either biblical scholars or the laity who had tasted the fruits of their research the pre-conciliar biblical famine that the Council had ended.

The third factor shaping post-conciliar Catholic biblical scholarship emerged very quickly after the Council. Catholic biblical scholarship was rapidly resituated in the larger secular academy. Many of those who would become the best Catholic biblical scholars of the first post-conciliar generation were being trained not only in the great theological faculties of Europe (e.g., Paris, Louvain, Tübingen, Oxford, Cambridge, the Pontifical Biblical Institute, the École Biblique in Jerusalem) but also in the great research universities in this country (Johns Hopkins, Yale, Harvard, Princeton, Stanford, Duke, Emory, the University of Chicago, and elsewhere).[7] The seminary, even with its

---

[7] For example, the three editors of *The Jerome Biblical Commentary*, Raymond E. Brown, Joseph A. Fitzmyer, and Roland E. Murphy, were examples of the ecclesially committed scholars who received excellent modern biblical educations in the immediate aftermath of the Council and went on to prepare not only the laity but successive

post-conciliar curriculum revised to centralize Scripture studies and with the recognition that Scripture was the soul of all theology (*Dei Verbum* 24), was no longer the only place to study the Bible, and there was general recognition that those who would teach Scripture in the seminary or Catholic universities and colleges needed doctoral-level preparation, much of which was, at first, available primarily only outside Catholic institutions in this country.

Immersion in the secular academy, often followed by active participation in professional societies that were not exclusively Catholic or even religious (such as the Society of Biblical Literature), exposed Catholic biblical scholars to the dynamics that were convulsing higher education in the 1960s and after. Increasingly, the religious sciences were being studied ecumenically and inter-religiously, and often enough even without explicit religious commitment on the part of professors or students. Interdisciplinarity was emerging as the hallmark of late modern and post-modern higher education. Women and other marginalized populations were being admitted for studies and, eventually, joining faculties bringing perspectives to biblical scholarship that had been simply non-existent for the first two millennia of the Church's engagement with the biblical text. These newcomers were bringing questions and answers that the establishment had no categories for handling. But once again, attempts to defend the academy against this novelty or to re-establish the patriarchal or hegemonic *status quo*, though painful, were ultimately futile.

The first and perhaps most noticeable effect of the relocation of Catholic biblical study and teaching from the enclosed confessional seminary into the mainstream of intellectual life in the centers of higher learning, was the methodological explosion within the discipline. Developments in secular historiography, archaeology, philology, literary studies, sociology and cultural anthropology, politics and economics, the physical sciences, linguistics, art, comparative literature, and aesthetics were increasingly seen as highly relevant to biblical interpretation, and their employment a source of new and exciting paths into heretofore unimagined realms of meaning and relevance. As members of marginalized groups, especially women, discovered

---

generations of biblical specialists who would keep the conciliar approach to biblical scholarship alive in the decades from the Council to the election of Francis.

that the Bible was not entirely liberating for them but, conversely, had functioned powerfully in the legitimation of their oppression in family, society, and Church, ideology criticism emerged.[8] As biblical scholars fanned out into these different fields and began to apply their findings in the task of interpreting the biblical texts, a wide range of new approaches, new forms of criticism, and new methods of exegesis emerged that went considerably beyond the classical historical and theological approaches of the pre-conciliar period. Of particular importance were literary methods such as narrative criticism, which was especially enriching because so much of both testaments is, in fact, narrative; a renewal of the engagement between biblical interpretation and spirituality which had been in abeyance since the Middle Ages; and the ideology criticism which became an important resource for liberation theologies of all kinds, from feminist to racial and ethnic, from first world to third world.[9]

A conundrum was developing during this time that would eventually lead to an engagement of biblical studies with philosophical hermeneutics: the more different methods refined and extended the quest of biblical scholars into the history of the biblical texts, the further away from the texts' message and meaning they got. Historical criticism has a built-in propensity for eternal regress. The answer to every historical question poses a new question about the even more remote history. But the whole point of studying sacred (that is, canonical) texts, as opposed to purely historical ones, is to "translate" these religiously normative texts into the lives of the people for whom they are religiously normative. "Translation" in this sense is not merely a linguistic transaction between different languages. It is an existential

---

[8] I have discussed this issue at considerable length as well as supplying some examples of feminist interpretation in Sandra Schneiders, "A Case Study: A Feminist Interpretation of John 4:1-42," in *The Revelatory Text: Interpreting the New Testament as Sacred Scripture*, 2nd ed. (Collegeville, MN: Liturgical Press, 1999), 180–99; Schneiders, "John 20:11-18: The Encounter of the Easter Jesus with Mary Magdalene—A Transformative Feminist Reading," in *What Is John? Readers and Readings of the Fourth Gospel*, ed. Fernando F. Segovia (Atlanta: Scholars Press, 1996), 155–68. For a more comprehensive study of the problem of patriarchal biblical language and imagery for God in the Bible as a whole, see Schneiders, *Women and the Word: The Gender of God in the New Testament and the Spirituality of Women* (New York/Mahwah: Paulist Press, 1986).

[9] I have treated this development at greater length in Schneiders, *The Revelatory Text*, esp. in chs. 4–5.

transaction between worlds. The question for the interpreter of a normative and authoritative sacred text (that is, a text regarded not merely as an historical record but as Scripture) is always and primarily not just what did this text mean to those who produced it, nor even what does this text mean in the abstract, but what does this text mean for the believing community in the present? In other words, the challenge is how to get the interpretive project going forward into the present and future of the community rather than simply backward into an ever-receding past.

Three Mediating Triads

Let me turn now from this rapid overview of factors influencing the development of biblical hermeneutics in the post-conciliar period to three other sets of pegs I want to set into the wall of our hermeneutical reflection. Each of the three sets has three pegs each. I hope these sets of interrelated concepts will help clarify later discussions.

The first triad is one that no one seems to be able to trace to its actual originator, although most scholars probably encountered it, implicitly or explicitly, in the writings of the French philosopher Paul Ricoeur.[10] (Some biblical scholars, especially the "new historicists," do not like it at all, but I think it is more clarifying than any alternatives I know.) It is the inter-related categories of the "world behind the text," the "world of the text," and the "world before or in front of the text." This is a heuristic schema, not a description of physical, historical, geographical, sociological, cultural, or any other kind of entity in the real world.

The world *behind the text* refers to what *produced the text*. There are at least two categories of such factors: first, the events (historical or meta-historical) to which the texts purport to refer (e.g., the exodus, the exile, the life and ministry of Jesus, the crucifixion, the resurrection and the experience of it by of the first disciples, Paul's ministry, the foundation of the early church); second, the agents who/which putatively or actually produced the text (e.g., Moses, the Deuteronomist,

---

[10] The most succinct treatment of this topic (although not explicitly under these three headings) is Paul Ricoeur's small *chef d'oeuvre*: *Interpretation Theory: Discourse and the Surplus of Meaning* (Fort Worth, TX: Texas Christian University Press, 1976).

Matthew's community, Paul or pseudo-Paul, an anonymous or pseudonymous redactor, or an oral or textual tradition). Notice that talking about the "world behind the text" does not involve any implication that a named event or agent ever happened or even existed. That is a different question. It means the researcher is choosing to investigate how, why, when, where, by what agency, etc., this text came to be, and that involves raising questions about all the theories or claims that can help give a plausible explanation of or answer to that question. This is the type of investigation that is usually subsumed under the collective heading of "historical criticism" and makes use primarily of historical methods. The historical critic will disassemble, deconstruct, analyze, compare the text with other texts and sources of historical data in the effort to elucidate its genesis and trace its development. This is essentially a diachronic process.

The world *of the text* refers to what *has been produced*, that is, to the literary entity in its integrity, e.g., this particular epic, psalm, gospel, pericope, parable, etc. Using primarily literary methods, both synchronic and diachronic, the investigator attempts to establish the nature or type or genre of this textual entity as it now stands, how it works linguistically and rhetorically, how it affects or intends to affect its audience. The primary interest is not who wrote it, when, where, and so forth, or even necessarily what it means in some singular or discursive way, but how it operates on its reader to produce meaning, which is virtually always multivalent. The literary critic works with the text as it now stands rather than with hypothesized earlier forms or editions—that is, with the final form of the text, and how readers, past and present, respond to it regardless of how the text came to be. For the literary critic the meaning is *in* the text, not behind it. Literary criticism is essentially a synchronic process.

The world *in front of* the text refers to what the *text produces* when text and reader interact. As we will see, this is the sphere of hermeneutics and it feeds into theological reflection, spirituality, pastoral engagement, social commitment, liberation theology, and so on.[11]

---

[11] I address these topics at some length in reference to the Fourth Gospel in Sandra Schneiders, *Written That You May Believe: Encountering Jesus in the Fourth Gospel*, rev. ed. (New York: Crossroad, 2003), esp. part 1, chs. 1–4.

In the actual work of biblical interpretation more than one of these areas is likely to be investigated and the results critically combined, but the interpreter is usually primarily concerned with one or the other.

Any serious biblical study is going to involve, in differing degrees and combinations, the categories of a second triad: exegesis, criticism, and interpretation which correspond roughly to historical, literary, and hermeneutical approaches. Exegesis, a term which was once thought to cover the whole scholarly enterprise of biblical interpretation, is actually primarily an effort to establish "what the text actually says," regardless of whether that is factually accurate, whether it is true, whether the exegete agrees with it, even whether it is moral or helpful, etc. The classical tools of historical criticism are the most useful for this task, but literary tools such as structural analysis, form criticism, rhetorical criticism, and so on are also useful and important. One of the major developments in post-conciliar biblical work has been the realization that exegesis is not synonymous or coterminous with interpretation. One cannot interpret a text until one knows what it says, but one can know quite well what it says without knowing what it means. (Parenthetically, this can be a hideout for an ecclesiastically threatened biblical scholar who says, "This is what responsible exegesis shows this text to be saying. Don't ask me whether it is true or what its implications are for the ordinary believer or how it does or does not relate to doctrine or magisterial positions.")

Criticism, which is an effort to analyze and evaluate the text's content in relation to the reader, that is, its meaning in and of itself, usually finds literary or sociological or psychological methods most useful. Again, criticism can be appreciative, highly reserved, or even practiced as rejection. The point is not the biblical scholar's reaction to what the text says or means but ascertaining how this text operates in relation to its readers or hearers. Thus, a feminist biblical critic might want to know whether John 20:1-18 actually presents Mary Magdalene as an apostle in the technical, theologically significant sense of the term, and (regardless of whether there ever was a Mary Magdalene or whether she did or said what the text presents her as doing and saying) how the answer to that question can be substantiated from the text, whereas an historical critic might be using the same passage in relation to its analogues in Matthew and Luke to determine whether the tomb was really empty on Easter morning.

Finally, interpretation, the full flowering of the hermeneutical project, which is an effort to assimilate the/a meaning of the text, involves the personal and transformative response of the reader or the reader's readers to what the text says and means. One's response may be positive or negative, accepting or rejecting, perplexed or challenging or argumentative or exhilarating. But the act of interpretation involves the reader personally with the text's meaning. Interpretation is the heart of the hermeneutical enterprise. It is where exegesis and criticism terminate in transformative appropriation.

In short, exegesis asks what the text says; criticism asks what the text means; hermeneutics engages the reader, individual and/or community, in the ongoing transformation that is required when one inhabits the text as Word of God.

In the period immediately following *Divino Afflante Spiritu*, Catholic biblical scholars reveled in the real, albeit limited, freedom to do actual exegesis, to really raise the question of what the biblical text says rather than starting with dogmatic answers and trying to find proof texts in the Bible to support those answers. Exegesis was the focus of their efforts, and historical criticism was seen by many Catholic biblical scholars at that time as the totality of the scholarly project. They left questions of meaning and implication to pastors or activists. In the wake of the Council, however, they became interested in the variety of critical methods that opened the text in exciting new ways for the life of the individual believer and the Church community. More synchronic methods such as semiotics, structuralism, and then deconstruction were investigated. Even more exciting approaches in the later post-conciliar period were literary methods, such as narrative criticism, and social scientific and psychological analysis. Most recently, praxis-oriented liberationist approaches such as ideology criticism and forays into the relationship between the biblical text and spirituality, social justice involvement, inter-religious dialogue, and the new cosmology have emerged. But as scholars saw how diverse were the results of this wide variety of critical methods, they found themselves increasingly aware of the necessity of finding some way to determine the validity of their interpretations and to adjudicate among conflicting results.[12] The issues were not purely technical or methodological. It

---

[12] I take up these hermeneutical questions in some detail in Schneiders, *The Revelatory Text*, 157–67.

is not necessarily the case that if one applies a method appropriately the resulting interpretation is valid. Scholars were beginning to see that different interpretations of the same text might be equally valid, that is, well-grounded in the text and methodologically justifiable, but not (or not equally) relevant or meaningful. The issue was not purely methodological or even epistemological. The issue was hermeneutical. Hermeneutics is the global enterprise of interpreting texts as meaningful and transformative of persons, social structures, intellectual commitments, and so on. Hermeneutics allows texts to transform "world," the imaginative reality constructions within which individuals and communities live, and thereby the readers who inhabit those worlds.

Not many biblical scholars were willing to engage this philosophical enterprise. Most were not philosophically trained, and, like many older scholars who had grown up intellectually in the over-specialized academy of the first half of the twentieth century, interdisciplinarity was intimidating. A "scholar" was, by definition, someone who had mastered his (and it was virtually always "his") field and respectfully left to other specialists things that were not part of his own specialization. But the intellectual world was changing. The days of total mastery of a single defined field, or even the existence of a methodologically defined "field" that was totally distinct from other fields, were over, if indeed such a situation had ever really existed.

Some twenty years ago, with a brashness that befitted and exposed my inexperience in regard to the conventions of the modern academy, I suggested in writing, to the combined vehement denials of some and shocked recognition of others in biblical scholarly circles, that we Catholic biblical scholars had become experts on how to do what we did without realizing that we did not really know what we were doing.[13] In other words, we had become highly proficient in the use of current exegetical and critical methodology but lacked a coherent hermeneutical theory to explain or justify our critical choices, exegetical practice, or even our interpretive success, to say nothing of how our approach to Scripture and its results fit into a coherent theology of revelation. There were a few of us, still unestablished enough in our fields to know that this was in fact the case and that biblical scholars had to venture into the philosophical thicket of theoretical hermeneutics just as we were venturing into the methods of

---

[13] Ibid., 21 (the comment had already appeared in the 1991 edition).

non-biblical fields such as literature, the social sciences, ideological analysis, and aesthetics. Biblical scholars had lived their way into and had to find their way through the problematic relation between validity of investigation (guaranteed by method) and meaningfulness of interpretation (truth).

The whole problematic was symbolically captured in the title of what was perhaps the most important book on the subject in the last half of the twentieth century, Hans-Georg Gadamer's *Truth and Method*, which, in fact, was really an attempt to challenge and reverse the accepted relationship between these two terms. According to Gadamer, method does not, as the high priests of the Scientific Revolution and then the Enlightenment would have us believe, control our access to truth nor determine the validity of our engagement with it. Rather, the hegemony of method is actually an obstacle to the search for truth, because it defines (and thereby limits) truth rather than using method to facilitate the quest for truth.[14] If one's method of investigation is a ruler, and that method is allowed to determine what questions can be asked and what answers are valid, only longitudinal measurements will count as truth. But if the most significant dimensions of the object of investigation far exceed linear measurement, then the hegemony of method rules out the real quest for truth. It is hard to exaggerate the radicalism of this proposal in an Enlightenment epistemological context. However, it has been generally recognized as valid even by those who do not fully subscribe to Gadamer's theory as a whole.

Hermeneutics, as applied to "texts" broadly understood, is the theory and practice of the complex process by which a text, through its engagement by interpretation, gives birth to understanding or life transforming appropriation of meaning. Hermeneutics, in other words, is critical to biblical scholarship's facilitation of the Bible becoming Scripture, that is, truly revelatory in and for the believing community. It is the bridge from "pure" exegetically based biblical criticism to preaching, to theology, to spirituality, to social commitment—indeed, the bridge from understanding our self and our world to changing them. The most important theorist of hermeneutics, writing at the

---

[14] See Hans-Georg Gadamer, *Wahrheit und Methode: Grundzüge einer philosophischen Hermeneutik* (Tübingen: Mohr, 1960); ET: *Truth and Method*, 2nd rev. ed., trans. Joel Weinsheimer and Donald G. Marshall (New York: Crossroad, 2006 [based on the 5th German ed., 1986]).

same time as Gadamer, was Paul Ricoeur, who produced an enormous corpus on the subject but whose theory of discourse under the conditions of inscription (i.e., textual discourse), which underlies his theory of biblical interpretation, is available in his small but dense work *Interpretation Theory: Discourse and the Surplus of Meaning*.[15]

In the last quarter of the twentieth century these two philosophical giants, neither of whom was a theologian or exegete by *métier* but both of whom were intensely interested in the role of texts in the human enterprise, especially those texts held sacred in societies, laid out the parameters of the hermeneutical project in which the field remains engaged. Gadamer attempted to develop an ontology of understanding, and Ricoeur a phenomenology of language, especially written language, that is, textual discourse. Together they provide, in my opinion, a theoretical model of what is involved in knowing when we interpret the Bible as Sacred Scripture, as the canonical revelatory text of the people of God. Scholars can and do disagree about the explanatory success of the particular theories of Gadamer and Ricoeur, and they have been much expanded since their first appearance. But these two scholars laid out the challenge to biblical studies to engage fully the task of developing an adequate hermeneutical framework for biblical interpretation, one that takes full account not only of exegetical and critical methods but also of the historical, literary, theological, and spirituality dimensions of the project. Such an integral theory of biblical interpretation is the *sine qua non* for achieving fully the task that the Council bequeathed to the biblical academy, namely, laying the table of the Word of God for the nourishment of the people of God in their task of transforming the world which God so loved as to give the only Son.

Where Are We Today?

So, where does this leave us? Catholic biblical scholarship today is polarized by, at one extreme, a Tridentine literalism that leans toward oppressive magisterial fundamentalism and, at the other extreme, a fascination with methodological experimentation, often for its own sake, that flirts with exoticism or even nihilism. In between are most

---

[15] See note 10.

serious biblical scholars who are doing yeoman service in and for the church in the quest for learning and faith, or indeed, a learned faith. We would be more effective, in my opinion, if we were more willing to risk deeper forays into hermeneutics in the strict sense of the word. This is the meeting ground between biblical scholarship and theology, which remains something of a "no man's land" when it could and should be the arena of fruitful mutuality. The two fields need each other both to neutralize the extremes and to maximize their contribution to the academy and the Church.

CHAPTER 2

Between Mountain Peaks and a Crumpled Handkerchief
Hermeneutics and Critical Theory

Francis Schüssler Fiorenza

The topic of hermeneutics and critical theory presents us with a dilemma. If one seeks to scan the wide diversity of the various theories, the danger of broad generalities exists. If one chooses one critical theorist or one significant debate to analyze in detail, another danger exists that the discussion will be so narrow that it will overlook significant topics and debates. In attempting to avoid these dangers, my *first section* touches on the classic German debate between Hans-Georg Gadamer, a hermeneutical theorist, and Jürgen Habermas, a representative of the critical theory of the Frankfurt School. The *second section* considers a North American debate by pointing to William E. Connolly's pluralist views and his critique of Charles Taylor's advocacy of a more hermeneutical philosophical position.

In these debates the hermeneutical positions seek to expand the reach and depth of hermeneutical theory. They look on the classics or outstanding literary and artistic productions of a culture as its high points or mountain peaks that express significant meaning and even truths about human existence and society. The critical theoretical framework, on the other hand, underscores the limits of hermeneutics. It uncovers the intertwinement of language and power and the interrelation between meaning and societal structures.

The difference between the two debates shows the changed constellation today. It establishes the background for an exploration of

Connolly's use of some contemporary French theorists in order to advance his ethos of a new pluralism. I use the metaphors of "mountain peaks" and a "crumpled handkerchief" to illustrate a difference between the more classical approach and Connolly's more contemporary approach, which depends on the topographical approach of Michel Serres. The *third and final section* of my paper briefly concretizes and applies the more theoretical analyses to the interpretation of Vatican II.

1. The "Classic" Debate between Gadamer and Habermas

The classic debate between Jürgen Habermas and Hans-George Gadamer remains significant for a couple of reasons. It took place among central figures of twentieth-century hermeneutics (Hans-Georg Gadamer and Paul Ricoeur, and in part Hans Robert Jauss) as well as a leading critical theorist of the Frankfurt School (Jürgen Habermas). It focused on the limitations of interpretation and the intertwinement of meaning with power. Habermas critically reviewed Gadamer's hermeneutics soon after *Truth and Method* was published.[1] He followed with an essay on the universality of hermeneutics that deepened the criticism. Gadamer responded to both essays, and Paul Ricoeur offered an alleged mediating position. Jauss's reception hermeneutic can be seen as a modification of Gadamer's position through his combination of synchronicity and diachronicity.[2]

Habermas argues that hermeneutics works out of a *translation model that assumes meaning*. When one translates, one assumes that the text is meaningful. If the result is not meaningful, one assumes that the translation is inadequate. A good example is our use of online

---

[1] Hans-Georg Gadamer, *Wahrheit und Methode: Grundzüge einer philosophischen Hermeneutik* (Tübingen: Mohr, 1960); ET: *Truth and Method*, 2nd rev. ed., trans. Joel Weinsheimer and Donald G. Marshall (New York: Continuum, 1989). See Jürgen Habermas, "A Review of Gadamer's Truth and Method," trans. Fred R. Dallmayr and Thomas McCarthy, and "The Hermeneutic Claim to Universality," trans. Josef Bleicher, in *The Hermeneutic Tradition: From Ast to Ricoeur*, ed. Gayle L. Ormiston and Alan D. Schrift (Albany: State University of New York Press, 1990), 213–44; 245–72. This volume also includes Gadamer's reply ("Reply to My Critics," trans. George H. Leiner, 273–97) and the intervention by Ricoeur ("Hermeneutics and the Critique of Ideology," trans. John B. Thompson, 298–334).

[2] Hans Robert Jauss, *Toward an Aesthetic of Reception*, trans. Timothy Bahti, Theory and History of Literature, vol. 2 (Minneapolis: University of Minnesota Press, 1982).

translations of foreign newspaper articles. Often the translated text is meaningful. But sometimes it is not; it appears as gibberish. Yet we do not think that the original article was nonsensical. Instead, we assume that a computerized translation does not yet have the necessary life-relation or background knowledge to translate. Often I have seen translations from Italian newspapers, translating and introducing some Vatican cardinal's pronouncement with the phrase "she said." (If only it were true!) Everyone with some background of Catholicism would know that such gendered linguistic form of "she said" does not correspond to present-day reality of church structures.

But Gadamer's approach is *much more fundamental than the translation model*. An adequate interpretation of Gadamer's hermeneutics has to take into account issues that go far beyond translation, as Habermas knows. Gadamer's hermeneutics appeals to Aristotle's practical philosophy and highlights, as Aristotle did, prudential (rather than axiomatic) judgments and the linking of interpretation with practical application. The latter two are done most readily in theology (for example, a sermon) or in law (where the interpretation of the law may revolve about its claim or applicability to the case at hand).

For Gadamer these aspects are interrelated such that one cannot understand one without the other: a text is understood only when one understands its practical application. This involves not an axiomatic judgment but a prudential judgment. Of course, one might disagree precisely about whether the text has a claim upon us today or whether a text is understood only or primarily when its claim is realized. For example, one might state that today one does not understand the Christian command to love one's enemies, or the parable of the Good Samaritan, or the Greek drama of Antigone with her transgression of Creon's decree to leave attackers of his state unburied, unless one realizes their application in practice today.

We understand these texts when we can appropriate them and apply them to us as making a claim upon today. Acknowledging the claim and understanding are interrelated. In the case of Tamerlan Tsarnaev, one of the bombers at the 2013 Boston Marathon, no one wanted to provide the grounds in which to bury him. Cemeteries refused to accept him; people protested outside of the funeral home, the mayor of Boston publicly announced he did not want him buried in Boston, the city manager of Cambridge said likewise, and the governor of

Massachusetts (like Pilate?) washed his hands of the case—a private matter not of his concern. Immediately after the events, Cardinal Sean O'Malley of Boston had preached urging forgiveness over vengeance, in the face of many calling for the death penalty (which was not possible under state law but was so under federal law). However, the Cardinal did not offer a Catholic cemetery as a place to bury him. Instead, Martha Mullen of Richmond, Virginia, a seminary school graduate and professional counselor, acted on Tsarnaev's behalf to have him buried: "My first thought was, Jesus says love your enemies and not hate them after they are dead."[3] What this particular case involves is an interpretation of Jesus as mirrored in the gospels that is brought to bear on a contemporary situation.

Gadamer's hermeneutical theory challenges how historical texts are read and interpreted. On the one hand, there is a challenge to a purely historicist reading of the text exclusively in terms of its context and particular addressee. For example, a historical interpretation of one of Paul's letters to the Corinthians would assert that it interprets its meaning primarily, if not exclusively, in terms of its meaning for its recipients in Corinth. Gadamer's theory of interpretation goes beyond such an historicist reading. On the other hand, although he is aware of the importance of the original context and horizon, he nevertheless affirms that understanding involves a fusion of horizons: the horizon of a past time, place, and culture, and the present horizon that frames our views. Such a fusion entails the expansion of our own horizons. In addition, Gadamer is conscious that we appropriate a tradition from a horizon of expectation that has been informed by the tradition or has in some way already understood the tradition.

Habermas offers yet another, more basic critique beyond the one of the translation model. This critique takes issue with the appeal to practical application that assumes that the tradition can be understood primarily in terms of having an authority or a claim upon us. Such an understanding, he believes, glosses over the hidden mechanisms of power. This fundamental critique goes against the universalism of

---

[3] Laura Vozzella and Frederick Kunkle, "Boston Bombing Suspect Buried in Virginia," *Washington Post* (May 10, 2013), https://www.washingtonpost.com/local/boston-bombing-suspect-buried-in-virginia/2013/05/10/6cd95482-b9ae-11e2-b94c-b684dda07add_story.html.

hermeneutics. Tradition not only expresses a meaning but also reveals and incorporates power and domination that are present in the hidden mechanisms and societal structures of the past and up to the present. Consequently, a need exists to critique the tradition through open discourse by all who are affected by the tradition. Habermas introduces the categories of the transcendental conditions of discourse that are counterfactual and consequently raises the possibility that every consensus can be revised and thrown into question. (In this respect, Habermas's counterfactual understanding of consensus brings him somewhat closer Jacques Derrida's "democracy to come" than is usually assumed.[4])

Gadamer's response to Habermas draws upon the tradition and its values.[5] Gadamer argues that any critique based on freedom and equality, such as Habermas's critique, *nolens volens* appropriates the very ideal and values of the tradition. Standards are not created *ex nihilo* but emerge as embedded within traditions. Therefore, Habermas is appealing to a tradition of freedom and equality in his very critique of dominative power within instances of the tradition. Paul Ricoeur, in assessing the debate between Habermas and Gadamer, argues for what he believes is a mediating position.[6] On the one hand, Ricoeur realizes that Gadamer's *Truth and Method* was misnamed—it should have been called "Truth or Method." Gadamer, in his view, should bring into his reflections on interpretation a greater sensitivity to method than he does. On the other hand, Ricoeur joins Gadamer against Habermas in arguing that the tradition provides the source and authority for the critique of the tradition.

---

[4] See Simon Critchley, "Remarks on Derrida and Habermas," *Constellations* 7, no. 4 (2000): 455–65. See also *Philosophy in a Time of Terror: Dialogues with Jürgen Habermas and Jacques Derrida*, interviewed by Giovanna Borradori (Chicago: University of Chicago Press, 2003); and Lasse Thomassen, ed., *The Derrida-Habermas Reader* (Chicago: University of Chicago Press, 2006).

[5] See Gadamer's responses to many reviews of the first edition of *Truth and Method*: "Reply to My Critics," and both the "Introduction" and "Foreword to the Second Edition," trans. Garrett Barden and John Cumming, in *The Hermeneutic Tradition*, 273–97, and 198–22, respectively.

[6] Ricoeur, "Hermeneutics and the Critique of Ideology," *The Hermeneutic Tradition*, 298–334.

If one steps back from this original debate between Gadamer and Habermas, three observations should be made: First, Gadamer, Habermas, and Ricoeur all have been influenced by a tradition of German philosophy stemming from Immanuel Kant that includes Georg Hegel, Edmund Husserl, and Martin Heidegger. Gadamer, appealing to Hegel and Heidegger, overcomes the transcendentalism of Kantian philosophy; Habermas is perhaps closer to the Kantians, as becomes more evident in his later writing.

Next, Gadamer is a classicist and stands within the tradition of German humanistic education. He assumes the normativity of the classics of this tradition of German education, going back to the ancient as well as modern classics. The classic is a particular instance of what is located in history and yet universal in its significance as an outstanding exemplification of understanding human existence.

It is interesting to observe that this fundamentally conservative or (more appropriately expressed) "traditional" stance of Gadamer gets a different twist in his reception elsewhere. When I began to teach Gadamer at the Catholic University of America, my colleague Avery Dulles viewed Gadamer more as a relativist than a traditionalist—not my view at the time. But Dulles's point becomes clear when one views the reception of Gadamer by Richard Rorty. He emphasizes the particularity of the culture that produces the classic. Hence societies with different classics have different norms. This comes to the fore in the debates over high school reading lists. Should we read Shakespeare in each year of high school or should we add (and even replace some works with) Geronimo's autobiographic *Story of His Life*, or Anne Frank's *The Diary of a Young Girl* or James Baldwin's *Notes of a Native Son* or Ursula Le Guin's *Left Hand of Darkness*? These classics represent values and traditions that the American high school canon had in previous generations not included. Today, some schools include them in their assigned readings, many others do not and may not even consider them to be classics.

My final observation about the debate between Gadamer and Habermas is that Habermas displays and acknowledges a certain traditional Enlightenment confidence in reason and rationality. His emphasis on the ability of reason and rationality to critique classics gives to reason and rationality an authority that the classic has for Gadamer. One sees this in his critiques when he labels some critical theorists (especially Michel Foucault) as neo-conservatives and when he argues that their own species of critique does not provide a normative basis for critique.[7] Habermas himself sees that emancipation as an ideal has its roots in the religious traditions of the West. In short, one can see that both Gadamer and Habermas belong to the West and even the classic modern German philosophical tradition.

2. William Connolly versus Charles Taylor

I move on to a more North American discussion between critical theory and hermeneutics, and focus on disputes between William E. Connolly and Charles Taylor. Taylor has clearly represented the hermeneutical tradition from his earliest writings on explanation and understanding and on Hegel, on up to his recent major works *Sources of the Self* and *A Secular Age*, as well as his many collections of essays.[8] Connolly, for his part, has been somewhat eclectic in his appropriation of sources, including not only North American philosophy but also recent French thought, including Foucault, Gilles Deleuze, and Michel Serres. In analyzing this debate, it is important to observe the difference in context and presuppositions between this North American debate and the more classical debate between Gadamer and Habermas.

The "confrontation" between Connolly and Taylor over Foucault that began with an exchange in *Political Theory* in 1985 has a different

---

[7] Jürgen Habermas, "Some Questions Concerning the Theory of Power: Foucault Again," in *The Philosophical Discourse of Modernity: Twelve Lectures*, trans. Frederick G. Lawrence (Cambridge, MA: MIT Press, 1987), 282–86. For a more nuanced critique, see Nancy Fraser, "Michael Foucault: A Young Conservative," *Ethics* 96, no. 1 (1985): 165–84. For a comparison between Habermas and Foucault, see David Ingram, "Foucault and Habermas," in *The Cambridge Companion to Foucault*, ed. Gary Gutting (New York: Cambridge University Press, 2003), 240–83.

[8] Charles Taylor, *Hegel and Modern Society* (New York: Cambridge University Press, 1979); Taylor, *Sources of the Self: The Making of the Modern Identity* (Cambridge, MA: Harvard University Press, 1989); Taylor, *A Secular Age* (Cambridge, MA: Harvard University Press, 2007); Taylor, *Philosophical Arguments* (Cambridge, MA: Harvard University Press, 1995); Taylor, *Liberal Politics and the Public Sphere* (London: Center for the Study of Global Governance London School of Economics, 1995). See his more recent collection of essays, Taylor, *Dilemmas and Connections: Selected Essays* (Cambridge, MA: Harvard University Press, 2014) and his discussion of human language in Taylor, *The Language Animal: The Full Shape of Human Linguistic Capacity* (Cambridge, MA: Harvard University Press, 2016). See also his collaboration with Hubert Dreyfus, *Retrieving Realism* (Cambridge, MA: Harvard University Press, 2015).

set of parameters than the Gadamer-Habermas debate.[9] Connolly's work continues to illustrate his fundamental philosophical and political disagreement with Taylor's much more traditional Catholic and transcendent vision. Connolly, of course, takes issue with Taylor's *Sources of the Self*, his work on multiculturalism, and his recent magnum opus, *A Secular Age*, by disagreeing not only with Taylor's hermeneutic positions and view of secularization, but more importantly with his underlying ontology, which in Connolly's view is much more teleological than pluralistic and has a nostalgia for attunement between being and society.[10] Connolly's critical theory represents an ontology of becoming that is pluralist and non-teleological. In many ways, he is somewhat eclectic in his amalgamated appropriation of Deleuze and Serres, along with elements of neuroscience and even William James. He offers a radical interpretation of immanence as well as transcendence in such a way that one could not place him in either camp without misunderstanding. Obviously, there is a wide range to Connolly's work, most recently featured in his book *Capitalism and Christianity*.[11]

In the 1985 exchange Connolly observes that, on Taylor's account, Foucault had indeed identified modes of subjugation that previous versions of critical theory had either not focused on or had not adequately articulated. However, Taylor maintains that the Nietzschean perspective that underlies Foucault's account eliminates precisely the moral or normative basis of any effort to minimize this subjugation or to improve the modern condition. While Connolly concedes that there is indeed in the abstract something accurate about Taylor's critique of Foucault, nevertheless the critique is basically flawed. When Taylor translates Foucault's arguments into Taylor's own formulations, in Connolly's view he obscures the very heart of Foucault's thought and

---

[9] William E. Connolly, "Taylor, Foucault, and Otherness," *Political Theory* 13 (1985): 365–76; and Charles Taylor, "Connolly, Foucault, and Truth," *Political Theory* 13 (1985): 377–85.

[10] See also William E. Connolly, "Catholicism and Philosophy: A Nontheistic Appreciation," in *Charles Taylor*, ed. Ruth Abbey (New York: Cambridge University, 2004), 166–86. See also his "Pluralism, Multiculturalism and the Nation State: Rethinking the Connections," *The Journal of Political Ideologies* 1, no. 1 (1996): 53–73.

[11] William E. Connolly, *Capitalism and Christianity, American Style* (Durham, NC: Duke University Press, 2008).

its distinctive characteristics. Connolly asserts that Taylor's critique of Foucault will be successful only to the extent that he can show that Taylor's own philosophical and historical construction are not undermined by the very criticisms he makes of Foucault.

"But I contend that those such as Taylor who seek to dismiss fundamental features of the project by showing it to be incoherent will find it more difficult to make that charge stick once they are not allowed to precede their critiques of Foucault's genealogy by a translation of it into the very formulations it seeks to interrogate."[12] Put more clearly, Connelly is arguing that by claiming that Foucault is incoherent, Taylor attempts to avoid Foucault's critique of Taylor's own positions, especially his theory of the expressive self. But, Connolly counters "first, that Foucault is not as vulnerable to these criticisms as Taylor makes him out to be and, second, that even though that charge is inflated, there still is a case to be made in favor of the modern subject."[13] It should be noted that Connolly is not without his own criticisms of Foucault for failing to deal with subjugation as a result of age, class, race, the surveillance of urban subgroups, and the lack of career possibilities as well as the necessary discipline for them.[14]

Taylor pushes Foucault aside as too Nietzschean, so that without a commitment to truth he cannot maintain the critique that he wants to have, whereas Connolly argues that Taylor misconstrues Foucault and does not provide an adequate response. In his view, even though Taylor criticizes the primacy of epistemology, rejects a correspondence theory of truth, and maintains that a hermeneutical circle for social theories entails their possible contestability, nevertheless Taylor has an expressive philosophy of language that cannot consistently co-exist with his more critical insights into the historical contingencies that Taylor himself acknowledges. In this sense, Taylor does not advance

---

[12] Connolly, "Taylor, Foucault, and Otherness," 369.

[13] Ibid., 374.

[14] See William E. Connolly, *A World of Becoming* (Durham, NC: Duke University Press, 2011), 53: "Foucault's description of disciplinary society does not deal adequately with differences in age, class, and race. There is today an urban underclass that is subjected to general strategies of urban containment and impersonal modes of surveillance in stores, streets, public facilities, reform schools, prisons and schools. There is also a suburban, career oriented, upper-middle class enmeshed in detailed disciplines in several domains, anticipating the day it rises above them."

a theory of truth that can be an alternative to Foucault's view while taking into account Foucault's insights. In Connolly's view, Taylor would have to modify his own theory of personal identity if he were to take into account Foucault's history of otherness. He questions whether Taylor's theory of the self can integrate Foucault's and postmodern understandings of otherness into a common will of rational community and whether it can allow otherness to be otherness. Finally, Connolly suggests that Taylor's views embody a type of commitment to a teleological ontology that Foucault's genealogical analyses have undercut, leading to the question of whether Taylor's ontology can be sustained.[15]

Connolly, in commenting on Taylor, on Habermas, and on hermeneutics in general, suggests that they have a similar weakness insofar as their hermeneutics ignore the body, and that they have basically a "pastoral" mode of hermeneutics.[16] Such a pastoral hermeneutics uses, but is not alone in doing so, metaphors of height and illumination. These metaphors are treated as media through which humans become "attuned" to the "harmonics" and order of being. He is convinced that the practitioners of pastoral hermeneutics seldom problematize explicitly the narrative and rhetorical frameworks governing their own texts. As he writes: "Each scheme of interpretation is necessarily invested with an ontopolitical position."[17] But none of these has at his or her disposal a consensual or transcendental strategy to refute their competitors.

2.1 Radical Pluralism as Critique of Consensus

Connolly's advocacy of pluralism has developed in such a way that it is possible to distinguish between two different conceptions of pluralism. In his initial approach to pluralism, Connolly primarily criticized the understanding of democratic pluralism that was prevalent in the political theories of Robert Dahl and Adolf Berle. Berle, for example, thought that democratic society could rely on an underlying public consensus of basic values that would give support to the federal

---

[15] Connolly, "Taylor, Foucault, and Otherness," 374–75.

[16] William E. Connolly, *The Ethos of Pluralization* (Minneapolis: University of Minnesota Press, 1995); see his essay "Nothing Is Fundamental," 1–40.

[17] Connolly, *Ethos of Pluralization*, 16.

28   *State of the Questions—Part 1*

government's regular business behavior. His notion of consensus does not take into account how certain groups, media, intellectual and political shape the agenda and thereby influence the regulation of power. Connolly argues certain groups have more power and are favored over against others, and his view on power is more complex than the reduction of power to class.[18]

2.2 Deep pluralism and the Multiplicity of Histories

However, Connolly's understanding of pluralism has become more complex as he has moved beyond his critique of liberal pluralism. His more developed view is often referred to as a "deep pluralism." It involves not only an emphasis on becoming and change rather than a teleological ontology but also an emphasis on the multiplicity of histories. In developing his deep pluralism, he takes over elements from diverse sources: William James, Michel Serres, and Gilles Deleuze. In appropriating James's notion of pluralism and bicameralism, Connolly notes in regard to the bicameral option that "deep pluralism within the academy and the culture pursues such a bicameral approach to existential differences. You advance your perspective without pretending you have demonstrated its necessity."[19] He also borrows from Serres's understanding of time and history. Serres deliberately distinguishes and employs topography over topology. If topology underscores connectedness and continuity by analyzing how properties are preserved despite various deformations or transformations, then topography maps out the local terrain in detail, showing its peculiarities, and with different shapes and features.

Connolly's appropriation of the understanding of history in Deleuze and Serres develops the concept of multiplicity and contrasts it with a traditional linear understanding of history.[20] One sees in both Deleuze and Serres what could be called a "spatial turn." Deleuze uses this turn to critique the nomos of the logos and to emphasize that every order

---

[18] David Campbell and Morton Schoolman, eds., *The New Pluralism: William Connolly and the Contemporary Global Condition* (Durham, NC: Duke University Press, 2008), 10.

[19] William E. Connolly, "The Power of Assemblages and the Fragility of Things," *British Journal of Politics & International Relations* 10 (2008): 241–50, at 242.

[20] See the analyses of each of Serres's works (from *Genesis* to the *Natural Contract*) separately on this topic by Maria L. Assad, *Reading with Michel Serres: An Encounter with Time* (Albany: SUNY, 1999).

rests on exclusion (a reference to Carl Schmitt) so that reason cannot out of logical reason attain to universalist status. He uses images from the sea to illustrate his spatial turn. Serres offers much more of a structural topology and, to explain Connolly's appropriation of Serres, the image of a "crumpled handkerchief" becomes important—a metaphor that they both use and appropriate.

3. From Mountain Peaks to Constituted Multiplicities to Crumpled Handkerchiefs

The metaphor of a "crumpled handkerchief" shows how time readily accommodates heterogeneous objects and how each of these different objects can be enclosed with opposite and opposing modes. Events that are very far apart in time also act as contemporary events. Serres uses the image of a "crumpled handkerchief" to suggest the non-linearity of time and the contemporaneity of past and present. The image suggests that time does not proceed like a linear superhighway, taking us as quickly as possible to our goal, but rather it moves in a series of "folds" or "twists." In addition to the image of a crumpled handkerchief, Serres uses the example of the brewing of coffee or the making of bread or an insect's flight. Consider these three examples: (1) Time does not so much flow as it percolates. Bubbles come to the fore and recede. It is this continued percolating of the water that has gone through the coffee that makes the taste of coffee. (2) How does one make bread? Anyone working with dough knows that there is a series of folding, stretching, doubling-back, squeezing, rolling, stretching again, folding again. Bread is not made in a flowing linear process from beginning to end. The word "process" is inadequate for what happens because it implies a simple movement forward. (3) Anyone who has tried to catch or swat a fly has noticed its sudden changes of direction, moving backward and forward without any pattern. All of which makes it all the more difficult to aim, because one does not have not the slightest idea in which direction the fly might move next.

Connolly notes that Eileen Joy, a medieval historian, expresses a similar point well when she notes the importance of using a model in historiography that understands that moments are inhabited by multiple and heterogeneous temporalities.[21] A similar point has been made

---

[21] Jane Bennett and William Connolly, "The Crumpled Handkerchief," in *Time and History in Deleuze and Serres*, ed. Bernd Herzogenrath (New York: Continuum, 2012),

in Reformation Studies by my late colleague, Robert Scribner, who has shown how many medieval Catholic practices were retained and practiced even in those areas and churches that had become Lutheran.[22]

A crucial question emerges from our survey: how does the emphasis on multiple histories or temporalities compare with the view of history in the hermeneutical tradition that came to the fore in Gadamer's hermeneutic theory or even in its critique by Habermas? It is clear that Gadamer makes a couple of moves. On the one hand, there is clearly a Gadamerian critique of scientism evident in the historical school. Gadamer's hermeneutics seeks to counter any formalist understanding of method. He employs Hegel against Kant, and there is clearly an anti-progressive element (vs. Hegel) insofar as Gadamer goes back to the classics of the tradition and the past and seeks a fusion of the past with the horizon of the present. Acknowledging and interpreting the claim of past classics upon the present is at the heart of his hermeneutical theory of understanding. The question of foreign cultures and spaces scarcely comes to the fore in Gadamer's work, although adapted in that way by Richard Rorty. Likewise, Ricoeur's monumental work *Memory, History, Forgetting* locates itself in the relation between memory and historical study.[23] In noting the interrelation between past, present, future, he is concerned that the relation to the past often overlooks the future, as his critique of Heidegger elaborates. Habermas's critique of the authority of the tradition in terms of either a critical rationality or a future counter-factual consensus with its emphasis on universality stands within this line. One could say that Gadamer's classics are located within the range of Western culture and civilization. They are outstanding examples—or, using the metaphor of mountain peaks, they represent those peaks of our tradition that we need to recognize, climb up to encounter, and interpret their significance for us today.

Clearly the emphasis on the multiplicities of histories and various topographies rather than topologies underscores the diversity and plu-

---

153–72. See Eileen Joy, *Cultural Studies of the Modern Middle Ages* (New York: Palgrave Macmillan, 2007).

[22] Robert W. Scribner and Trevor Johnson, *Popular Religion in Germany and Central Europe, 1400–1800* (New York: St. Martin's, 1996); Robert W. Scribner, *Popular Culture and Popular Movements in Reformation Germany* (Ronceverte, WV: Hambledon, 1987).

[23] Paul Ricœur, *Memory, History, Forgetting*, trans. Kathleen Blamey and David Pellauer (Chicago: University of Chicago Press, 2004), 346–52.

ralities of historical events and spaces. It underscores their non-linear and almost chaotic character. The metaphor of a crumpled handkerchief challenges a linear view of history and points to the multiplicity of fusions and intertwinements that takes place between past and present. The question that the early Gadamer-Habermas debate does not really engage is the question of the multiplicities of pluralism. Nor does Charles Taylor in his writings on Hegel, modern society, and the secular age, though he acknowledges and outlines diverse types of secularism.[24] Even Foucault writes of discourse and history in terms of the development of modern institutions, discourses, or orders of knowledge, though his later writings admit the linkage between modern understandings of the self and the Christian tradition.[25] However, he challenges us to go beyond an understanding that uses categories of unilineal historical development when considering the relation between the historical past and the challenges of the present.

Quite often, a unilinear version of history contains evaluative judgments, and these judgments are based on the directionality of history rather than the modal view suggested by a "crumpled handkerchief." Take, for example, the history of the movement from medieval to Enlightenment, conceived unilaterally in terms of "dark ages" versus "the age of light" (Enlightenment). Or take the development of modernity considered in categories of technocratic control or secularization without openness to transcendence—again there is a unilateralism and unidirectionality. The same narrative of progression is evident. There is often reference to first-, second-, third-, and even fourth-wave feminism in the twentieth century, as if one has moved past the outdated position of the previous wave without considering that the issues of each wave still need to be addressed. One could apply a typology and

---

[24] See the essays in Michael Warner, Jonathan Van Antwerpen, and Craig Calhoun, eds., *Varieties of Secularism in a Secular Age* (Cambridge, MA: Harvard University Press, 2010); and the analysis by James K. A. Smith, *How (Not) to Be Secular: Reading Charles Taylor* (Grand Rapids, MI: William B. Eerdmans, 2014).

[25] Michael Foucault, *About the Beginning of the Hermeneutics of the Self: Lectures at Dartmouth College*, ed. Henri-Paul Fruchaud and Daniele Lorenzini, trans. Graham Burchell (Chicago: University of Chicago Press, 2016), esp. 53–92. Foucault, however, has a critical aim to develop a hermeneutics of the self "not as it was in the case of early Christianity, on the sacrifice of the self but, on the contrary, on a positive, on the theoretic and practical emergence of the self" (75).

ask what are the advantages or disadvantages of each, while a supposed unilinear development tends to eviscerate that consideration. Finally, take the discussion of modernity and postmodernity. Obviously, for postmoderns, modernity is outdated and wrong in many respects. But what that position overlooks is that postmodernity overlays modernity to such a degree that it cannot be considered independently.

In underscoring some of the important contributions of Connolly's views of pluralism and history, I do not want to overlook the serious challenges and criticisms that can be raised against them. Obviously, in the debate between Connolly and Taylor, there are the issues of Connolly's advocacy of an immanence over transcendence (though some commentators see him as closer to Spinoza).[26] In addition, Lois McNay makes the important point that Connolly's view of social pluralism downplays the role of social structure. Connolly's emphasis on non-identity and on the contingency of social existence, along with his celebration of the pluri-potentiality of social pluralism, tends to emphasize "the plurality of struggles per se rather than the consideration of how some struggles may go further than others in challenging deep-seated asymmetries of power."[27]

It is in this regard that Habermas's linkage of critical theory with a theory of discourse and a communicative ethics may ultimately be superior. In that he has come to develop two tracks, public and official discourse along with diverse discourses of individual groups.[28]

---

[26] Mark Wenman argues that the notion of agonistic respect plays such an important role in his thought that one august suggestion is that Connolly's thought "retains fairly thick traces of Spinoza pan-theism, in the sense that he imagines the forms of regularity and order tend to emerge *spontaneously* from the immanent movement of social and cultural forces" ("William E. Connolly: Pluralism without Transcendence," *British Journal of Politics & International Relations* 10, no. 2 [2008]: 156–70, at 157). In his response in the same issue, Connolly takes issue with this interpretation ("The Power of Assemblages and the Fragility of Things," 241–50).

[27] Lois McNay, *The Misguided Search for the Political* (Malden, MA: Polity, 2014), 169.

[28] Francis Schüssler Fiorenza, "The Church as a Community of Interpretation: Political Theology between Discourse Ethics and Hermeneutical Reconstruction," in *Habermas, Modernity, and Public Theology*, ed. Francis Schüssler Fiorenza and Don Browning (New York: Crossroad, 1992), 66–91. See Jürgen Habermas, *Between Facts and Norms: Contributions to a Discourse Theory of Law and Democracy*, trans. William Rehg (Cambridge, MA: MIT Press, 1996); Nancy Fraser, "Abnormal Justice," *Critical Inquiry* 34, no. 3 (Spring 2008): 393–422.

He seeks to develop a communicative ethics that acknowledges the importance of the institutional and legal and is also conscious that all discourse takes place under limited conditions and power.

4. Some Reflections on Vatican II

In contrasting these debates and the different viewpoints of the different sides, my intention was not to take one side over the other or one debate over the other. Instead, it was to underscore the issues of conflicting views of interpretation, history, power, and pluralism. In concluding, I would suggest that these two debates are relevant to the ongoing interpretation and understanding of Vatican II,[29] a topic of much discussion in recent Catholic theology and one of the catalysts for the discussions in this volume.

4.1 Inadequacy of Translation Model

The Vatican II documents deal with crucial and decisive issues of Roman Catholic theological and religious traditions. In their interpretations a creative newness and difference from the tradition emerges. However, at the same time there is a strong affirmation of identity with the tradition. To interpret Vatican II adequately one has to take into account both the decisive differences from the tradition and at the same time also similarities and identities.[30] There are indeed important new affirmations or changes on significant theological issues. However, there are also places in those texts where contradictory statements are placed side by side, or where one affirmation is followed by a contrasting affirmation. It has been central to the hermeneutical theories of both Gadamer and Ricoeur that one should not limit the meaning of the text merely to the intention in the mind of the author, or to

---

[29] See *History of Vatican II*, ed. Giuseppe Alberigo and Joseph A. Komonchak, trans. Matthew J. O'Connell, 5 vols. (Maryknoll, NY: Orbis Books; Leuven: Peeters, 1995–2006). John W. O'Malley, *What Happened at Vatican II* (Cambridge, MA: Harvard University Press, 2008).

[30] Francis Schüssler Fiorenza, "Vatican II," in *The Routledge Companion to Modern Christian Thought*, ed. Chad Meister and James Beilby (London and New York: Routledge, 2013), 364–75.

the authorial experience which led to the text (as proposed by the hermeneutics of the Romantic period).[31]

The situation is further complicated by the process of composing the texts that issued from Vatican II, where the various drafting committees sought formulations and compromises in order to get a majority of votes. A singular or unified determination of meaning does not clearly exist. In cases where differing or contrasting statements stand side-by-side, for example, one can only make coherent sense out of the paragraph when one assumes that the text seeks to bring a diversity and plurality of meanings to the fore. An affirmation is often qualified by an ensuing affirmation or negation. In this respect, Habermas's caution against assuming the universality of hermeneutics is well taken. A translation model that assumes a unitary meaning or that equates meaning with authorial intention overlooks the complexity of the text and the independence of meaning from intentionality.

In addition to the problems of interpreting individual passages within the various documents of Vatican II, there is also the problem of the interpretation of the meaning as well as significance of a whole document. The interpretation of *Gaudium et Spes*, which is in many ways the culmination of the council's work, has been open to diverse and conflicting interpretations. Does it betray a too optimistic worldview? Or does it take into account the failures of modern society? How does it stand in relation to Pope John XXIII's encyclical, *Pacem in Terris*, in its acceptance of human rights, an acceptance that goes beyond the church's criticisms of human rights in its past centuries?[32] Here one can also learn from the discussions on the ethos of pluralization that Connolly's work has provoked.

---

[31] See Friedrich Schleiermacher, *Hermeneutics and Criticism and Other Writings*, trans. and ed. Andrew Bowie, Cambridge Texts in the History of Philosophy (Cambridge: Cambridge University Press, 1998). Ricoeur often emphasizes that Gadamer's interpretation of Schleiermacher in terms of authorial intent should be counterbalanced by statements in Schleiermacher that underscore the grammar and vocabulary of the text itself.

[32] Francis Schüssler Fiorenza, "*Gaudium et Spes* and Human Rights," in *The Church and Human Freedom: Forty Years after* Gaudium et Spes, ed. Darlene Fozard Weaver (Villanova, PA: Villanova University Press, 2006), 38–65; Fiorenza, "Freedom and Human Rights: The Cosmopolitan Context for the Justification of Human Rights in Roman Catholicism," in *Quests for Freedom: Biblical—Historical—Contemporary*, ed. Michael Welker (Neukirchen-Vluyn: Neukirchener, 2015), 360–89.

4.2 Radical Pluralism

The point of my discussion of Connolly was to highlight his affirmation that, despite the claim of many authors, the world has not become more "alike" or more "homogenized." The "modern"—the word itself implies a unity or position not applicable to all places—has multiple minorities. These multiple minorities are not organized as individual self-enclosed groups. Instead, they are organized among several different layers and dimensions, crisscrossing in their identities.[33] They face the task of either continuing in their hostility toward one another or to learning to interact with mutual respect. As Connolly puts it, "We inhabit a world in which most territorial regimes find themselves under intense pressure either to negotiate a multidimensional diversity of faiths, gender practices, sensual affiliations, family structures, primary language, and ethnicities in more noble ways or to erect new barriers against these very negotiations."[34]

Karl Rahner, in one of his most famous essays (originally given as a talk at Weston School of Theology), developed the notion that the church after Vatican II had become a world church.[35] Almost fifty years later, Cardinal Walter Kasper, in his interpretation of Vatican II, has spelled out some of the changes and complexities in the becoming of a "world church."[36] He underscores the fact that today the Church has become a world church not only because the majority of Christians live outside of Europe but also because there is increasing growth in those areas. The question now becomes whether a hermeneutical model that seeks to merge the horizon of the non-West with the West

---

[33] Connolly confesses that he remains "uncertain about the breath of his [Taylor's] commitment to deep pluralism" and observes that much of Taylor's appreciation for multicultural diversity deals with "territorial concentrated constituencies within a state, such as the Quebecois and the Intuit in Canada." See Connolly, "Catholicism and Philosophy: A Nontheistic Appreciation" [n. 10], 173; 185 n. 24.

[34] Connolly, *A World of Becoming*, 84.

[35] Karl Rahner, "Towards a Fundamental Theological Interpretation of Vatican II," *Theological Studies* 40, no. 4 (1979): 716–27.

[36] Walter Kasper, "Renewal from the Source: The Interpretation and Reception of the Second Vatican Council," in *Speaking Truth in Love: The Theology of Cardinal Walter Kasper*, ed. Kristin M. Colberg and Robert A. Krieg (Collegeville, MN: Liturgical Press, 2014), 278–95; Kasper, "Vatican II: Toward a Multifaceted Unity," *Origins* 45, no. 9 (2015): 153–60.

is adequate.[37] And more presently challenging us is the question of whether the insights of postcolonialism, critical theory, and a topography of diversity point to a much more radical challenge that Vatican II itself did not come close to articulating or raising.

4.3 Experience as a Crumpled Handkerchief

The notion of a "crumpled handkerchief" is relevant because it underscores that the past is not "past" in the sense that there is a linear path between the past and the present. Rather, like a crumpled handkerchief, the past and the present are folded over onto one another. Scholars often love to divide time and history into periods, linearly and developmentally. There is past, present, and future. There is the ancient church, the medieval church, the Reformation churches, Counter-Reformation church, and so on. One can describe the church in history as "pre–Vatican II" and "post–Vatican II." But is such a linear conception of church history adequate? An analysis of Vatican II shows how much it should be understood not as linear development but rather much more along the lines of the overlapping or folding together of the past and the present. If one separates the past and the present as two distant horizons, then one fails to grasp that at Vatican II, divergent historical and geographical currents came together, percolated in the debates, and have continued to interact ever since.[38]

Take, for example, Vatican II's liturgical reforms. In many ways they are products of the liturgical movement of the twentieth century. That movement, spearheaded in monasteries and some churches, was a contemporary activity in the twentieth century, but at the same time that movement has to be seen as a *ressourcement*, an attempt to go back to the early church and the liturgical practices that eventually became narrowed or fossilized in the post-Tridentine period. In short, the liturgical reforms resulted from the intertwinement of the

---

[37] Francis Schüssler Fiorenza, "Pluralism: A Western Commodity or Justice for the Other," in *Ethical Monotheism, Past and Present: Essays in Honor of Wendell Dietrich*, ed. Theodore M. Vial and Mark A. Hadley (Providence, RI: Brown Judaic Studies, 2001), 389–424.

[38] Francis Schüssler Fiorenza, "Vatican II and the *Aggiornamento* of Roman Catholic Theology," in James Livingston and others, *Modern Christian Thought*, vol. 2: *The Twentieth Century*, 2nd ed. (Minneapolis: Fortress Press, 2006), 233–71.

past and the present up to the time of the council. It involved both retrieval of ancient traditions and meeting the challenges of churches in contemporary societies, their practices and cultures.

Take as another example the emphasis on Scripture in Vatican II's discussions on revelation, Scripture, and the relation between Scripture and tradition.[39] Giving Scripture a primacy in the church and declaring it "the soul of sacred theology" (*Dei Verbum* 24) shows an attempt to go back to the earliest testimony of the Scriptures and emphasize their importance for the church, in contrast to some post-Tridentine theologies. Yet this move also represents the present, insofar as it is part and parcel of the development toward a contemporary understanding of Scripture that took place in various developing statements of the biblical commission and papal encyclicals that underscored the importance of literary forms and the knowledge of the original languages. In addition, it was influenced much by the modern awareness of the importance of historical research. The search for the historical Jesus and for the different theologies of the various biblical authors is a distinctly modern phenomenon. At the same time, it also acknowledges the importance of the plurality of senses or meaning of the Bible. As a result, in Roman Catholicism today historical-critical approaches co-exist alongside different approaches and readings of the Scriptures.

We can look at Vatican II both as an ongoing event for us today and as an event in the past. I have students in my classes whose parents were born after Vatican II, and they have no idea what the phrase "Tridentine Mass" even refers to. Yet for some of us who are older, Vatican II and the Catholic world from which it issued were very personal elements of our lives. I still remember my first seminar with Joseph Ratzinger in Münster when he brought into class the recently approved document on the church (*Lumen Gentium*) and had a discussion on it. The German students, not sharing my pious and reverential background, tore into the text: its use of Scripture, its metaphors, its contradictions. They claimed it did not fully take into account modern historical exegesis. Ratzinger smiled and tried to answer all their questions and point to an understanding of the text

---

[39] Second Vatican Council, Dogmatic Constitution on Divine Revelation (*Dei Verbum*), November 18, 1965, http://www.vatican.va/archive/hist_councils/ii_vatican_council/documents/vat-ii_const_19651118_dei-verbum_en.html.

that included diverse meanings. My experience in Ratzinger's seminar shows the intertwining of diverse religious (and indeed Catholic) contexts, interpretations, and receptions that were beginning to emerge even before the text had been officially dispersed.

The constitutions and decrees have already achieved the status of normative classics for Roman Catholics today. Many are alive who witnessed the council and its proceedings. Yet many (the overwhelming majority) Roman Catholics have been born in the generations following the Council. At the same time, the issues that are present today have become more complex and varied. It is no longer the historical question of opening the windows of Catholicism to modernity while looking at the failures of modernity, as *Gaudium et Spes* does when it underscores that the advances in technology and communications co-exist with the increase in poverty and inequality. The past issue of the divisions within Christianity and especially the relation to the Protestant reformation still exists but the relation to other religions which was present in *Nostra Aetate*[40] has moved much more to the forefront as comparative religious issue and as intermarriages have increased. The issues of postmodernism, postcolonialism, and even "posthumanism" have come much more sharply to the fore. It is these questions that theories of interpretation (hermeneutical), critical theory (especially the Frankfurt School), new understandings of power and subjugation (Foucault), and pluralism (Connolly) increasing engage us and will engage the Roman Catholic Church in the future. The "mountain peaks" of our tradition will remain as challenges for us to take up as we realize that the search for meaning exists only in the crumpled "foldings" where past, present, and future come together to create the context in which we live as church. Recently, a journal of medieval studies was established with the intention of asking how premodern historical periods can help to address and adjudicate the troubling contemporary questions that postmodern and posthuman discourses address.[41] In doing that we have to ask how our contemporary is-

---

[40] Second Vatican Council, Declaration on the Relation of the Church to Non-Christian Religions (*Nostra Aetate*), October 28, 1965, http://www.vatican.va/archive/hist_councils/ii_vatican_council/documents/vat-ii_decl_19651028_nostra-aetate_en.html.

[41] Eileen A. Joy and Craig Dionne, "Editors' Introduction: Before the Trains of Thought Have Been Laid Down So Firmly; The Premodern Post/human," *Postmedievel: A Journal of Medieval Cultural Studies* 1, nos. 1–2 (2010): 1–9.

sues and challenges move us beyond merely translating or applying the past to the present, but engaging in a critical dialogue that takes into account our experiences and retroductive warrants drawn from them.[42] Such a critical dialogue involves a discourse that is public and sacramental.[43]

---

[42] Francis Schüssler Fiorenza, "From Interpretation to Rhetoric: The Feminist Challenge to Systematic Theology," in *Walk in the Ways of Wisdom*, ed. Shelly Matthews, Cynthia Briggs Kittredge, and Melanie Johnson Debaufre (Philadelphia: Trinity Press International, 2003), 17–45; Fiorenza, "The Conflict of Hermeneutical Traditions and Christian Theology," *Journal of Chinese Philosophy* 27 (2000): 3–31.

[43] See Francis Schüssler Fiorenza, "Faith and Political Engagement in a Pluralistic Word: Beyond the Idols of Public Space," in *The Task of Theology: Leading Theologians on the Most Compelling Questions*, ed. Anselm K. Min (Maryknoll, NY: Orbis Books, 2014), 93–125; Fiorenza, "Foundational Theology as Political and Sacramental Public Theology," *Louvain Studies* 39 (2015–2016): 119–38.

CHAPTER 3

Emerging Forms of Intercultural Hermeneutics

Robert J. Schreiter

Introduction

Interest in intercultural hermeneutics—or, critical reflection on interpretation as it occurs across cultural boundaries—began to emerge in the 1980s. Within its origins in the West, it grew out of the same matrix as the then-emerging concerns for difference as manifested in the focus on gender, race, and class. To be sure, awareness of the impact of cultural difference goes back far in Western history. One detects it already in the *Histories* of Herodotus, with its accounts of the ways and customs of peoples in the Eastern Mediterranean. As a category of difference, what we now call "culture" has been found in many forms. In the nineteenth and early twentieth centuries, especially in the English-speaking world, the term "race" was used to describe ethnic differences. Hastings's *Encyclopaedia of Religion and Ethics*, first published in 1908, devotes nine pages to "race," with no entry at all for "culture." "Race"—as indicative of certain physiological phenotypes, as we know it today—was then just emerging in the racial theories being developed in France and England.[1] It would take the development of the so-called "modern" sense of culture in the social sciences—beginning in the second half of the nineteenth century and

---

[1] For this history, see Robert J. C. Young, *Colonial Desire: Hybridity in Theory, Culture, and Race* (London: Routledge, 1994).

coming to full form in the twentieth—to provide the groundwork on which a critical understanding of communication across cultural boundaries could be built.

This chapter gives a general and brief account of where intercultural hermeneutics in theology has come since the 1980s, by situating it in the larger field of intercultural studies, and offering some indications of where it is going and perhaps also needs to go in the immediate future. I will do this in three steps. The first looks at intercultural theological hermeneutics within the larger field of intercultural studies as it is developing today. The second step examines the principal domains within theology where intercultural hermeneutics is currently most salient. In a third step, the two principal philosophical frameworks of intercultural hermeneutics today will be noted, followed by an exploration of what would appear to be the major growing edge of a critical intercultural hermeneutics.

1. Intercultural Hermeneutics with the Field of Intercultural Studies

Intercultural Studies has become a feature of many disciplines in the humanities, the social sciences, and theology. One could not even begin to give a comprehensive view of the field here. But before beginning to sketch out a crude map of its various forms, so as to situate intercultural theological hermeneutics within it, something has to be said about its two defining units: "inter" and "cultural."

"Inter" and "Cultural"

As one looks across the field, the prefix "inter" takes on two meanings that are often conflated. "Inter," on the one hand, defines a single site of boundary crossing between two distinguishable cultures. The point of interest lies in the specificities—both commonalities and differences—of the respective cultures. On the other hand, "inter" can point to generalizations that can be drawn from a number of different intercultural encounters; "inter" in this sense attempts to point to a larger pattern in such encounters. In the literature of the 1970s, for example, the term "cross-cultural" also appears. "Cross-cultural" referred to both kinds of intercultural encounters just presented. In more recent literature in the social sciences, "intercultural" is reserved for the specific encounters between two cultures, while "cross-cultural" is used for generalizations about such boundary-crossings. In the humanities, "intercultural" covers both the categories of specifying and generalizing. This is largely also the case in theology.

Inasmuch as the aim of hermeneutics is to derive general rules for communication and quests for meaning, intercultural hermeneutics will tend to move especially toward the second understanding of intercultural.

"Cultural" too is not a univocal term. It is clearly intended to be a category of difference, but beyond that there is little general consensus as to what it means. Indeed, it is used to cover a wide range of phenomena. Within theology, at least, "culture" has come to stand for any of three social configurations, usually designated now as "classical," "modern," and "postmodern" forms.[2] "Classical" understandings of culture point to the highest artistic and literary achievements of a people: their music, their art, their poetry, and the like. These are seen as defining a people in a distinctive way, yet communicating universal values and themes. The "modern" sense of culture began to emerge in the Romantic movement of the eighteenth century. Culture in this sense focused on specificity. J. G. Herder saw culture as the unity of three things: language, custom, and territory. Whereas classical understandings of culture limited the concept to referring to an educated elite of a society, everyone has "culture" in the modern sense of the term. This modern sense of culture informs most of the understanding of culture in the humanities and the social sciences today. It is the "culture" that most people see in the discipline of cultural anthropology, for example.

A third concept of culture began to emerge in the 1980s, now commonly called the "postmodern" concept of culture. It recognizes that migration and urbanization have meant that territory is no longer an ongoing basis of identity for a people. Globalization has had a strong impact on both language and custom. Western concepts of postmodernity that refer to the loss of a master narrative, along with the general fragmentation of life, require a new understanding of culture. This new concept of culture might best be defined as a kind

---

[2] For an elaboration on these three, see Kathryn Tanner, *Theories of Culture* (Minneapolis: Fortress Press, 1997).

of force-field where identities are negotiated, drawing on fragments of erstwhile narratives, customs, and other forms of identification to form a tentative, ever-shifting whole.[3] This third concept of culture has been embraced especially in postmodern and postcolonial thinking. How to incorporate and negotiate this notion of culture in intercultural hermeneutics is one of the major challenges for theology today.

Intercultural Studies in the Social Sciences and the Humanities

I turn now to a brief look at Intercultural Studies in the social sciences and the humanities. I begin with the social sciences, since it is here that the language of the intercultural first appeared in the 1960s. In the social sciences, the intercultural first manifests itself in the study of communication, that is, how cultural difference affects communication and the transmission of meaning between two individuals or groups. The impulse for this came from two sectors: the business world and education. As businesses became more transnational, the challenge of communication became a crucial point for success. In education, as the pupils in classrooms in urban settings came to represent more and more cultural backgrounds, teachers had to grapple with how this was challenging pedagogy. Consequently, a great deal of research began to go into what is now called "intercultural communication competence," how to communicate effectively across cultural and linguistic differences. This constitutes an indispensable part of what an intercultural theological hermeneutics needs to do, as it affects all forms of human communication.[4]

In the humanities, intercultural hermeneutics has been most in evidence in two areas: reading and translation, and comparative studies. In terms of reading and translation, a closer attention to the worldviews shaped by culture (in both the classical and the modern senses) helps in understanding a text. Translation is an inexact science, since semantic domains signified by words inevitably vary. Hence, a closer attention to culture helps in both reading and in translation. Comparative studies in

---

[3] I have called this third understanding of culture a "globalized" concept of culture. See Robert J. Schreiter, *The New Catholicity: Theology between the Global and the Local* (Maryknoll, NY: Orbis Books, 1997).

[4] For a good summary of the state of the field, see Darla Deardorff, ed., *The Sage Handbook of Intercultural Competence* (Thousand Oaks, CA: Sage Publications, 2009).

literature have been enhanced by greater attention to culture as well. In terms of an explicit attention to culture in both of these areas, the German-language literature has been perhaps the most extensive to date, although there is an abundant literature in English, French, and other languages as well.

Both of these concerns with intercultural hermeneutics are relevant to theological study. "Inculturation" is, when seen from this perspective, one form of translation. And the growing field of comparative theology, reading texts from two different religious traditions side by side, has much it can learn from comparative studies of literature.

There has been considerable reflection in philosophy on intercultural hermeneutics since the 1980s as well. I will defer that until the third part of this paper, since it has been with philosophy that most theological intercultural hermeneutics has been engaged. But the three developments from the social sciences and the humanities sketched here—communication, reading and translation, and comparative studies all are important to the theological forms of intercultural hermeneutics, to which I now turn.

2. Intercultural Hermeneutics in Theology

One can delineate two major streams of work in intercultural hermeneutics within systematic theology.[5] The first has to do with efforts to develop a theology of inculturation; the second, with interreligious dialogue and comparative theology.

Theologies of inculturation found their beginnings in the years immediately prior to the Second Vatican Council. The beginning point is usually traced back to the publication of a set of papers by young African theologians studying in Paris in the 1950s under the title *Des*

---

[5] Following what had been said in the previous section, one might want to make a case for translation as important. See in this regard Norbert Hintersteiner, *Traditionen überschreiten. Angloamerikanische Beiträge zur interkulturellen Hermeneutik* (Vienna: Wiener Universitätsverlag, 2001). Most recently, departments of missiology have been renaming themselves as departments of "intercultural studies." This development will not be taken up here. My own sense is that this has been done to rescue missiology as a (inter)disciplinary site of study without considering the consequences of such renaming. For a critique of this move, see Robert Schreiter, "Verbreitung der Wahrheit oder interkulturelle Theologie? Was meinen wir, wenn wir heute von Mission sprechen?" *Interkulturelle Theologie/ Zeitschrift für Missionswissenschaft* 36 (2010): 13–31.

prêtres noirs s'interrogent.⁶ In these essays, they voiced their dissatisfaction with the theology they were learning, calling instead for a theology that was more attuned to the realities of contemporary Africa. The Second Vatican Council, soon after, encouraged closer attention to culture, both in the Pastoral Constitution on the Church in the Modern World, *Gaudium et Spes*, and the Decree on Missionary Activity, *Ad Gentes*. Pope Paul VI's visit to Africa in 1966 provided a further impulse. By the mid-1970s, these efforts in Catholic circles were being gathered under the rubric of "inculturation." More theorizing on the state of intercultural hermeneutics itself with theologies of inculturation came later in the 1980s and 1990s.⁷ Parallels can be found in ecumenical circles as well. In 1995, a workgroup of the World Council of Churches produced a statement on intercultural hermeneutics.⁸ Most recently, a more thoroughgoing review of the literature on intercultural theology, viewed critically through the lens of hermeneutics, has been published by the German theologian Volker Küster.⁹ All of these raise questions about how the Christian message interacts with the cultures it encounters, especially through the culture(s) in which the message is transmitted. We will turn to the meta-questions that shape the formal hermeneutics of this interaction in the following section.

Interreligious dialogue has raised questions about intercultural hermeneutics as well. In the first instance, culture was not an explicit category, but its role was just below the surface. The work of Raimon Panikkar comes to mind in this regard.¹⁰ In more recent years, the

---

⁶ Albert Abble, ed., *Des prêtres noirs s'interrogent*, Coll. Rencontres, 47 (Paris: Editions du Cerf, 1956). There are many histories of the development of inculturation within Catholic theology. For a recent example, see Gerald Arbuckle, *Culture, Inculturation, Theologians* (Collegeville, MN: Liturgical Press, 2010).

⁷ See, e.g., Robert J. Schreiter, *Constructing Local Theologies* (Maryknoll, NY: Orbis Books, 1985); Aylward Shorter, *A Theology of Inculturation* (Maryknoll, NY: Orbis Books, 1989); Stephen Bevans, *Models of Contextual Theology* (Maryknoll, NY: Orbis Books, 1992); Schreiter, *The New Catholicity*. Important also for our purposes here is Orlando Espin, "Toward an Intercultural Theory of (Catholic) Tradition," in *Grace and Humanness: Theological Reflections Because of Culture* (Maryknoll, NY: Orbis Books, 2007), 1–50.

⁸ "On Intercultural Hermeneutics," *International Review of Mission* 85, no. 337 (1996): 241–52.

⁹ Volker Küster, *Einführung in die interkulturelle Theologie* (Göttingen: Vandenhoek & Ruprecht, 2011.)

¹⁰ See, e.g., Raimon Panikkar, *The Intrareligious Dialogue*, rev. ed. (Mahwah, NJ: Paulist Press, 1999).

relations between intercultural and interreligious communication has come under more investigation.[11] When one looks at what intercultural hermeneutics may bring to interreligious dialogue, one finds perspectives on both the nature of the concept of religion and of the concept of culture. That "religion" is a Western concept that does not translate easily into non-Western settings has become a truism. The interaction of "religion" and "culture" in Asian and Muslim settings where Hinduism, Buddhism, and Islam are majority religions further complicates even the usefulness of these concepts. Translating the results of these interactions into other settings only deepens the hermeneutical challenges involved.

The new "comparative theology," as articulated by Francis Clooney, James Fredericks, and others, has opened yet another vista for theological hermeneutics.[12] From a hermeneutical perspective, the method involves setting texts from different religious traditions side by side and allowing them to "speak" to each other. Scholars working in comparative theology emphasize an openness on the part of the reader so that the reader might be addressed by these texts in their own respective idioms. As a method of reading, the more acquaintance one has with each of the traditions, the more fruitful the reading will be. These scholars emphasize an overcoming of presuppositions and prejudices that will allow the texts to be able to speak with integrity. What have been particularly useful, from a hermeneutical point of view, are the actual parallel readings that are done; theorizing, to this point, has been kept to a minimum. As the results of such readings accumulate, comparative theology may be able to make some distinctive contributions to theorizing about intercultural hermeneutics for theology.[13]

---

[11] See, e.g., Robert J. Schreiter, "The Possibilities (and Limits) of an Intercultural Dialogue about God," in *The Concept of God in Global Dialogue*, ed. Werner Jeanrond and Aasulv Lande (Maryknoll, NY: Orbis Books, 2005), 19–31; Schreiter, "Intercultural and Interreligious Dialogue about God Revisited," in *Thinking the Divine in Interreligious Encounter*, ed. Norbert Hinstersteiner and François Bousquet (Amsterdam: Rodopi, 2012), 303–19.

[12] For an introduction to comparative theology, see Francis X. Clooney's introduction to the subject in his *Comparative Theology: Deep Learning Across Religious Borders* (Chicester: Wiley-Blackwell, 2010), and Clooney, ed., *The New Comparative Theology: Interreligious Insights for the Next Generation* (London: T. & T. Clark, 2010).

[13] In the readings in the collection just cited, *The New Comparative Theology*, one can see such potential.

This has been a very summary overview of the areas in theology where intercultural hermeneutics is being explored and elaborated. Rather than going further into specific points regarding inculturation, interreligious dialogue, and comparative theology, I would like to move to the third part of this presentation to propose three ways of understanding the current state of intercultural hermeneutics as it manifests itself in systematic theology today.

3. Three Approaches to Intercultural Hermeneutics in Theology Today

In discussing intercultural studies in the social sciences and the humanities, I did not refer to the extensive literature in philosophy. As one might expect, there is a significant literature here to be considered, a literature that intersects quite directly with theological concerns. Some of this literature addresses very specific concerns, such as understanding the stranger—a kind of variant on the literature on alterity, but one with a focus on the intercultural dimension.[14] What I wish to highlight here, however, might be called two approaches or frameworks to intercultural hermeneutics, along with an emerging third one. All three of these, and especially the first two, are philosophical frameworks that in turn either directly have been translated into theological work or are suggestive of how theological thinking may be taken further. I am calling them here a hermeneutics of commonality, a hermeneutics of difference, and a hermeneutics of globality.

A Hermeneutics of Commonality

The first approach or framework is a hermeneutics of commonality. In crossing cultural boundaries, this hermeneutics seeks out commonalities in the worlds of its interlocutors. The commonalities provide the basis for intercultural dialogue.

Perhaps most prominent in this hermeneutics have been the German-Indian philosopher Ram Adhar Mall and the Austrian philosopher

---

[14] See, e.g., the extensive writings of the German philosopher Bernhard Waldenfels, especially his *Der Stachel des Fremden* (Frankfurt: Suhrkamp, 1990), as well as the theological explorations of the German theologian Theo Sundermeier, as seen in his *Den Fremden verstehen* (Göttingen: Vandenhoeck & Ruprecht, 1996).

Franz Martin Wimmer.[15] In differing ways, both have sought out commonalities on which to build: Mall, with his concept of an "analogical hermeneutics"; and Wimmer, with his concept of a "polylogue."

A hermeneutics of commonality is at its most evident in some forms of interreligious dialogue. The soteriological focus so common in Christian interlocutors especially lends itself to seeking soteriological analogues in the other religious traditions. Since about 1990, the search for a global ethic among the religious traditions has prompted closer attention to common ethical mandates in the traditions. The growing ecological crisis has intensified finding common ground even further. And now, too, seeking ways of interreligious cooperation to promote peace and social development has added yet a third element to this growing concern.

Seeking commonalities, then, has an important role to play as a framework for intercultural hermeneutics. Through the years it has grown increasingly sophisticated, trying to distance itself from some of the critiques that have been raised against such a hermeneutical approach. It distinguishes itself from a hermeneutic of "sameness" that can result in homogenizing similarities and creating a hegemonic rather than a dialogical relationship between the two. The universalism of Western Enlightenment thinking that has served imperial and colonial interests of Europe is something this hermeneutics of commonality seeks to avoid. Navigating a way between universalism and commonality, therefore, is one of its important challenges and tasks. It seeks too to distance itself from a rationalist and an idealist mode of philosophy that does not pay attention to context and social location. These are all not easy tasks to undertake and sustain. But given the ethical necessity of finding ways to come together—especially through the mediation of religion—this mode of intercultural hermeneutics has become vital to our planet's future.

A Hermeneutics of Difference

A hermeneutics of difference derives from a number of sources. One of the most important has been the rise of "standpoint" philos-

---

[15] See, e.g., Ram Adhar Mall, *Philosophie im Vergleich der Kulturen* (Darmstadt: Wissenschaftliche Buchgesellschaft, 1996); Mall, *Interkulturelle Logik* (Paderborn: Mentis, 2009). Of interest here also is Mall, *Gadamers Hermeneutik interkulturell gelesen* (Nordhausen: Bautz, 2005). For Franz Martin Wimmer, see his *Interkulturelle Philosophie*, 2 vols. (Vienna: Passagen, 1990f.), as well as Franz Gmainer-Pranzl and Anke Graness, ed., *Perspektive interkulturellen philosophierens: Beiträge zur Geschichte und Methodik von Polylogen: Für Franz Martin Wimmer* (Vienna: Facultas, 2012).

ophies highlighting social features that had been ignored in traditional hermeneutics, such as gender, race, and class. In doing this, it was both a reaction to the homogenizing and hegemonic character of Western hermeneutics of the first half of the twentieth century, which attempted to marginalize, suppress, or even erase differences that disturbed master narratives. As such it opened up discourse to voices not heard before and gave new agency to women, to oppressed and silenced peoples, and to minorities of all types.

A second source has been the attempts to come to terms with otherness or alterity. A growing awareness that there were features of the "other" that could not be reduced to a oneness prompted great difficulties for a philosophical mind-set that was monologic in nature. It continues to haunt this kind of thinking: how to conceive of unity that does not require uniformity.

A third source has been the engagement with the plurality and diversity that otherness implies. Here both modern and postmodern attempts can be found: modernity, as it were, continuing to seek a unity; postmodernity, on the other hand, acknowledging and even celebrating diversity and fragmentation. This is especially evident in the concepts of culture, called "modern" and "postmodern" above.

Pursuit of a hermeneutics of difference has enriched the scope and texture of intercultural hermeneutics immensely. Indeed it is hard to imagine what a return to a previous state of some four decades ago might even be. Important has been how difference now no longer means variation in peripheral dimensions of experience or discourse; difference can shift the framework of experience and discourse qualitatively.[16]

As interreligious dialogue has expanded its scope, Christians have taken on a wide range of themes. Most notably in recent times there have been moves beyond soteriological concerns to include a general sense of openness.[17] This allows for following the leads of a hermeneutic of difference in more detail.

In the theologies of inculturation mentioned above, a hermeneutics of difference has played an enormous role in their development. In the early stages, inculturation often meant asserting cultural difference

---

[16] See, for example, Susan Abraham's chapter in this collection.

[17] Marianne Moyaert, "Recent Developments in the Theology of Interreligious Dialogue: From Soteriological Openness to Hermeneutical Openness," *Modern Theology* 28 (2012): 26–41.

as a basis of identity for colonized and marginalized groups. In a later stage, inculturation was seized upon for renewal of societies in the Christian-majority countries of the Global North and the reconstruction of the post-communist societies of Central and Eastern Europe. Today, it has taken on a third dimension of a critical building of culturally diverse societies.[18]

As with any hermeneutical framework, a hermeneutics of difference has its limitations as well. There are three such limitations that stand out especially. First of all, if difference becomes the principal defining characteristic in intercultural hermeneutics, one can end up with a world of "others" that do not share sufficient characteristics to permit dialogue and exchange. Anselm Min has explored this feature especially in investigating postmodern thinking about difference. In such an extreme setting, solidarity that permits interaction of any kind becomes an extrinsic "add-on" that may or may not compromise difference.[19] When there is near incommensurability, how can there be *intercultural* interaction?

Second, Latin American thinkers such as Cuban philosopher Raul Fornet-Betancourt have noted that the emphasis on difference and fragmentation can lead to an abdication of ethical responsibility. Because I am different, how can I take any responsibility for the other, or the other for me? Fornet-Betancourt points to the political and ethical problems this raises for an intercultural hermeneutic.[20] The kind of solipsism that can grow out of this, coupled with the hegemonic power that the West still enjoys, makes Western varieties of this kind of postmodern form of thinking potentially quite destructive of intercultural interaction and discourse.

Third, an overemphasis on "standpoints" (e.g., gender, race, class) can lead to an essentialization of these categories, which ends up undermining the pursuit of difference that the introduction of these concepts tried to achieve in the first place.

---

[18] I have explored this in greater detail in Robert J. Schreiter, "Mission in der Spannung von universalem Anspruch und partikularem Kontext," in *Kontextualität des Evangeliums: Weltkirchliche Herausforderungen der Missionstheologie*, ed. Markus Luber (Regensburg: Friedrich Pustet, 2012), 51–67.

[19] Anselm Kyongsuk Min, *The Solidarity of Others in a Divided World: A Postmodern Theology after Postmodernism* (New York: T. & T. Clark International, 2004).

[20] See the discussion of his and other Latin Americans' reflections on this in Espin, "Toward an Intercultural Theology of (Catholic) Tradition," 19–21.

A Hermeneutics of Globality

I turn now to a potential third framework for an intercultural hermeneutics. As a third form, it seeks to acknowledge both the strengths and the weaknesses of the hermeneutics of commonality and the hermeneutics of difference. But at the same time, it should not be seen as a sublation of those two forms. It is also "potential" in the sense that its development still leaves a lot to be done. It is the "emerging form" of the title of this chapter. I call it here a hermeneutics of globality.

In *The New Catholicity*, I spoke of "integrated" and "globalized" concepts of culture.[21] "Integrated" coincided largely with what have now come to be called "modern" concepts of culture. "Globalized" concepts as presented there have many similarities with "postmodern" concepts but reach beyond them in an important way by taking the paradoxes and ambivalences of globalization—rather than some form of late modernity—as their frame of reference.[22] Globalization, I believe, changes the context for the monological framing of a hermeneutics of commonality and the late-modern context of a hermeneutics of difference (in either its postmodern or postcolonial form). Globalization carries deep ambivalences which, I think, cannot be overcome by patterns of dialectical thinking but rather need to be confronted with paradox as a mode of engagement.

Here I have found Latin American thinking of greatest value. I have already mentioned the Cuban philosopher Raul Fornet-Betancourt, who brings a decided ethic and political reading to postmodern thinking and to the consequences of globalization.[23] In arguing for what he terms "interculturality" instead of "inculturation," Fornet-Betancourt outlines a mode of dialogue that seeks to overcome hegemonic holds on the discourse from erstwhile colonizers. In significant ways, his proposal looks like what Jürgen Habermas has called "communicative action,"[24] but with a more conscious and explicit gesture toward the

---

[21] Schreiter, *The New Catholicity*, 46–61.

[22] Espín, "Toward an Intercultural Theory of (Catholic) Tradition," 8–15, follows this train of thought in his own way.

[23] See ibid., 15–25, where Espín gives a very good summary of his thought. More recent work by Espín includes *Interculturalidad, critica y liberación* (Aachen: Mainz Verlag, 2012) and *Interkulturalität und Religion* (Aachen: Mainz Verlag, 2012).

[24] Jürgen Habermas, *The Theory of Communicative Action*, 2 vols., trans. Thomas McCarthy (Boston: Beacon Press, 1984, 1987).

ethical and political implications. Another source that I have found helpful has been the decolonial writing of the Argentinian philosopher Walter Mignolo.[25] I would like to summarize under five headings the elements that I think go into an intercultural hermeneutics of globality.

The first heading is *globality*. I am suggesting this term over "universality" or "commonality" as a frame of reference. Globality evokes globalization that is our inevitable context (at least for now) for any intercultural endeavor. Globality, as does globalization, suggests a wide spread of certain phenomena, even as that spread is uneven and can evoke very opposing reactions. This is evident, for example, in the way religion has come to be seen in the public forum, the ethnification of cultural identities that did not exist previously, and reactions that reflect the asymmetries of power. Globality reflects too what has happened to worldwide communication in so many (but not all) parts of the world, and the unexpected agency it has given to oppressed people. The very unevenness of globality mirrors better the diversity that remains even under the most persistent homogenization that may be taking place.

The theological counterpart to globality is "catholicity," itself a potentially comprehensive but also uneven and at times oppressive reality. Catholicity holds together from a theological point of view both local integrity and the interactive nature of global communion.[26]

The second heading for this intercultural hermeneutical proposal is *paradox*. Methodologically, paradox is a call to embrace the ambivalences and interconnectedness of seeming opposites in order to articulate meaning in intercultural encounter. It is the methodological acknowledgment of diversity and complexity. Much thinking in globalization has been more characterized by reverting to dialectic, itself a useful tool of analysis. But the bifurcations that the latter term implies can stand in the way of what Fornet-Betancourt would call a genuine interculturality.

---

[25] See Walter Mignolo, *The Darker Side of Western Modernity: Global Futures, Decolonial Options (Latin America and Otherwise)* (Durham, NC: Duke University Press, 2011); Mignolo, *Local Histories/Global Designs* (Princeton, NJ: Princeton University Press, 2012).

[26] I have explored further the ambiguities of the concept of the global, especially as it impinges upon theology, in Robert J. Schreiter, "Globalität als theologischer Begriff," in *Globalität und Katholizität. Weltkirchlichkeit unter den Bedingungen des 21. Jahrhunderts*, ed. Christoph Böttigheimer (Freiburg: Herder, 2016), 17–30.

Closely related to paradox is the third heading of this proposal: *resilience*. Much attention has been paid to *resistance* as an important form of agency of the oppressed and subjugated in postmodern and postcolonial theory. It has been a very useful way of exploring the dynamics of the subaltern and the colonialized. I am not suggesting discarding resistance in a consideration of an intercultural hermeneutic but rather adding another dimension which has been gaining more ground on a variety of fronts, namely, resilience. Resilience, too, is a form of agency that examines how a population maintains its integrity in face of adversity and how it adapts to maintain that integrity in changed circumstances. It has become an important category in biology and ecological studies, but also in the social sciences, as populations face catastrophe and long-term subjugation.[27] For such populations, one ritual exercise that has proven important is the recitation of the founding narrative of a people that includes how adversity has been faced in the past. As an example, after the murder of six Sikhs in their *gurdwara* in Oak Creek, Wisconsin, in 2012, members of the Sikh community gathered to recite their holiest Scripture, the *Guru Granth Sahib*, from beginning to end—a ritual that takes two days. In so doing they reaffirmed their identity, values, and ideals as Sikhs in the face of the attack upon them. The series of readings that make up part of the Catholic Easter Vigil service can be seen to function in much the same way for Christians.

Work on the psychological and social aspects of resilience is still being done, but the capacity of resilience to hold together both resistance (which can end up being defined by the outside aggressor) and the ongoing integrity of the community fits well into a method of paradox and a frame of globality. Work on this topic in theology is now also underway.[28]

The fourth heading is *aesthetics*. Alongside the obvious insistence on ethics and the political implications that flow from it, aesthetics—at least of a special kind—comes more to the fore. In this regard I am not speaking about an aesthetics that advocates withdrawal from critical

---

[27] See, e.g., Steven Southwick and Dennis Charney, *Resilience: The Science of Mastering Life's Greatest Challenges* (Cambridge: Cambridge University Press, 2012).

[28] See, e.g., Clemens Sedmak, *Innerlichkeit und Kraft. Studie über epistemische Resilienz* (Freiburg: Herder, 2013); David Carr, *Holy Resilience: The Bible's Traumatic Origins* (New Haven, CT: Yale University Press, 2014).

thinking and ethical commitment, but one along the lines suggested by the work of the late Cuban American scholar Alejandro García-Rivera, who developed an aesthetics growing out of communities of the marginalized and the wounded.[29] Art—and an aesthetics that articulates it in a verbal medium—is one of the principal ways we can give expression to paradox and the complexities and contradictions of existence. In a globalized world, art in all its forms—writing, painting, sculpting, filmmaking, drama, and dance—can capture these complexities and communicate them in a special way. I am thinking here too of those forms of art and aesthetics of those who experience the ambivalences of globalization in the most acute way.[30]

The fifth and final heading has to do with the cultivation of intellectual and spiritual disciplines needed to engage in a hermeneutics of globality. Here Bernard Lonergan's definition of conversion comes to mind.[31] It is a conversion that permits one to experience and see the world differently. It is a conversion that calls for action and solidarity. It is a conversion that lures us more deeply into God's design for healing and reconciling the world.

These five headings suggest an outline for the development of the next phase of intercultural hermeneutics, representing the results of efforts that have been made to this point to define the field, with an eye toward the immediate issues pressing now upon us. To what extent these challenges will be taken up remains to be seen in the coming years.[32]

---

[29] Alejandro García-Rivera, *The Community of the Beautiful* (Collegeville, MN: Liturgical Press, 1999); García-Rivera, *A Wounded Innocence: Sketches for a Theology of Art* (Collegeville, MN: Liturgical Press, 2003). See also John Thiel's chapter in this collection.

[30] As an example of theology and film, I think of the work of Antonio Sison. See his most recent book, *World Cinema, Theology and the Human: Humanity in Deep Focus* (New York: Routledge, 2012).

[31] See Bernard J. F. Lonergan, *Method in Theology*, 2nd ed. (1973; reprint, Toronto: University of Toronto Press, 1990), 237–43.

[32] Mihai Spariosu, "Some Observations on the Prospects of Intercultural Hermeneutics in a Global Framework," in *The Agon of Interpretations: Towards a Critical Intercultural Hermeneutics*, ed. Ming Xie (Toronto: University of Toronto Press, 2014), 170–209, argues for many of these same points in setting up an intercultural hermeneutics in a global context: the global-local frame of reference, the non-linear forms of thinking, the re-mapping or fusion of horizons, and the place of aesthetics. He also brings forward a critique of the "critical" when applied to intercultural hermeneutics. If "critical" means the neo-Marxist thinking associated with Habermas, then it will remain locked in a Western, Enlightenment worldview.

Coda: A Theological Postscript

In trying to sketch out the current domain of intercultural hermeneutics and suggest some new directions in it, we keep in mind of course that this is a *theological* hermeneutics. Up to this point, the two principal areas of doctrine that have been the most helpful in articulating a theological basis for an intercultural hermeneutic have been the Trinity and the Incarnation. The Trinity has played an increasingly important role in articulating a theology of religious pluralism that will support interreligious dialogue. Likewise, a theology of the Holy Spirit within the doctrine of the Trinity continues to open new vistas for dealing with pluralism in general. The Incarnation has created a kind of theological warrant for seeing how the Gospel message might take root in all human cultures. It certainly is central to the teaching of the Second Vatican Council on culture and what has come to be known as inculturation.

Perhaps we might consider a third area of theology that will be helpful in the further elaboration of an intercultural hermeneutics. I am thinking here of the discussions in the first half of the twentieth century on nature and grace, and the relation of the natural to the supernatural. Might those discussions not help us see better, in our discussions both of religious pluralism and of interreligious dialogue, the presence of God beyond the confines of our own points of view? Might the struggle to overcome extrinsicism in those debates help create the interculturality that Fornet-Betancourt is proposing? It's just a thought—and something to explore further at another time.

CHAPTER 4

The Aesthetics of Tradition and Styles of Theology

John E. Thiel

Hans Urs von Balthasar's impressive achievement in *Herrlichkeit* has led theologians to appreciate the value of aesthetics for theological interpretation.[1] Balthasar's magnum opus draws on the category of beauty in order to contemplate God's divine life as beauty itself and the incarnation as the consummate revelation of finite beauty. The subplot of *Herrlichkeit* unfolds in an extended meditation on modernity's loss of a faithful sensibility for the beauty of the incarnate form, a reflection on the insidiousness of sin viewed through the lens of aesthetics. The richness of Balthasar's multivolume work appears in a plethora of discrete studies that advance an accomplished argument for the divine glory as the plenitude of beauty, of which, he insists, modern theologians are as obliged to take account as the ancients were.

Balthasar's work has since prompted interest in putting the category of beauty to theological service, even if not necessarily in the manner of his particular project. Richard Viladesau, for example, has proposed a transcendental argument that finds God's infinite beauty posited in the conditions for the possibility of beauty's finite apprehension.[2] Alejandro García-Rivera has developed a Latino theological

---

[1] Hans Urs von Balthasar, *Herrlichkeit: Eine theologische Ästhetik*, 7 vols. (Einsieseln: Johannes Verlag, 1961–69); ET: *The Glory of the Lord: A Theological Aesthetics*, 7 vols., ed. Joseph Fessio and John Kenneth Riches (San Francisco: Ignatius Press, 1984–91).

[2] Richard Viladesau, *Theological Aesthetics: God in Imagination, Beauty, and Art* (New York: Oxford University Press, 1999).

aesthetics that sees the beauty of a faith-filled community in its capacity to appreciate difference, including cultural difference, within the unity of God's redemptive order.[3] Mirjam-Christina Redeker has offered a theological aesthetics that understands itself as a perception theory of faith, keen to explain both the beautiful and truthful nuances of the human relation to God that the act of faith grasps.[4]

In the pages that follow, I would like to join the company of these aesthetical-theological interpreters, albeit in a much more limited and modest way, by bringing an aesthetic perspective to bear on the theological concept of tradition itself. A number of monographs on tradition have appeared in recent years, and none has parsed the notion of tradition by appeal to the category of aesthetics.[5] The advantage of such a perspective is that it will elucidate different kinds of Catholic sensibilities about the nature of doctrinal truth, clarify an aesthetic dimension to contemporary disagreement in the Church about the authentically Catholic, and also provide understanding about competing notions of the proper task of theology in our present ecclesial moment. We live in a time in which Catholic theology is polarized by traditionalist and progressive sensibilities that both rather facilely valorize their own approach to theology as though it were exclusively authentic. Indeed, I want to warn my readers at the outset that they will be tempted judgmentally to do just this in making their way through my account of the two Catholic aesthetics of tradition that are respectively associated with more conservative or more liberal

---

[3] Alejandro García-Rivera, *The Community of the Beautiful: A Theological Aesthetics* (Collegeville, MN: Liturgical Press, 1999). See also Roberto S. Goizueta, *Christ Our Companion: Toward a Theological Aesthetics of Liberation* (Maryknoll, NY: Orbis Books, 2009).

[4] Mirjam-Christina Redeker, *Wahrnehmung und Glaube: Zum Verhältnis von Theologie und Ästhetik in gegenwärtiger Zeit* (Berlin: Walter De Gruyter, 2011).

[5] Kathryn Tanner, *Theories of Culture: A New Agenda for Theology* (Minneapolis: Fortress Press, 1997); David Brown, *Tradition and Imagination: Revelation and Change* (Oxford: Oxford University Press, 1999); David Brown, *Discipleship and Imagination: Christian Tradition and Truth* (New York: Oxford University Press, 2000); John E. Thiel, *Senses of Tradition: Continuity and Development in Catholic Faith* (New York: Oxford University Press, 2000); Terrence W. Tilley, *Inventing Catholic Tradition* (Maryknoll, NY: Orbis Books, 2000). Brown's volumes might seem an exception to my judgment that none of these works examines tradition through the lens of aesthetics, since he attends to art as a dimension of the content of tradition. Yet, in Brown's work, aesthetics is not invoked as a perspective for appreciating the beauty of tradition itself.

approaches to theology, namely, the classical aesthetics of tradition and the developmental aesthetics of tradition. I, however, assume that both of these aesthetics present the "Catholicly beautiful," as do the theological styles that serve these two aesthetics. My aim in this chapter is irenic. Hence my goal is to cultivate a deeper appreciation of the range of the Catholicly beautiful and, through it, to offer a more welcoming understanding of how theologians might represent it well, even when capturing its beauty from different perspectives.

Tradition and Aesthetics

Catholic belief has long held that the act of faith encounters God's revelation in Scripture and tradition, even if this particular way of conjunctively formulating the belief only appeared in the aftermath of the Reformation. According to the Council of Trent (1545–1563), Jesus Christ is the one source of the truth of the gospel message that was faithfully promulgated to the Church by his apostles. Yet this saving "truth and rule [of conduct] are contained in written books and in unwritten traditions which were received by the apostles from the mouth of Christ himself, or else have come down to us, handed on, as it were, from the apostles themselves at the inspiration of the holy Spirit."[6] The pressing concern for the council fathers at Trent was to define the Catholic teaching on divine revelation in the face of Luther's claim that God's revelation was communicated in Scripture alone, and that ecclesiastical tradition was humanly invented corruption and nothing more than the popery Luther identified with all that was wrong with the Church of Rome. In defining a dimension of revelation that exceeded the biblical page, the council fathers found expression for the medieval Catholic belief that the truth of God's revelation appeared in the teachings of ecumenical councils, whose definitions were inspired by the Holy Spirit, in papal teachings, and in the writings of recognized, orthodox theologians who, it was assumed, pronounced on dogmatic loci with unwavering agreement that reflected the unity

---

[6] Council of Trent, Session IV, First Decree: Acceptance of the Sacred Books and Apostolic Tradition (April 8, 1546), in *Decrees of the Ecumenical Councils*, 2 vols., ed. Norman P. Tanner (Washington, DC: Georgetown University Press, 1990), 2:663. For a more detailed discussion of the Catholic belief in the authority of tradition as a mode of revelation, see Thiel, *Senses of Tradition*, 13–25.

of divine truth. This tradition of *sacra scriptura* was complemented further in the teaching of Trent by all the time-honored beliefs and practices that did not take written form but that, invested with the authority of apostolic teaching, communicated the truth of the gospel.

In the aftermath of Trent, Catholic theologians advanced the distinctiveness of the Tridentine teaching against the Protestant Scripture principle by accentuating both the truth and authority of Catholic tradition as a mode of revelation. As time passed, this accent resulted in the development of a theology of the magisterium that found a proliferating content for its interpretation in a marked increase in the publication of papal encyclicals since the late eighteenth century and the definition of the dogma of papal infallibility at Vatican I (1870). Thus, tradition achieved a certain integrity in Catholic belief that prevented its reduction to Scripture or even to the history of the interpretation of Scripture, even to the point that tradition could sometimes be understood as partly conveying God's revelation that was partly conveyed as well in the Bible. This "partly . . . partly" (*partim . . . partim*) conceptualization of the relationship between Scripture and tradition was considered by the fathers at Trent and rejected for its disjunctive implication that there were two sources for the truth of revelation which remained incomplete in each.

Yet, as late as the initial draft of Vatican II's *Dei Verbum* (Dogmatic Constitution on Divine Revelation), this "partly . . . partly" formulation was still seriously considered by its authors as a viable way of insisting on the integrity of tradition as a distinct dimension of God's revelation. Continued dissatisfaction with this schema, however, led the Council Fathers to approve a much-revised final version of *Dei Verbum* that insisted that "sacred tradition and Scripture . . . are bound together in a close and reciprocal relationship," that they "both flow from the same divine wellspring, merge together to some extent, and are on course towards the same end." The "partly . . . partly" conceptualization was excised from the final text of *Dei Verbum* since "tradition and Scripture together form a single sacred deposit of the word of God, entrusted to the church." This teaching of Vatican II on the unity of revelation in the truthful coherence of Scripture and tradition does not mean that tradition can be reduced to the reception of Scripture's truth in the history of faith and its transmission. Moreover, the Council affirms that "the church's certainty about all that is revealed is not drawn from holy Scripture alone" but also from sacred tradition. Thus, repeating the teaching of the Council of Trent, *Dei Verbum* teaches that "both Scripture and tradition are to be accepted and honored with like devotion and reverence."[7]

It is this integrity of tradition in Catholic belief that I wish to explore through the interpretive lens of aesthetics. And since this lens can register a broad, visual range, I would like to focus the aesthetic perspective that will be put to hermeneutical use here.

Any number of ancient and medieval philosophers and theologians addressed aesthetic issues and questions, but the appearance of the discipline of aesthetics as a dimension of philosophical inquiry is usually dated from Alexander Baumgarten's 1735 dissertation *Meditationes philosophicae de nonnullis ad poema pertinentibus*, which addressed the poem as a work of art. This work introduced the word "aesthetics," which Baumgarten defined as "a science of how things are to be known by means of the senses,"[8] a formulation he would expand some years later in his 1750 work *Aesthetica* to include the phrase "the art of thinking beautifully."[9]

The epistemological orientation of Baumgarten's early definition has ever remained a concern for philosophers interested in aesthetics, though the discipline has since developed to include an extensive range of issues. Writing a generation before Baumgarten, Anthony Ashley Cooper, the third earl of Shaftesbury, and Frances Hutcheson strove to describe the nature of beauty itself, as well as its proper regard by human sensibility. Growing attention in the eighteenth century to the workings of creativity and genius led to the inclusion of these themes in the scope of aesthetic concerns, the most systematic treatment of which appeared in Kant's *Critique of Judgment* (1790), specifically in part one, which advances a "critique of aesthetical judgment."[10] The concerns of the philosophical subdiscipline widened further under the influence of Hegel's judgment that beauty appears most truthfully not

---

[7] Second Vatican Council, The Dogmatic Constitution on Divine Revelation (*Dei Verbum*), §9, in *Decrees of the Ecumenical Councils*, 2:974–75.

[8] Quoted in Paul Guyer, "The Origins of Modern Aesthetics: 1711–35," in *The Blackwell Guide to Aesthetics*, ed. Peter Kivy (Malden, MA: Blackwell, 2004), 15.

[9] Alexander G. Baumgarten, *Ästhetik: Lateinisch-Deutsch*, trans., intro., annot. Dagmar Mirbach (Hamburg: Felix Meiner, 2007), 1:11.

[10] Immanuel Kant, *Critique of Judgment*, trans. J. H. Bernard (New York: Hafner, 1951), 37–202.

in natural phenomena but in works of art that manifest the movement of Spirit in history. Hegel's influence has led to the consideration of aesthetics as a discipline devoted to the criticism of art and artistic judgment.[11] With the advent of the avant-garde in various forms of modern art, the scope of aesthetics widened further as artists intentionally eschewed responsibility for representing the beautiful, and the aesthetic task turned to explaining exactly what made art art.

In these pages I will focus on aesthetics as a theory of the beautiful. My goal is not to define the nature of the beautiful as an objective state. Aesthetic thought has long recognized in the notion of taste that aesthetic judgment is pluralistic and, as a consequence, that there are differing perceptions of the beautiful and the qualities that configure it. Along similar lines, I argue that there are different Catholic perceptions of the beauty of tradition and that these differing perceptions are grounded in different Catholic sensibilities about the beauty of God and the believer's encounter with that divine beauty in faith. I wish to reiterate, by way of introduction, that in the next two sections I describe sensibilities in the Catholic imaginary, and I attempt to describe them in a manner faithful to their own particular values, without offering criticisms of their limitations. Talk of limitations appears in my concluding discussion of how these aesthetics are appropriated theologically.

A Classical Aesthetics of Tradition

A classical Christian aesthetics measures any instance of the beautiful against faith's affirmation that God is consummate beauty itself. Christian aesthetic judgment, however, is always exercised in the midst of the created conditions of existence where experiences of beauty offer imaginative entry to transcendent beauty. Thus, in faith, created beauty is judged to be so because it participates in the divine beauty. Even more pointedly, qualities that faith ascribes to the divine nature will be qualities judged to be beautiful in God's creation. Divine qualities like mercy and love can be found in the realm of human virtue where they may be judged beautiful not only because they are emotionally poignant and relationally redemptive but also because human mercy and

---

[11] Mary Mothersill, *Beauty Restored* (Oxford: Clarendon Press, 1986), 388.

love share finitely in the beauty of these qualities as divine attributes. The divine attribute of goodness behaves like the moral attributes of mercy and love, not only in the sense that it admits of analogical construal, but also to the degree that faith finds goodness beautiful, a judgment affirmed most strikingly by both Pseudo-Dionysius and Thomas Aquinas who agreed that goodness and beauty are the same.[12]

Not all divine qualities, however, admit of this analogical translation as readily as others, and, as a consequence, they resonate less aesthetically in the Christian imagination. God's power and presence are examples of attributes that resist analogical construal and so elude Christian appreciation as the beautiful. Medieval Christian theology held that all created being possesses the transcendental qualities of oneness, truth, goodness, and beauty since these are qualities of the Creator. All being as being is beautiful, as are the conditions under which being appears, such as its power or presence. Yet, power and presence are not moral qualities like mercy, love, and goodness. The power and presence of finite being stand less easily in analogical relationship to the utterly divine qualities of omnipotence and omnipresence, even to the point that Christian discourse would be disinclined to speak specifically of creaturely power and presence as beautiful.

At first glance, it would seem that much the same could be said of the divine attribute of immutability. Like omnipotence and omnipresence, divine immutability does not easily admit of analogical translation to creaturely existence, which is enmeshed in time and change. Nevertheless, it is this divine attribute more than any other that epitomizes God's beauty in the Christian imagination.[13] God's immutability offers no homology to the created conditions of temporality and marks the divine transcendence with the absolute perfection that changelessness and timelessness logically require. True analogy may fail between the beauty of eternal perfection and the vagaries of created time, and yet classical Christian definitions of beauty readily imagine the qualities of beauty against the backdrop of divine immutability. Aquinas, for ex-

---

[12] See Viladesau, *Theological Aesthetics*, 115.

[13] One of the most famous testimonies to this classically aesthetical judgment is found in Augustine's account of the mystical experience of God's timelessness that he and his mother Monica shared in Ostia shortly before her death, as recorded in the *Confessions* 9.10.

ample, delineates three conditions that characterize beauty: "clarity," "proportion or harmony," and "integrity or perfection" (*integritas, sive perfectio*).[14] The perfection he ascribes to finite beauty, though, cannot approach the perfection of the immutable God and conveys much more an aesthetic sense of the "wholeness" of what is judged beautiful. Too distant a comparison to be judged analogy in any strict sense, the aesthetic quality of *perfectio* dimly hints at the divine quality most attractive to Christian aesthetic judgment. However much some divine attributes susceptible to analogical construal encourage the believer to find some limited coherence between finite and infinite beauty, the attribute of immutability captures the Christian imagination with a divine beauty marked by its utter difference from all that is worldly.[15]

Having offered such judgments about the attribute of immutability, I wish to make a qualification that has some bearing on our present topic. As we have seen, Catholic belief maintains that tradition, along with Scripture, is a mode of divine revelation, the means by which God has chosen to communicate the sublime and saving truth of the Christ event to the world. In a classical aesthetics of tradition, the doctrines and practices that make up tradition possess a definitiveness that defies time, since they are imagined to be—in the words of the fifth-century monk Vincent of Lérins—what has been believed "everywhere, always, and by all."[16] It is Vincent's "always" that carries the banner of immutability onto the field of tradition. Tradition, of course, is in time and, as the very process of "handing down" the faith, is characterized by change. Yet, a classical aesthetics of tradition finds the beauty of tradition in its abiding truth as divine revelation. The teachings and practices of tradition identified as the apostolic heritage are seen in this sensibility as fixed. The words of the Nicene Creed, for example, are as permanent as the truths about the nature

---

[14] Thomas Aquinas, *Summa theologiae*, I, q. 39, a. 8, in *Summa theologiae*, trans. Thomas Gilby et al., 61 vols. [Blackfriars edition] (London: Eyre and Spottiswoode; New York: McGraw-Hill, 1964–76), 7:132–33. Hereafter cited parenthetically as ST, along with the volume and page(s).

[15] See the discussion of the beauty of God's unchanging perfection in David Bentley Hart, *The Beauty of the Infinite: The Aesthetics of Christian Truth* (Grand Rapids, MI: Eerdmans, 2003), 178–249.

[16] Vincent of Lérins, *Commonitorium* 2.3, in *Documents of the Christian Church*, 4th ed., ed. Henry Bettenson and Chris Maunder (Oxford: Oxford University Press, 2011), 89.

of God and the saving drama they express. The practice of the eucharistic real presence is timelessly repeated in the devout reception of the sacrament. Papal infallibility ensures the certainty of those dimensions of tradition that are not subject to change and so, in the judgment of the Church's teaching authority, are worthy of the entire Church's appreciation as the timeless truth of revelation. Since revelation, and thus tradition as revelation, communicates God's providential plan to save the world, and since that plan issues from God's eternal love and unchanging will, tradition, of all that dwells in the creaturely realm, can be represented in faith as a finite reflection of the divine immutability. Its beauty, like God's, lies in its difference from the ordinary conditions of temporality that, in this Catholic sensibility, are saturated with relativity and doubt.

Immutability as a quality of God's being by definition transcends anything in creation including tradition, which as a dimension of divine revelation must conform to the human capacities for its subjective recognition and reception, and so must be enmeshed in time and culture. Tradition cannot be immutable in any strict sense. For a classical aesthetic sensibility, though, its beauty lies in its ability to capture a sense of God's unchanging truth, the very content of divine revelation. In this respect, tradition's unchanging truth possesses a beauty that is more distinctive than the unchanging truth of Scripture. Christians believe that the inspired words of the Bible convey God's timeless truth. The revelatory power of Scripture *and* tradition, however, is a peculiarly Roman Catholic belief. Moreover, the immutability of a classical aesthetics of Scripture appears not only in its unchanging content but also in the fixed character of the words on the page, ever the same and ever conveying the once-and-for-all events of the Savior's life that bring the world to redemption. Tradition, though, offers itself in a great variety of aesthetic forms that capture the Catholic sense of tradition's permanence, itself a reflection of God's unchanging beauty. Tradition appears in such literary forms as the teachings of ecumenical councils, papal encyclicals, and the writings of authoritative theologians. Tradition appears in such unwritten forms as the celebration of Mass, Marian devotions, and the pastoral leadership of the local bishop. This variety, which includes so many other manifestations of tradition, extends the permanence of traditional truth into every dimension of Catholic life, unifying the experience of the traditionally beautiful. In this classical aesthetics, the transcendental quality of beauty radiates in tradition in a way that illuminates the other transcendental qualities of tradition—its unity, truth, and goodness.

Beauty functions mimetically in this classical aesthetics of tradition. Early in its history, Christian theology embraced the Platonic categories that served as the intellectual *lingua franca* of the Mediterranean world, and that satisfied the Christian desire to think and speak well of God's otherness. Like the Platonic forms or ideas, the divine nature transcends time and change and dwells in a state of metaphysical perfection. For Plato, the things of this world are merely shadowy copies of the supersensible ideas. They stand in mimetic relationship to the eternal truths to which they correspond. Yet, the absence of a doctrine of creation in ancient Greek philosophy makes this mimesis disappointing. Mimesis registers its imitation in the ambit of physicality. It implicates the senses, which distract the intellect from the true objects of knowledge. Plato expresses this misgiving about mimesis most notably in Book X of the *Republic* where Socrates advocates the censoring of art in the ideal state on the grounds that, as a physical imitation of a physical imitation, it lures the mind away from the contemplation of the immutably true and beautiful.[17]

Christian mimesis transforms these Platonic categories in every respect by ascribing immutability and its consummate beauty to the Creator God and by positing a rich correspondence between the physical universe and its Creator. This transformation was facilitated all the more in the late antique world as Plotinus's later interpretation of Platonism was appropriated theologically by Augustine and through his influence came to be embraced as normative in the medieval theological tradition. This variety of Platonism eschewed Plato's disjunctive regard for the relationship between the visible and invisible worlds and saw finite being as sharing in the power and qualities of consummate being itself, a metaphysical resonance most acceptable to the Christian affirmation of the goodness of being and God's providential presence to creation.[18] Mimesis in this Christian ontology is enabled by the participation of created being in the uncreated being of God.

---

[17] Plato, *Republic*, Book 10, 595a–608a, in *Plato: The Collected Dialogues, including the Letters*, trans. Lane Cooper et al., ed. Edith Hamilton and Huntington Cairns (Princeton, NJ: Princeton University Press, 1961), 819–33.

[18] See Stephen Halliwell, *The Aesthetics of Mimesis: Ancient Texts and Modern Problems* (Princeton, NJ: Princeton University Press, 2002), 313–43.

The exercise of sensibility in this kind of mimesis can be an occasion of sin, since the reflection of eternal being in finite being could be idolatrously distorted by human volition.[19] But even while susceptible to sinful corruption, Christian mimesis properly falls within the scope of creation's sacramentality in which finite being is metaphysically receptive to, and conveys the graceful presence of, God.

A classical aesthetics of tradition presupposes this understanding of Christian mimesis, regarding finite beauty as a mirroring of God's beauty facilitated by its created participation in the fullness of being. A classical perspective on Christian mimesis assumes that this finite mirroring of the divine beauty occurs statically, since tradition reflects the divine immutability. This stationary beauty of tradition appears in interesting ways—in commonly affirmed iterations of the Creed, in the iconic lives of the saints, and in the repetition of the sacramental life of the Church. In each of these examples and all the others that might have served, the Catholic imagination delights in the immovability of tradition's mimesis, ever the same in its mirroring of the divine immutability. This static mimesis is truly beautiful as a representation of what is authentically Catholic and of what enduringly abides as the apostolic faith of the tradition.

As we have seen, mimesis implicates the senses, and in Christian mimesis the senses, responding well to grace and resisting the pitfalls of sin, are the experiential modes of apprehending sacred beauty. Catholic Christianity richly appreciates the role of sensibility in religious experience and in that respect is especially open to the aesthetic dimensions of the encounter with God. In a distinctly Catholic aesthetics, all the senses have a share in the experience of created beauty and its transcendent arc toward eternal beauty, at least to the degree that the senses mutually draw each other into the apprehension of the world. Aquinas, though, argued that of all the senses those most cognitive—seeing and hearing—especially apprehend the beautiful. The beautiful, he claims, "is that which calms desire, by being seen or known," and it is the senses of sight and hearing that particularly minister to reason, the

---

[19] In her study of Augustine's aesthetical thought, Carol Harrison highlights Augustine's abiding concern that the materiality of finite beauty easily becomes a source of sinful temptation. See Carol Harrison, *Beauty and Revelation in the Thought of Augustine* (Oxford: Clarendon Press, 1992), 271.

faculty that conceptually grasps the beautiful. Thus, he observed, "we speak of beautiful sights and beautiful sounds," but "we do not speak of beautiful tastes, and beautiful odors."[20] Although Thomas singled out the senses of seeing and hearing as inclined to the experience of the beautiful, it is interesting to note that vision has a prominence in this aesthetic grouping. Early in the *Summa theologiae*, Thomas defines beauty as that which "consists in due proportion" and beautiful things as "those which please when seen [*quae visa placet*]."[21]

Aquinas voices widely held Catholic assumptions in the aesthetic primacy he assigns to the sense of sight. Of all the senses, vision has pride of place in a classical Catholic aesthetics. The sense of sight unifies the other senses by construing possible objects of experience, and so of aesthetic experience, in a spatial field, there to be engaged by the other senses. Viewed as a theater of creation, this field offers a host of images upon which faith-filled vision might gaze in order to contemplate the mimesis of divine beauty. Unlike a Protestant aesthetic sensibility, which is iconoclastically wary of the visual and far more attracted to the beauty of a faith that comes from hearing the Word of God purely preached (*fides ex auditu*), a Catholic aesthetics turns to the visual apprehension of creation—in Aquinas's apt phrase "*intellectum nostrum . . . convertendo se ad phantasmata*"[22]—in order to behold finite concresences of divine beauty, an optics supported by

---

[20] ST I–II, q. 27, a. 1 (19:77). If the project here were a fully developed theological anthropology, then I would be obliged to give account of the aesthetical dimensions of all the senses and the ways each contributes to the experience of God. My project, however, is not anthropology but aesthetics. I have chosen to focus here on a theological aesthetics of seeing and hearing, not only because, following Aquinas, I judge these senses to be aesthetically paramount, but also because an aesthetics of these senses captures the ecclesial aesthetics that flourish in the Church today. Nevertheless, as I note above, all the senses have a share in the experience of created beauty and, through it, in the apprehension of divine beauty.

[21] ST I, q. 5, a. 4 (2:72). The priority accorded to vision as the aesthetical sense also stems from the medieval belief that color is the cause of beauty. See Umberto Eco, ed., *History of Beauty*, trans. Alastair McEwen (New York: Rizzoli, 2010), 99–129. See also Eco's detailed study *The Aesthetics of Thomas Aquinas*, trans. Hugh Bredin (Cambridge, MA: Harvard University Press, 1988).

[22] ST I, q. 84, a. 7 (12:40–41). Even though Aquinas speaks more generally in this article of sense images, it is interesting to note that visual experience prevails in the examples he offers of how the senses inform acts of understanding.

the ancient Christian claim that God is light (1 John 1:5). A Catholic visual aesthetics embraces the values of an Orthodox theology of the icon, which sees the static, painted image as a window to eternity and the supernatural mysteries of the faith. Latin Catholicism, however, widens this window and with it the religious efficacy of vision by regarding three-dimensional objects—religious statuary and the crucifix—as its conventional art forms that represent the sacred for visual apprehension, an aesthetic commitment that reflects a readiness to find the divine beauty in the wider realm of ordinary physical things. The openness of Roman Catholicism to the reality of extraordinary visionary events, of appearances of the Savior, the Virgin, or the saints to believers, bespeaks the primacy of vision in a classical Catholic aesthetics, as does the more ordinary Catholic experience of gazing in veneration at the consecrated bread and wine elevated by the celebrant at the ritual climax of the Mass and in the exposition of the Blessed Sacrament.[23]

A classical Catholic aesthetics values all of the senses in grasping the specific beauty of tradition, though here again the sense of sight has prominence. The Christian paradigm of visual beauty is the beatific vision, the consummation of eschatological meaning in the vision of God. Paul spoke of this visual experience movingly early in the tradition, expressing for the first time the aim of Christian yearning: "For now we see in a mirror, dimly, but then we will see face to face" (1 Cor 13:12; NRSV). Pope Benedict XII articulated the hope of believers more fully in his fourteenth-century teaching that the souls of the blessed in heaven "see the divine essence with an intuitive vision" immediately, even before the resurrection of the body and its future reuniting with the soul at the end of time, and that in this vision God is seen "nakedly, clearly, and openly" so that in the vision the theological virtues of faith and hope disappear.[24] In remarkable poetry, Dante captures the hope of believers for this wondrous sight as he recounts the final

---

[23] Caroline Walker Bynum notes an extreme form of this pious practice in late medieval German devotion. In the practice of what scholars have come to call *Schaufrömmigkeit* (visual piety), some believers were satisfied to "receive" the Eucharist simply by encountering the host visually. See Bynum, *Wonderful Blood: Theology and Practice in Late Medieval Northern Germany and Beyond* (Philadelphia: University of Pennsylvania Press, 2007), 10.

[24] Pope Benedict XII, Constitution *Benedictus Deus* (January 29, 1336), in *Enchiridion symbolorum definitionum et declarationum de rebus fidei et morum*, ed. Heinrich Denzinger

steps of his heavenly ascent in the *Paradiso*: "Thus my mind, all rapt, was gazing, fixed, motionless and intent, ever enkindled by its gazing. In that Light one becomes such that it is impossible he should ever consent to turn himself from it for other sight; for the good, which is the object of the will, is all gathered in it, and outside of it that is defective which is perfect there."[25] In Dante's supernatural imaginary, which articulated the very Christian assumptions it both confirmed and profoundly influenced, it is the beauty of the divine immutability that brings the believer to rapture, a finite state that shares in the immutability of God. Dante describes this heavenly participation by portraying his mind as "motionless" (*immobile*), transfixed by the vision of the impassible God. It is the sense of sight in its eschatological register that enjoys this redemptive encounter with the glory of God that radiates from the unchanging perfection of the divine nature.

This most profound of Christian hopes finds an analogue in the visual apprehension of the many forms of tradition, which offer a beautiful mimesis of the divine immutability. Catholic belief in the permanence of tradition encourages this connection, as does the status of tradition as a dimension of divine revelation itself. Like great works of visual art, the forms of tradition endure, defying effective change. Their beauty lies not only in their capacity to please when seen but also in their timeless availability to sight, to be seen and to please in the unchanging beauty of their sacred form again and again. Great works of visual art, of course, are only imaginatively and not literally timeless. They can be diminished in their beauty, much in the manner of Michelangelo's Sistine Chapel ceiling fresco that had been sullied in its appearance with the passage of time. Corruption here is put right through restoration, in the recovery of the most beautiful original by erasing the deleterious effects of time. Along similar aesthetic lines, the forms of tradition possess the perfection of orthodoxy that presents itself in all its clarity before the devout eyes of believers, its beauty appearing in the abiding and ever-familiar doctrinal formulations, rituals, beliefs, practices, and authorities that convey the saving truth of redemption. Corruption in this classical aesthetics is deviation from

---

and Adolfus Schönmetzer, 34th ed. (Freiberg im Breisgau: Herder, 1967), 297 (DS 1000–1001).

[25] Dante Alighieri, *Paradiso*, vol. 3, of *The Divine Comedy*, 6 vols. in 3, trans. Charles S. Singleton (Princeton, NJ: Princeton University Press, 1975), Canto 33, 377.

the beauty of orthodox perfection, itself a reflection of God's unchanging being. And here too, heterodox corruption can only be addressed through restoration, in the recovery of the beautiful original by erasing novel interpretations that occasionally claim false authority, disrupting the familiar field of tradition's fixed, observable beauty.

A Developmental Aesthetics of Tradition

Before considering the features of a developmental aesthetics of tradition, I would like to state that my identification of this sensibility does not assume that the two aesthetics are mutually exclusive, as though commitment to one necessarily precludes a commitment to the other. Each of these aesthetics can accommodate the values of the other. Nevertheless, a classical Catholic aesthetics is basic to Catholic sensibilities. Any other Catholic sensibility is a variation on its theme and issues from a sense of compatibility with it. Compatible tastes, though, often proceed from an experience of preference and the same typically applies to these kinds of Catholic taste. Moreover, any kind of taste can be held so strongly that it judges its grasp of the beautiful alone to be adequate to its object and so rejects other aesthetic judgments that claim validity. These various allegiances and alignments of Catholic taste present themselves in the encounter between a classical and a developmental aesthetics of tradition.

A developmental Christian aesthetics of tradition has only appeared in the modern period as a post-Enlightenment sensibility. It is a recent arrival in the history of Catholic taste and for that very reason is regarded suspiciously by the classical sensibility. A product of historical consciousness, a developmental aesthetics of tradition finds divine beauty in the providential unfolding of events in time that slowly clarifies the fullness of tradition's truth. Beauty in this aesthetics is judged by believers to dwell not only in the truthful content of tradition but also in the process that brought it to be and also too in the anticipation that this process is occurring now in the present moment.

This sensibility was first expressed theologically in the notion of the development of doctrine that first appeared in the early nineteenth century, initially in the work of the Protestant theologian Friedrich Schleiermacher (1768–1834) and then, through his influence, in the work of Catholic theologians at the University of Tübingen, most notably in the early writings of Johann Sebastian von Drey (1777–1853). All of these theologians, Protestant and Catholic, found in the theological principle of doctrinal development an effective response to the historical-critical interpretation of Scripture and the history of doctrine that Enlightenment and post-Enlightenment thinkers presented as proof of Christianity's falsity. Historical-critical interpretation exposed all the differences in Scripture that a canonical reading of its pages easily glossed over. Historical-critical interpretation of the history of doctrine likewise demonstrated that the earliest Christian Church—the foundation of what Christians devoutly called the apostolic tradition—was characterized by a vast plurality of beliefs that settled on orthodox unity only over the course of centuries of Christian infighting and through the vagaries of historical events. In these respects, historical-critical interpretation, motivated by Enlightenment disdain for Christian meaning, was a direct assault on a classical aesthetics of Scripture and tradition that delights in what it judges to be the lovely permanence of Christian mimesis. The principle of doctrinal development enabled theologians to acknowledge the facts of historical data marshaled against Christianity by its "modern cultured despisers" while yet interpreting the facts theologically to demonstrate the ways the tradition gradually came to its orthodox clarity, the development itself now placed within the ambit of divine providence at the prodding of the Holy Spirit.

Johann Sebastian von Drey sketched the first Catholic understanding of developing tradition in his brief work on theological method, *Kurze Einleitung in das Studium der Theologie* (1819). Here Drey averred that conceptualizing the system of doctrine "not as a dead tradition from a time gone by" but instead "as the development of a living tradition" requires thinking of it as defined by two dialectically related elements: one that is *fixed* (ein *"fixes"*) and one that is *mobile* (ein *"bewegliches"*).[26] The fixed element takes shape as dogma, which Drey portrayed as "the single objectively . . . valid criterion of Christian

---

[26] Johann Sebastian von Drey, *Kurze Einleitung in das Studium der Theologie mit Rücksicht auf den wissenschaftlichen Standpunct und das katholische System*, ed. Max Seckler and Winfried Werner (Tübingen: Francke, 2007), 133 (§256). To clarify the quotation's orthography: in Drey's text, *fixes* and *bewegliches* are italicized. Translations of this text are mine.

truth."²⁷ The fixity of dogma is a function of its truth being "closed" or "completed," not from any privileged state of giveness but only, Drey insisted, through a process of doctrinal development in which the finally settled state of dogma has been proven in the abiding faith of the Church. This mobile element of doctrine ever dwells in the ongoing life of the Church as a quality of engaged faith that "in the development . . . is still conceiving [doctrinal truth]."²⁸

For Drey, an authentic understanding of tradition is one in which the fixed signposts of dogma guide the proper development of doctrine in consonance with the orthodox past. This direction, however, does not produce an utterly reflexive mimesis of authoritative dogma. Even when it lacks the recognized validity of orthodoxy, the mobile element in doctrine "can yet be Christian truth that has not yet developed to the level that can be recognized generally as such."²⁹ Indeed, Drey pointed out that truthful tradition can be misrepresented through the error of "hyperorthodoxy," which "finally denies any mobility" to doctrine.³⁰ In an astonishing judgment expressing the Romantic assumptions that enabled this modern conception of tradition, Drey observed that persons can "distance themselves from the truth either by falling away from it or by lagging behind it [*Zurückbleiben hinter ihr*]." The latter prospect, he continued, is "inertia, a consequence of the expiring activity of the (religious) principle in its progressive development."³¹ For Drey, this developmental understanding of history is the only legitimate way of rendering the mystery of God's presence to tradition, so much so that "any historical conception and account of the [temporal] appearances of Christianity that proceed from a principle different from [a developmental one] contradicts Christianity, is unchristian and untheological."³²

The next generation of Tübingen theologians appropriated Drey's historical understanding of tradition, most notably his influential student Johann Adam Möhler (1796–1838) who favored the imagery of organic growth for the development of tradition in his early work

---

²⁷ Ibid., 134 (§258).
²⁸ Ibid., 133 (§256).
²⁹ Ibid., 134 (§258).
³⁰ Ibid., 135 (§260).
³¹ Ibid., 127 (§240).
³² Ibid., 97 (§175).

Unity in the Church.³³ It was John Henry Newman's *Essay on the Development of Christian Doctrine* (1845), however, that brought the notion of developing tradition into the theological mainstream. Throughout the *Essay*, Newman compared the development of doctrine to the mental clarification of an idea. In this noetic analogy, the content of the idea represents the truth of the apostolic deposit of faith which, like any objectively true idea, is always complete in itself. Yet, like any idea of depth, the apostolic tradition, as expressed in a variety of authoritative doctrines, comes to be believed, appreciated, and understood gradually in the conditions of time and culture. "This process," Newman claimed, "whether it be longer or shorter in point of time, by which the aspects of an idea are brought into consistency and form, I call its development, being the germination and maturation of some truth or apparent truth on a large mental field."³⁴ Like Drey, Newman thinks that the established doctrinal tradition provides an authoritative heuristic for development. And yet, like Drey, Newman regards historical development as the means by which established orthodoxy itself came to take shape, the means by which it is meaningfully enlivened in every present moment, and the means by which a presently obscure and only latent orthodoxy achieves clarity and manifest recognition.

Even though the notion of a developing tradition fell under the suspicion of Church authorities during the Modernist crisis in the early years of the twentieth century, its integrity has come to be regarded as axiomatic since the Second Vatican Council. In his famous address convening the Council on October 11, 1962, Pope John XXIII himself referred to the work of the Council as an exercise in re-interpreting and so developing the ancient faith for the present moment, a conceptualization of the workings of tradition that gave magisterial voice to this modern understanding:

> But from the renewed, serene, and tranquil adherence to all the teaching of the Church in its entirety and preciseness . . . , the

---

³³ See Bradford E. Hinze, "The Holy Spirit and the Catholic Tradition: The Legacy of Johann Adam Möhler," in *The Legacy of the Tübingen School: The Relevance of Nineteenth-Century Theology for the Twenty-First Century*, ed. Donald J. Dietrich and Michael J. Himes (New York: Crossroad, 1997), 79–87.

³⁴ John Henry Newman, *An Essay on the Development of Christian Doctrine*, 2nd ed. [1878], (Notre Dame, IN: University of Notre Dame, 1989), 38.

Christian, Catholic, and apostolic spirit of the whole world expects a step forward toward a doctrinal penetration and a formation of consciousness in faithful and perfect conformity to the authentic doctrine, which, however, should be studied and expounded through the methods of research and through the literary forms of modern thought. The substance of the ancient doctrine of the deposit of faith is one thing, and the way in which it is presented is another.[35]

Although John XXIII was reflecting here on the task of the Council fathers, the understanding of doctrinal development that he articulated—what we might call the reception model—has come to be accepted as the normative way of imagining the changeability of tradition. Catholic theologians have come to understand their interpretive efforts as possible contributions to the development of doctrine that offer new ways of imagining both how the ancient truth of tradition might be received meaningfully in the present moment and how novel developments might themselves take shape as future orthodoxy. Even more broadly, this reception model envisions every believer's act of faith as a hermeneutical site for meaningfully reconciling the truth of ancient doctrine and the truthfulness of contemporary experience in the ongoing life of the Church.

In considering the aesthetics of this conception, it is important to note that the explicit sense that developing tradition is beautiful first requires awareness that tradition is developing, and such an explicit awareness presumes knowledge of the historicity of doctrine that can be acquired only through education. This is not to say that believers who have not been educated in the historicity of doctrine are incapable of the implicit awareness that the truth of the faith develops in their lives and in the life of the Church. The ongoing experience of deeper conversion into the mysteries of the faith is a good example of implicit awareness of development that believers share as a matter of course, especially as conversion is consciously shaped by events in life that are

---

[35] Pope John XXIII, "Opening Address to the Council," in *The Documents of Vatican II*, ed. Walter M. Abbott (New York: America Press, 1966), 715. John XXIII's formulation has since been supported by a teaching of the Congregation for the Doctrine of the Faith, *Mysterium Ecclesiae* (June 24, 1973); see Congregation for the Doctrine of the Faith, *Declaration in Defense of the Catholic Doctrine on the Church against Certain Errors of the Present Day* (June 24, 1973), esp. no. 5, http://www.vatican.va/roman_curia/congregations/cfaith/documents/ rc_con_cfaith_doc_19730705_mysterium-ecclesiae_en.html.

surprisingly transformative and prompt a sense of change. This kind of experience in turn can be broadened imaginatively to the entire Church throughout its history, so that this implicit sense of development extends beyond the life circumstances of the believer to tradition as such. Moreover, believers who are not educated in the historicity of doctrine often have the sense that the Holy Spirit is at work in their lives and in the Church in unprecedented ways. An implicit sense of development does not require education in the historicity of doctrine. Yet, this understanding of tradition, however it be aesthetically judged, most commonly comes through education and even specifically theological education. Aesthetic judgments about a developmental understanding of tradition, whether appreciative or unappreciative, are typically offered by those who are theologically literate.

Those who judge the developing tradition of the Church to be beautiful do so in a number of ways. If a classical aesthetics of tradition is inclined to identify the transcendental qualities of the beautiful and the good, a developmental aesthetics of tradition is inclined to identify the transcendental qualities of the beautiful and the true. Believers attracted to this modern aesthetics find special beauty in the developing conception's capacity to reconcile faithful claims for tradition's truth and the historical evidence of the how doctrine actually developed. From the perspective of this Catholic taste, there is no opposition between truthful secular knowledge and the sacred knowledge that resides in the deposit of faith. The unity of truth enables the believer to embrace, rather than resist, the factual record of Christian events and yet to affirm authentic continuity amid what might otherwise be seen as time's corrosive threat to tradition.[36] This sensibility, then, finds beauty in the eventfulness of tradition imagined as a different kind of Christian mimesis, one that regards the development of doctrine as an ever-changing reflection of the eventfulness of the divine life, particularly in its providential outreach to the temporality of creation. This divine eventfulness mirrored in tradition can be imagined as the perichoretic dynamism of the divine life itself, as ways in which the impassible God may yet mysteriously move and be moved in love, or as the event of incarnation that unfolds in the life, death, and

---

[36] On traditional continuity through the vagaries of time, see John E. Thiel, "The Analogy of Tradition," *Theological Studies* 66 (2005): 358–80.

resurrection of Jesus Christ. Typically, though, a developmental aesthetics locates God's beauty in the many ways the Holy Spirit is believed to be eventfully present to time, and so accentuates the pneumatological immanence of God in history. The surprising ways the Spirit brings the world to sanctification is the imagined object of this kind of Christian mimesis, and mimesis reflects the eventfulness of divine providence.

In this aesthetics, the beauty of eventfulness also appears in the way that the notion of a developing tradition enlivens the Council of Trent's teaching on the cooperative role of human agency in the encounter with divine grace. In its Decree on Justification, Trent formally defined the long-standing Catholic belief in the responsibility of free choice in accepting the offer of divine grace, and so affirmed the indispensability of human agency in contributing to the believer's justification.[37] Drawing on this Catholic anthropology, an aesthetics of development finds beauty in the ways that believers engage the presence of the Holy Spirit in the Church to enact both the recognized truth of tradition and the truth of tradition that has yet to be fully grasped. Believers are perceived by those attracted to this aesthetics as the receptive means through which the Holy Spirit works in bringing to fruition the beliefs and practices that take shape as tradition in the course of time. But more, believers are perceived as gracefully endowed with a supernatural *sensus fidei* that enables them to discern and articulate the truth of sacred tradition that both they and the Holy Spirit bring to reality, albeit in extraordinarily unequal ways.[38] Catholic mimesis in this aesthetic style appreciates the way the very temporality of tradition captures the truth of the economy of salvation that eventually unfolds on this side of the Last Judgment.

Whereas the classical aesthetics of tradition privileges the sense of sight and imagines the objects of tradition beautifully visible in a field of sacred space, the developmental aesthetics of tradition values the sense of hearing, which apprehends the sound of traditioning in the sequence of sacred time. In a reflection on Catholic aesthetics, one might assume too quickly that the aural dimensions of tradition

---

[37] Council of Trent, Session VI: Decree on Justification (January 13, 1547), in *Decrees of the Ecumenical Councils*, 2:671–78.

[38] Second Vatican Council, Dogmatic Constitution on the Church (*Lumen Gentium*), §12, in *Decrees of the Ecumenical Councils*, 2:858.

would be bound up in some way with the art form of sacred music. In point of fact, there are different styles of liturgical music that are more or less compatible with each of the two aesthetic sensibilities of tradition. The sound of tradition valued in the developmental aesthetics of tradition is the resonance of believers' voices giving expression to their faith, of talk in the Church about how the truth of the Holy Spirit takes shape as tradition. Often, this talk expresses the common faith of the Church, as happens in creedal recitation or in the prayer of the Mass. As much as the developmental aesthetics attends to the Church's common voice and finds its resonance beautiful, it finds beauty also in the sound of faithful voices expressing new perceptions of the Spirit's presence to the present moment and, through this act of hearing, finds beauty as well in the process of doctrinal development that faithful listening grasps and discerns.

These voices express themselves in different patterns of discourse that are heard in the Church in somewhat different registers of the traditionally beautiful. One common ecclesial discourse expresses a sense of what we might call "development-in-continuity," the customary reception of the age-old faith of the Church in the most recent circumstances of time and culture by which the tradition develops slowly and even imperceptibly, as past and present meanings encounter one another in the act of faith and prove to be mutually enlivening. At times, though, the voices that the community hears make claims to the faith that are strangely novel, since they are unfamiliar and even at odds with what has long been recognized and held as the orthodox tradition. For those inclined to the developmental aesthetics, such voiced claims are contributions to a genuine ecclesial dialogue about the Spirit's truthful presence, a dialogue judged to be beautiful even when, and perhaps even because, some of its voices clamor for the disruption of the traditionally given. In this dialogue, listening and speaking are practices that enhance an appreciation for the beauty of tradition that has been and will always be, as well as for tradition that may be in the process of coming to be.[39] Like any authentic conversation, this ecclesial dialogue is unpredictable in its direction and characterized by all sorts of twists and turns that authentic openness to the truth requires. For

---

[39] On dialogue in the Church, see Bradford E. Hinze, *Practices of Dialogue in the Roman Catholic Church: Aims and Obstacles, Lessons and Laments* (New York: Continuum, 2006).

those whose Catholic taste is inclined to the developmental aesthetics of tradition, this truth-seeking conversation itself is beautiful both in its devoted efforts to name the purposes of the Spirit at work in time and, when truthfully founded on the *sensus fidei*, as a possible mimesis of God's revelation in and through sacred tradition.

Catholic Aesthetics and Theological Styles

Whereas the classical aesthetics of tradition is quite old, extending from the early medieval period to our day, the developmental aesthetics of tradition is a relatively recent arrival in Catholic history, appearing initially in the nineteenth century but not flourishing until the time of Vatican II. Thus, the effective engagement of these Catholic sensibilities is a post–Vatican II phenomenon. As we have seen, these aesthetics are not mutually exclusive. Contemporary Catholics who are especially inclined to the classical aesthetics often recognize and embrace the truth and beauty of the developmental aesthetics. The foundational status of the classical aesthetics ensures that its values are affirmed and appreciated by believers inclined to the developmental aesthetics. And yet, at times how these aesthetics are practiced in ecclesial life can become occasions for forming Catholic identities that are factional and exclusive. In such cases, they tragically reduce an encounter with the beauty of tradition and, through it, an encounter with the beauty of God to a fetish that is configured to represent all that is authentically Catholic.

Theologians share these same Catholic tastes and adopt interpretive styles that express their sensibilities. Those attracted to the classical aesthetics are drawn to a theological style that finds edification in the close description of the traditionally valorized reception of Scripture and tradition. In this approach, tradition itself becomes a kind of canonical structure that sets the boundaries for legitimate theological reflection. Theology in this style judges the tradition to be so beautiful that any other possible theological resource is at best distracting and at worst a deviation from its sacred truth. The tradition within which theology reflects is regarded as ostensible in its clarity, its teaching as manifestly visible as the revelatory genre itself. Theology in this style is configured as a mimesis of tradition's unchanging permanence, the beauty of its constructive art defined by its meticulous faithfulness.

Those attracted to the developmental aesthetics are drawn to a theological style keen on exploring the truthful relations between Scripture and tradition, on the one hand, and the changing circumstances of history and culture on the other. In this approach, the theologian often chooses some dimension of worldly wisdom judged to be truthful as a means of elucidating the meaningfulness of tradition for the present moment. This theological act of mediation is interpretively dialogical. It purports to capture the ecclesial dialogue about the Spirit's immanence to which the whole Church listens and whose truth the theologian tries to discern, in order to articulate the authentic development of doctrine. The Spirit's activity and its moving mimesis in the life of the Church is what is judged beautiful in this aesthetics, and the beauty of theology in this style lies in the degree to which its constructive art captures the truthful dynamism of the Spirit's presence in developing tradition.

These theological styles, quite like the aesthetics they express, all too easily become markers of Catholic difference, and this is especially so among the theologically literate—theologians, the magisterium, and educated Catholics—whose knowledge of the historicity of tradition is a prerequisite for making explicit judgments about the comparative value of these aesthetics and their accompanying theological styles. Conflict between the styles emerges when one regards the other as deficient in principle simply because the style negatively judged is not the one prioritized. The ancient status of the classical aesthetics and its foundational character in Catholic sensibility makes it especially susceptible to this sort of exclusive judgment, though both the classical and developmental aesthetics, each in its own way, can be myopic in their regard for the full range of the traditionally beautiful.

At its best, the classical aesthetics highlights the beauty of the Christ event, which is the source of the very divine revelation that theology interprets. But this dedication to the clarity of the Christ event itself can sometimes lead to impatience with the ambiguous dimensions of a tradition that courses through time and so does change. This impatience can be and has been exercised in a variety of ways that attempt to reduce tradition's temporality, plurality, and ambiguity to a permanence, singularity, and clarity that it does not and should not have. These failures of the classical aesthetic take shape theologically in the expectations that authentic theology will be classically homogeneous and not pluralistic, that it will conform to the focused lucidity of the propositional formulae of the *Catechism of the Catholic Church*,[40] and that the faithful work of the theologian involves explaining and defending the current state of the *Catechism* and the pronouncements of the magisterium. At its best, the developmental aesthetics of tradition appreciates the beauty of the Spirit's ongoing presence to the Church and the world, as well as the beauty of the graceful discernment of that presence by the community of believers. But this attunement to the mysterious character of tradition's truthful change that unfolds in ecclesial dialogue can sometimes lead to impatience with the clearly visible parameters of the ancient tradition, in which what was once dialogue has now become devout recitation. This impatience can be and has been exercised in a variety of ways that imagine the truth claims of the present moment to supersede the authority of proven tradition simply because of their contemporaneity, as though the permanence of tradition in its temporal expanse could be instantly eclipsed by the most recent novel claim for traditional truth. These failures of the developmental aesthetics take shape theologically in the expectations that human experience is the preeminent source of theology, that sinfulness is endemic in principle to the visible and hierarchical structures of the Church, and that the magisterium's conservative voice cannot find a place in the kind of dialogue that this theological style judges to be beautiful.

As Elaine Scarry has observed: "Beauty, sooner or later, brings us into contact with our own capacity for making errors. The beautiful, almost without any effort of our own, acquaints us with the mental event of conviction, and so pleasurable a mental state is this that ever afterwards one is willing to labor, struggle, wrestle with the world to locate enduring sources of conviction—to locate what is true."[41] Often, though, the pleasure of conviction leads those who enjoy it to narrow their conceptions of the true and the beautiful for the sake of a skewed sense of their complete capture, a state of affairs that unfortunately prevails as much in the Church as it does in the world. The failures of each Catholic sensibility explain much of the polarization

---

[40] *Catechism of the Catholic Church*, 2nd ed. (Vatican City: Libreria Editrice Vaticana; Washington, DC: United States Catholic Conference, 2000).

[41] Elaine Scarry, *On Beauty and Being Just* (Princeton, NJ: Princeton University Press, 1999), 31.

in the Church between believers, and the ways these failures manifest themselves theologically explain much of the polarization in the Church between theologians, and between theologians and the magisterium. All of these parties—which is to say the entire community of faith—would do well to reflect on how these failures, as errors of aesthetic reductionism, are detrimental to the rich unity of the Church that appears only in the wholeness of tradition's beauty grasped by each Catholic sensibility in its own limited way.

Perhaps the analysis of Catholic taste offered here can be helpful in embracing the aesthetic pluralism that does indeed exist in the Church, the deep Catholic desires for the beauty of tradition and finally for the beauty of God that both aesthetics share, and the obligation on the part of each sensibility, pressed upon it by its Catholic commitment to the one body of Christ, to value the other sensibility and its theological style as a perspective on sacred tradition without which the Church's appreciation for tradition's goodness and truth would be diminished. There is an ecclesial need in our day for believers to reflect on how the Catholic sensibilities and theological styles can and should be sources of mutual appreciation rather than markers of division.

We have seen that each of the two Catholic aesthetics prioritizes a particular sense experience to which it accords special powers in apprehending sacred beauty—seeing for the classical aesthetics and hearing for the developmental aesthetics. Aquinas, we should recall, concluded that the two senses of seeing and hearing are aesthetic by nature in their shared capacity to apprehend beauty, an ability that directly eludes the other senses. As senses in the service of an aesthetics of tradition, seeing and hearing turn to different kinds of objects in order to appreciate sacred beauty that is imagined in different ways. Yearning for the consummate sight of the beatific vision, the eyes of faith anticipate its beautiful and unchanging perfection in the permanence of tradition that appears in the space of tradition's sacred visibility. Enamored of the Spirit's living presence, the ears of faith strain to hear how God moves the Church in time, changing it—sometimes slowly, sometimes suddenly—ever toward the fulfillment of the kingdom of God that will eschatologically encounter the depth of the divine mystery. Finally, faithful seeing and hearing apprehend the same divine beauty in the same sacred tradition and are engaged interpretively in the same theological task. The Church would be the poorer were it to lack one of these aesthetics, just as it would be poorer were it to lack either of the styles of Catholic theology that serve these sensibilities. The Church is poorer now to the extent that these Catholic tastes tend to regard each other suspiciously rather than appreciate how each sensibility complements the other and how both together apprehend the beauty of tradition much more fully than either may alone.

As an aid in fostering this broader appreciation, I propose the fifth-century teaching of the Council of Chalcedon as a rule of faith that extends analogously beyond the nature of the incarnation to the proper relationship between the two Catholic aesthetics. The Chalcedonian decree condemned the christological belief of the monophysites who believed that only the immutable divine nature of Christ defined his person to the exclusion of his full humanity. The monophysites were scandalized by the thought that the Savior's unchanging divinity could dwell in real relationship to a created nature that was completely human, coursing in the finite conditions of time and change. In response, Chalcedon sanctioned the fourth-century Cappadocian theology that insisted on the hypostatic union of complete divinity and complete humanity in the incarnate person of Christ.[42] We might very well view the beauty of tradition and of its theological interpretation in a similar way. The beauty of tradition lies in the mysterious union of its permanence and its development, of its unchanging and changing dimensions that together comprise the living unity of tradition. In much the same manner, the theological styles interpretively inclined to each of these traditionally beautiful qualities are themselves only dimensions of the unity of the theological task.

Even though the teaching of Chalcedon defines the orthodox faith on the person of Christ, many Christians throughout the centuries have been tempted to imagine the Savior in the manner of the monophysites, as fully divine but not as fully human. To some degree, this latent monophysitism stems from the status of divine immutability as an aesthetic paradigm in Christian imagination. Just as the tradition long resisted the notion that divine immutability enters the creaturely realm divorced in the person of Christ from the definitively human,

---

[42] Council of Chalcedon, "Definition of the Faith," in *Decrees of the Ecumenical Councils*, 1:86–87.

so too should contemporary believers resist an aesthetics of tradition that finds beauty only in its permanence at the expense of its development. The theological styles inclined more or less to a classical or developmental aesthetics of tradition are obliged to foster an appreciation for both senses of Catholic beauty in their theologies, for only through such a comprehensive aesthetics can they do justice to what is beautifully old and beautifully new in tradition and, through it, all that is old and new in our encounter with the beauty of God.[43]

---

[43] I am grateful to Roger Haight, SJ, Jeannine Hill-Fletcher, Bradford Hinze, Paul Lakeland, Elena Procario-Foley, Michele Saracino, and John Slotemaker for their criticism of this article in its draft stages.

PART 2

Disputed Questions

CHAPTER 5

From Dialectic to Disjunction
A Paradigm Shift of Catholic Interpretations of Secularism

Dominic Doyle

  This chapter explores some of the hermeneutical issues surrounding discussions of the notions of the secular, the post-secular, and the post-Christian. Its goal is twofold: first, to identify some clarifying developments in the understanding of the process of secularization; second, in light of these developments, to advance an original theological response. The clarifying development centers on the influential use of the interpretative lens of "disjunction" in the discourse on secularity—in particular, in terms of the contradictions (a) within Christian life and thought and (b) between regressive aspects of Christian identity and more progressive, broadly accepted goods of modern culture. The theological response consists in a reformulation of standard accounts of theological virtue ethics, indebted to but different from the standard Thomistic account—and so hopefully more adequate to the task of addressing and reversing contemporary disbelief.
  Two arguments are advanced to attain these goals. (1) The hermeneutics of "disjunction," as a way to give a theological interpretation of some of the issues surrounding the phenomena of a post-Christian society, is an advance on the notion of "dialectics" as used by mid-twentieth-century Catholic thinkers such as Bernard Lonergan. (2) Nonetheless, the term "dialectics," understood in a more flexible and, especially, reflexive sense (i.e., as applying to the subject—in this case, the church and believers), remains a serviceable term that in fact

provides greater control over the theological discourse on secularization. The theological virtues function as a kind of test case that gives greater theological content to the discussion.

Why focus on the theological virtues? The selection of this topic is fitting because it is a striking example of one of the common theological responses to the rise of secularization: namely, the reaffirmation of Christian identity through the proclamation of distinct beliefs and the cultivation of distinct traits. (The other major response, one could say, is to seek points of contact with the secular culture through dialogical correlation.[1]) Throughout the tradition, the theological virtues have been identified as a clear, summative way to express the heart of Christian identity, for example, in Augustine's *Enchiridion* and Thomas Aquinas's *Compendium theologiae* (indeed, these virtues form the basis of Aquinas's more systematic presentation in the *secunda secundae* of the *Summa theologiae*). Most recently, these three virtues of faith, hope, and charity have been the subject of three of the encyclicals (*Deus Caritas Est*, *Spe Salvi*, and, for the most part, *Lumen Fidei*) written by Pope Benedict XVI, whose papacy was desirous of reaffirming Christian identity in an increasingly secular Europe.[2] The focus on the theological virtues, then, is a time-honored strategy for expressing the heart of Christian thought and life. It is therefore no surprise to see their re-articulation at the center of Joseph Ratzinger/Pope Benedict's contribution to the intellectual renewal of the church.[3]

---

[1] This standard, broad-stroke picture often invokes contrasts between thinkers such as, on the one hand, Karl Barth and Hans Urs von Balthasar and, on the other, Paul Tillich and David Tracy.

[2] Pope Benedict XVI, Encyclical *Deus Caritas Est* (December 25, 2005), http://w2.vatican.va/content/benedict-xvi/en/encyclicals/documents/hf_ben-xvi_enc_20051225_deus-caritas-est.html; Encyclical *Spe Salvi* (November 30, 2007), http://w2.vatican.va/content/benedict-xvi/en/encyclicals/documents/hf_ben-xvi_enc_20071130_spe-salvi.html; Pope Francis [and Pope Benedict XVI], Encyclical *Lumen Fidei* (June 29, 2013), http://w2.vatican.va/content/francesco/en/encyclicals/documents/papa-francesco_20130629_enciclica-lumen-fidei.html.

[3] For an earlier example of Ratzinger's exposition of the theological virtues, see Joseph Ratzinger, *Aus Christus Schauen: Einübung in Glaube, Hoffnung, Liebe* (Freiburg im Breisgau: Herder, 1989); Ratzinger, *To Look on Christ*, trans. Robert Nowell (New York: Crossroad, 1991), republished as *The Yes of Jesus Christ: Spiritual Exercises in Faith, Hope, and Love* (New York: Crossroad, 2005).

Inspired by and indebted to this tradition, I want to argue for a new understanding of the relationship between the theological virtues in the context of a secular age. This attempt to construe a new account of the nexus of faith, hope, and love ultimately issues from the conviction that it is not possible to summon these virtues out of their revered place in the tradition and simply use them as a powerful rallying cry that presents the core of Christian identity to a post-Christian culture. They are not timeless instruments that can be picked up from the theological toolbox and set to work for the purposes of re-building the church in an increasingly secular culture. Rather, as these virtues are invoked, experienced, and understood within that secular culture, they themselves undergo significant changes. It is for this reason, developed below, that I propose an understanding of the theological virtues that attempts to do justice to the fact that Christian thought and practice—whether it likes it or not, or even whether it sees it or not—is already deeply entangled in the dynamics of secularization. For even the most recent and traditional reaffirmation of the theological virtues in Pope Benedict's triad of encyclicals has as its proximate context the reassertion of Christian identity precisely as threatened by the surrounding secular culture. Thus, even the very decision to select and privilege the theological virtues as worthy of communication is already implicated in the broader discourse on disbelief.

The original contribution of this chapter will be to make explicit and incorporate centrally the experience of disbelief in the very experience of these core markers of Christian identity. In other words, the new account of the theological virtues that I am advancing here recognizes from the outset the impact of secularization on theological discourse. Indeed, it incorporates the rise of disbelief as one of the key dynamics for how to understand the experiential unfolding of these three traits of faith, hope, and love at the core of Christian identity. The end result of this argument will be to understand how the theological virtues are not simply representative of one standard response to secularization (namely, the reaffirmation of identity) but rather include the seemingly contrasting theological strategy of seeking relevance through dialogical engagement.

Context

Before spelling out this argument, it is helpful to give some of the proximate context of this discussion: a research project called "Faith in a Secular Age" sponsored by the Catholic University of America's Council for Research in Values and Philosophy (CRVP). It began in 2012 under the leadership of George McLean (president of the CRVP), José Casanova, and Charles Taylor and generated over a dozen research groups from around the globe that met numerous times over the next few years. Some of its impressive fruits have already been published in *Church and People: Disjunctions in a Secular Age*, which includes essays by Taylor, Casanova, Danièle Hervieu-Léger, Tomáš Halík, and Francis Oakley.[4] If *A Catholic Modernity?* gave Taylor an opportunity to expand on the implicit theological commitments that were operative yet undeveloped in *Sources of the Self*, then this volume (shepherded by another impressive, bridge-building Catholic public intellectual-cum-entrepreneur) gives Taylor an opportunity to expand on the nascent ecclesiological commitments operative yet undeveloped in his more explicitly theological reflection on secularization in *A Secular Age*.[5]

This research project initially focused on four areas identified by Taylor that exhibit a disconnect between, on the one hand, the teaching and communicative style of the magisterium and, on the other, the culture and aspirations of contemporary Western culture. (It is worth noting that this diagnosis was made in 2010, well before the resignation of Pope Benedict XVI.) These disjunctions between "church and people" are as follows:

(1) The cultural attitude of spiritual seeking and its attendant proliferation of questions and questioning, in contrast to the magisterial assertion and reassertion of already formulated answers, with the attendant message of a seeming inability or unwillingness to listen.

---

[4] Charles Taylor, José Casanova, George McLean, eds., *Church and People: Disjunctions in a Secular Age* (Cardinal Station, Washington, DC: Council for Research in Values and Philosophy, 2012).

[5] Charles Taylor, *A Catholic Modernity? Charles Taylor's Marianist Award Lecture, with Responses by William M. Shea, Rosemary Luling Haughton, George Marsden, and Jean Bethke Elshtain*, ed. James L. Heft (New York: Oxford University Press, 1999); Taylor, *Sources of the Self: The Making of the Modern Identity* (Cambridge, MA: Harvard University Press, 1989); Taylor, *A Secular Age* (Cambridge, MA: Belknap Press/Harvard University Press, 2007).

(2) The recognition in Western polities of the importance of devolution and personal responsibility, in contrast to the centralization of power within the institutional church and the concomitant lack of transparency and emphasis on obedience.

(3) The growing cultural acceptance of greater diversity in terms of sexual ethics and gender roles and, more broadly, the recognition of the historical and sometimes fallible nature of moral convictions, in contrast to magisterial formulations of gender identity and sexual ethics on the basis of essentialist, ahistorical, and non-revisable appeals to nature and natural law categories.

(4) The recognition of many different and authentic forms of spirituality in contemporary culture, not only in other religions but also outside official religious allegiance, all of which invites respectful dialogue and can enrich the church's own spiritual traditions, in contrast to an overly critical attitude to alternative modes of spirituality and the implication of the completeness of Christian spirituality.

These disjunctions, one may surmise, play no small role in contributing to the high rate of attrition of Catholics from the Church in the contemporary West. More basically, they also capture the often startling contradiction between official Church teaching and the actual practice of the majority of the faithful. One of the most striking examples of this, of course, is the fact that 87 percent of US Catholics think that the use of artificial contraception—condemned as "intrinsically evil" by the magisterium—is "morally acceptable."[6] These are the disjunctions Taylor diagnosed in 2010 and that generated an impressive research project.

At its conception, this project might have been described as a theological version of the owl of Minerva—surveying the various ways in which the Catholic Church was precipitating its own decline. With the election of Pope Francis, however, the project conveys the sense of not so much taking flight at dusk as preparing to greet a new,

---

[6] The phrase "intrinsically evil" occurs in US Catholic Conference, *Catechism of the Catholic Church* (New York: Doubleday, 1994), section 2370 (although it does not appear in the encyclical passage there cited, *Humanae Vitae* 14, which instead uses the term "intrinsece inhonestum"). The poll on Catholics and artificial contraception that used the phrase "morally acceptable" was Gallup's 2012 Values and Beliefs survey; a summary can be found here: http://www.gallup.com/poll/154799/americans-including-catholics-say-birth-control-morally.aspx.

long-awaited dawn. To put it more prosaically, the tenor of the project evolved from a retrospective, cautionary, even somewhat gloomy survey, into a more hopeful attempt to articulate new directions for those "new itineraries" commended by Taylor in *A Secular Age*. In other words, the project has taken on a more optimistic turn from identifying hardened disjunctions to articulating new visions. As a result, there was increased positivity in its more recent work, an international conference co-sponsored by the Center for Research in Values and Philosophy and the Pontifical Gregorian University titled "Renewing the Church in a Secular Age: Holistic Dialogue and Kenotic Vision" (held in Rome in March 2015). This conference included presentations from Charles Taylor, José Casanova, Hans Joas, and William Desmond and advanced a fourfold vision of the church (somewhat related to the four disjunctions above): (1) attentive to the experience of the laity (2) engaged in discernment about its collective future, and therefore (3) encouraging and welcoming the spiritual seeker and (4) in a pluralistic context. In the spirit of the origins of this research project, scholars across the world (but mainly from North America and Europe) were invited to collaborate in their own regions in order to advance the shared goal of the renewal of the church in a way that squarely faces its manifold challenges.

Such is the remote context of this essay. I now offer a modest contribution to this goal. The value of the contribution lies in offering a theological language with which to understand, express, and do justice to the penetrating and sometimes uncomfortable insights of recent accounts of the historical sources of secularization.

From Dialectics to Disjunction

In the mid-twentieth-century heyday of the "Catholic moment" in the United States, leading Catholic thinkers such as John Courtney Murray and Bernard Lonergan gave rhetorically persuasive and philosophically compelling Christian responses to modern secularization. At the climax of Lonergan's *Insight*, for example, and also in his *Method in Theology*, this response was made through a powerful appeal to the redemptive value of faith, hope, and charity in countering (respectively) the ideology, despair, and hatred that were judged to be the fruits of atheistic thought that by 1945 had resulted in the collapse of European civilization. Thus, in the final chapter of *Insight*, Lonergan arranges the "heuristic structure of the solution" to the problem of evil in terms of the theological virtues. Beginning with charity, a virtue present in the will, Lonergan draws heavily on the notion of dialectic and makes a clarifying comparison with the intellectual process of dialectics:

> Now the will can contribute to the solution of the problem of the social surd inasmuch as it adopts a dialectic attitude that parallels the dialectical method of intellect. The dialectic method of intellect consists in grasping that the social surd neither is intelligible nor is to be treated as intelligible. The corresponding dialectical attitude of the will is to return good for evil. For it is only inasmuch as men are willing to meet evil with good, to love their enemies, to pray for those that persecute and calumniate them, that the social surd is a potential good.[7]

Echoes of this dialectic process are found in his account of the theological virtue of hope. This virtue "will take issue with the conflicting tendencies and considerations. On one hand, then, it will be a decision against man's despair. . . . On the other hand, it will be a decision against presumption."[8] Finally, Lonergan presents the virtue of faith in the more standard terms of dialectic, namely, reversing false positions and promoting true ones.[9]

> There is needed in the present a universally accessible and permanently effective manner of pulling men's minds out of the counterpositions, of fixing them in the positions, of securing for them the certitude that God exists and that he has provided a solution which they are to acknowledge and to accept.[10]

In all of these three presentations of the theological virtues, it is striking to see how Lonergan expresses the nature and purpose of each virtue (either explicitly in terms of faith or implicitly but clearly in terms of faith, and implicitly in terms of hope) in the language of dialectics.

---

[7] Bernard J. F. Lonergan, *Insight: A Study of Human Understanding* (Toronto: University of Toronto Press, 1992), 721.

[8] Ibid., 723.

[9] On the nature of dialectic as developing positions and reversing counter-positions, see Bernard J. F. Lonergan, *Method in Theology* (Toronto: University of Toronto, 1990), 249–50.

[10] Lonergan, *Insight*, 725.

Later, in *Method in Theology*, the proximate context of the discussion of the theological virtues focus shifts *from* the discussion of the unrestricted desire to know *to* the more practical question of the cultural mediation of religion. Hence, Lonergan gives a more integrated and urgent statement of the role of the theological virtues in reversing cultural decline.

> Decline disrupts culture with conflicting ideologies. It afflicts on individuals the social, economic, and psychological pressures that for human frailty amount to determinism. It multiplies and heaps up the abuses and absurdities that breed resentment, hatred, anger, violence. It is not propaganda and it is not argument but religious *faith* that will liberate human reasonableness from its ideological prisons. It is not the promises of men but religious *hope* that can enable men to resist the vast pressures of social decay. If passions are to quiet down, if wrongs are not to be exacerbated, not ignored, not merely palliated, but acknowledged and removed, then human possessiveness and human pride have to be replaced by religious *charity*, by the charity of the suffering servant, by self-sacrificing love. Men are sinners. . . . They have to learn with humility that religious development is dialectical.[11]

In this way, Lonergan advances the classic Thomistic understanding of the theological virtues as an organic development (or "generation") of faith, hope, and charity that perfect the natural desire of the intellect and will for wisdom and love.[12] That classic position is summarized by Aquinas as follows: "Faith shows the end, hope moves to the end, charity unites with the end."[13] Insofar as this model conveys the sense of a gradual and linear unfolding, it differs quite considerably in tone

---

[11] Lonergan, *Method in Theology,* 117–18 (emphasis added).

[12] For a brief overview of Thomas Aquinas's understanding of the difference and relation between the theological virtues, see Dominic Doyle, *The Promise of Christian Humanism: Thomas Aquinas on Hope* (New York: Crossroad, 2012), 80–94.

[13] "Fides autem ostendit [finem], spes facit tendere in eum, caritas unit" (*Commentary on 1 Timothy*, Caput I, Lectio II in *Opera Omnia*, Parmae, 2nd ed. [New York: Musurgia Publishers, 1949], 587). The context of this lapidary quotation reads: "Virtutes autem theologicae ultimum finem habent pro objecto; aliae autem sunt circa ea quae sunt ad finem. Virtutes ergo omnes respiciunt theologicas sicut finem. Inter theologicas vero illa plus habet rationem finis quae propinquius se habet ad ultimum finem. Fides autem ostendit eum, spes facit tendere in eum, caritas unit. Ergo omnes ordinantur ad caritatem; et sic dicitur caritas finis praeceptorum."

from Lonergan's description. That historically minded account presents these virtues not so much as the elevating perfection of a faculty psychology but as an escalating conflict with a cultural reality.[14] This dramatic antagonism Lonergan described as "dialectical" because it involves a "concrete unfolding of linked but opposed principles of change" (that is, between faith/hope/charity and ideology/despair/hatred).[15] In a more general way, Murray too shared in this robust theological engagement with modern secular culture, likewise advocating the reversal of secular principles by theological ones. Something of Murray's more triumphalist spirit can be seen in his confident assertion that the purpose of theology is to mount "a triumphantly argumentative defense of the faith against error."[16]

Today's situation is different. In light of the continued decline of Christian belief in the West, the non-materialization of the hopes expressed by a Murray or a Christopher Dawson for the revival of the Catholic Christian foundations of Western civilization, and, further, in light of the damning evidence of scandalous internal shortcomings with the Church itself, many leading Catholic thinkers talk less of dialectical opposition with modern secular culture and opt instead for a diagnosis of disjunctions between the Church's official teaching and its actual life, or, more broadly, between what the Church offers and what the people it serves seek.

These disjunctions have been diagnosed in a wide range of areas. Two recent and prominent examples in the area of the historical study of secularization are provided by Michael Buckley and Charles Taylor. Buckley gives an account of modern atheism as arising from the contradiction between an apologetics that used the *impersonal* evidence of physics to prove the existence of a *personal* god and, the further contradiction between its philosophic form of argumentation and the religious nature of the experience that it purported to defend. Taylor's account focuses on the origin of an exclusive humanism in the very reforming impulses of late medieval and early modern Christian

---

[14] He does, though, note the perfective element in his recognition of the "genetic" nature of charity. "As genetic process, it develops generic potentiality to its specific perfection" (*Insight*, 722).

[15] *Insight*, 242.

[16] John Courtney Murray, "Towards a Theology of the Layman," *Theological Studies* 5, no. 1 (March 1944): 43–75, at 62.

movements. One could note analogous patterns of internal contradictions within Christianity that gave rise to disbelief. Buckley cites James Turner's *Without God, Without Creed: The Origins of Unbelief in America* and Alan Kors's *The Orthodox Sources of Disbelief* as historical studies that resonate with his thesis.[17] In light of this recent and compelling body of evidence, it is worth developing a theological response.

If we now turn from the historical contradictions that seeded secularization and focus on the contemporary contradictions that threaten belief, perhaps the most insightful commentator is Taylor himself. As noted, he sees several such disjunctions (that are the focus of the CUA think-tank mentioned earlier). To recall just two examples, there exists, according to Taylor:

> (1) a disjunction between, on the one hand, the spiritual seeking that is widespread in the West and, on the other, the clearly defined answers delivered in magisterial documents
>
> (2) a disjunction between, on the one hand, a media-exacerbated centralization of power in the papacy and, on the other, the need to realize the Second Vatican Council's desire for the Church to draw more moral authority and practical wisdom from the local bishops[18]

These historical and contemporary examples show an important trend in Catholic intellectual life: Catholic identity is no longer straightforwardly discussed in terms of dialectical opposition with secular culture but rather in terms of (in the past) internal tensions within Christian life and thought that generated atheism and (in the present) sharp contradictions between what the church offers and what many in the secular West seek. This shift—*from* dialectical opposition against secular culture *to* a reflexive awareness of the internal contradictions within Catholicism as it dwells within (and even in some way has brought about) a secular culture—this shift, from dialectics to disjunction, constitutes a significant development in Catholic theological attempts to understand the reality of secularization. And, indeed, this preference for disjunction over dialectic can be seen in other chapters of this book. For example, in the context of reconciliation studies, Robert Schreiter in this volume

---

[17] Michael J. Buckley, *Denying and Disclosing God: The Ambiguous Progress of Modern Atheism* (New Haven, CT: Yale University Press, 2005), 29.

[18] Cf. Taylor, Casanova, and McLean, *Church and People*.

has noted his preference for paradox, as contrasted with a Hegelian sense of dialectic that sees the absolute Geist working through history.[19]

In passing, it is worth noting that the deep philosophical influence behind these interpretations is Hegel rather than Aquinas (both Buckley's and Taylor's early work engaged Hegel).[20] This seems appropriate because Hegel provides tools that are absent in the Thomistic tradition, such as an analysis of the social formation of identity through shared forms of life, and the historical transformation of identity through the outworking of conflict and tension. It should also be noted, of course, that Lonergan was enormously influential for Catholic thought and did not hesitate to critique inadequate practices and thought-patterns within Catholicism. It therefore follows that I should emphasize that my reservations about Lonergan's use of dialectic arise from the fact that he applied it to the theological virtues in a non-reflexive way that simply opposed cultural decline. My purpose here could be seen as simply applying Lonergan's own critique of internal shortcomings to his account of the theological virtues.[21]

How does this "disjunction model" interpret the theological virtues, given its more sober and chastened acknowledgment of the origin, spread, and hold of secularization? We can begin to glean an answer to this question from one (newly famous) member of CUA's Council for Research in Values and Philosophy, Tomáš Halík, the Czech priest and winner of the 2014 Templeton Prize, who, living under communist rule, has experienced more than most of us what secularization means. I will briefly present his position and then offer some suggestions for how to develop and reframe his basic insights. Halík was drawn to

---

[19] See also in this volume Francis Schüssler Fiorenza's exploration of William Connolly's image of a crumpled handkerchief, as distinct from mountain imagery of peak experiences.

[20] Charles Taylor, *Hegel* (New York: Cambridge University Press, 1975) and *Hegel and Modern Society* (New York: Cambridge University Press, 1979). Michael Buckley, *Motion and Motion's God: Thematic Variations in Aristotle, Cicero, Newton, and Hegel* (Princeton, NJ: Princeton University Press, 1971).

[21] Lonergan clearly recognized decline within the church, and so it is consistent with his thought to apply the notion of dialectic internally (e.g., *Method*, 291: "As there is decline, there is also the problem of undoing it . . . not only in the world but also in the church"). But, to my knowledge, he does not take this route by applying it to our understanding of the theological virtues specifically, unless that is his meaning in his discussion of "imperfect" theological virtues (*Insight*, 748–50).

Christianity because, in his words, "it was a religion of paradoxes."[22] In his popular book *Patience with God*, he accordingly describes faith, hope, and love as "three forms of patience for confronting the absence of God."[23] More radically, Halík offers a new interpretation of Thérèse de Lisieux's experience of unbelief as a "solidarity with unbelievers [that serves as] a hermeneutic key *toward new theological reflection on present-day society, its spiritual climate, and the church's mission at the present time.*"[24] As faith and hope fall away—she literally "died without faith"—all that remains is total reliance upon divine love alone. From this reading of Thérèse, Halík asserts the following paradox: "Faith can overcome unbelief only by embracing it."[25]

This is a radical interpretation, born of a deep spirituality that is keenly attuned to the disjunctions and paradoxes of contemporary Christian life in the secular West. Nonetheless, it seems to me that some elements of this disjunctive interpretation render the theological virtues unintelligible, or at least unrecognizable (for example, the literal removal of faith, or faith as an embrace of unbelief). So, in the next section, I will explore how one can (to adapt Augustine) "embrace the unbeliever, not the unbelief." Or, in other words, how one can avoid Halík's conflation of epistemic states (which differ between believer and unbeliever) with ethical stances or sense of spiritual quest (which can overlap to some degree).

Reconsidering Dialectic

In order to do this, we must first consider a slightly different meaning of the word "dialectic." As we saw, Lonergan defined dialectic as "a concrete unfolding of linked but opposed principles of change." Another meaning, though, that avoids both this oppositional sense and the fundamentalist Hegelian vision of absolute *Geist* unfolding in history is Michael Buckley's rendition of dialectic as, simply, a way of inquiry that "moves through negation to resolve contradiction in a

---

[22] Tomáš Halík, *Patience with God: The Story of Zacchaeus Continuing in Us* (New York: Doubleday, 2009), 26.
[23] Ibid., ix.
[24] Ibid., 36.
[25] Ibid., 31, 35.

higher unity."²⁶ This understanding of dialectic, as we have seen, lies at the root of his and Taylor's interpretation of modern disbelief: in that they both identify internal tensions or contradictions within past Christian thought or life that generated atheistic denials, but, further, that those atheistic denials can in turn be denied, insofar as they create the conditions for a deeper and more authentic appropriation of faith. Thus, what Taylor calls the "fragility" of belief or Buckley calls the "finitude" of religious ideas are not necessarily reasons to permanently reject belief (although they are often taken that way) but rather can be seen as stages in the dialectical deepening of a person's belief.²⁷

It is this sense of dialectic, I believe, that can generate a new understanding of the theological virtues as they are received and experienced in a secular culture.²⁸ This position incorporates the spiritual insight of how faith is remoulded amid the disjunctive and fragilizing conditions of contemporary belief (as Taylor would have it) but without too quickly—or even unintelligibly—appealing to paradox. In this reading of the theological virtues, one begins by acknowledging two key internal tensions in faith:

(1) between the strong *conviction* faith imparts and the slim *evidence* it possesses; and,

(2) if that first tension is denied and its attendant difficulties suppressed, there arises a deeper tension between, on the one hand, the consequent rigidity that clings to this or that partial aspect of the faith and, on the other, the pilgrim life faith is meant to begin.

These internal tensions give rise to a certain inquietude or restlessness within faith. Contradiction, as Aristotle long ago observed, generates movement.²⁹ And so the very nature of faith, as well as the sometimes inauthentic ways one clings to it, involves contradiction or at least an

---

²⁶ Michael Buckley, *At the Origins of Modern Atheism* (New Haven, CT: Yale University Press, 1987), 23. See also further discussion in Buckley, *Denying and Disclosing God* and Buckley's response there to John Milbank's criticism (28–29).

²⁷ For Taylor on the fragilization of belief, see *A Secular Age*, 303–4. For Buckley on the "finitude" of religious ideas, see chapter 5 of *Denying and Disclosing God* ("The Radical Finitude of Religious Ideas: Atheism and Contemplation").

²⁸ I have developed this argument at greater length in "The Dialectic Unfolding of the Theological Virtues," *Gregorianum* 92, no. 4 (2011): 687–708.

²⁹ Aristotle, *Physics* 1.7.191a3-22.

inner tension that gives rise to a movement or a searching that seeks to resolve that tension.

The partial resolution of this tension happens when the believer becomes a pilgrim—that is, when the first theological virtue opens up into the second theological virtue, hope. The advent of this second virtue brings into human experience its central features of movement or pilgrimage. It also enables the person to find a greater capacity to face difficulty and suffering. The classic definition of hope, after all, is the movement toward a future, difficult, yet possible good. Hope is therefore the virtue that is particularly well suited to undo any rigid or triumphal dogmatism of "bad faith" that results from the suppression of painful (and painfully obvious) disjunctions of contemporary belief. Hope thus negates the contradictions that arise when faith fixates on beliefs as a marker of a cultural boundary rather than as the beginning of eternal life.[30] But hope itself remains incomplete, for it only moves toward the goal but does not unite the person with it. Also, insofar as its motion refers only to the subject moved and his or her goal of eternal life, it contradicts the agapic, other-focused impulse of the gospel. And thus insofar as hope emphasizes transcendence toward eternity, it is brought back to earth by charity's participation in God's love for the world. Thus, just as faith is dialectically reworked by hope, so the imbalances that attend hope are dialectically reworked into a higher, more stable unity by charity. It is precisely the strength of a dialectical patterning of inquiry to hold with a higher viewpoint an evolving and complex intelligibility that cannot be reduced to a single term.[31] And so just as Christian life involves differentiated elements of intellectual assent, volitional seeking, and affective union, all of which are historically conditioned and, in a secular age, culturally fragile, so the corresponding mode of Christianity's theological expression of its

---

[30] See Aquinas's reformulation of Hebrews 11:6 into a precise definition of faith as "a habit of the mind whereby eternal life is begun in us, making the intellect assent to what is not seen" (*Summa theologiae* II-II, q. 4, a.1, my translation), http://www.corpusthomisticum.org/sth3001.html. See also *De Veritate*, q. 14, a. 2.

[31] "That is why Hegel holds that the ordinary viewpoint of identity has to be abandoned in philosophy in favour of a way of thinking which can be called dialectical in that it presents us with something which cannot be grasped in a single proposition or series of propositions. . . . The minimum cluster which can really do justice to reality is three propositions" (Taylor, *Hegel and Modern Society*, 15).

core identity must be dialectical. In fact, it is precisely the experience of disjunction that warrants the hermeneutics of dialectics for Christians trying to make sense of their identity in a secular age.

Conclusion

In this chapter, I have tried to identify a significant hermeneutical shift in Catholic interpretations of secularism *from* dialectic opposition *to* the diagnosis of self-defeating disjunctions that impair the Church's effective engagement with secularity. I then offered a coda that argued the term "dialectic" can be retrieved in a way that both avoids oppositional triumphalism and includes the insights of this new "disjunctive" hermeneutic. To illustrate this argument, I charted differing conceptions of the theological virtues, ending with a new account that sees them not only as transformative *ad extra* but also corrective *ad intra*.

This new interpretation, I believe, can mediate between two classic and differing theological responses to secular modernity, mentioned at the start of the this paper: identity or relevance. The focus on identity is one response and it was exemplified by Benedict XVI's encyclicals on the theological virtues. But if the focus on identity avoids institutional self-criticism, it invites suspicion. See, for example, Lieven Boeve's speculations that Benedict resigned because of the cognitive dissonance—i.e., disjunction—between his idealized view of the Church's identity and the sorry state of some of its actual life.[32] There may well be truth in this particular speculation and, more likely, in the general caution about idealized appeals to the Church's distinct identity. But be that as it may, we now need a way to reconceive of Christian identity *simultaneously* in terms of its key identity markers *and* in terms of the solvent effects of secularization. That is why I have argued that we should interpret the church's key identity markers—the theological virtues of faith, hope, and charity—not as an ideal type of a Christian virtue ethic that stands above the corrosive effects of secularization, but as itself already implicated in, and challenged by (and hopefully even deepened through), these inescapable but not permanent experiences of disjunction.

---

[32] Lieven Boeve, "Conversion and Cognitive Dissonance: Evaluating the Theological-Ecclesial Program of Joseph Ratzinger/Pope Benedict XVI," *Horizons* 40, no. 2 (2013): 242–54.

CHAPTER 6

A Theological Reading of Scripture?
Critical Problematic and Prophetic Vision in the Aftermath and Crossroads of Disciplinary Transformation

Fernando F. Segovia

Biblical studies today stands in the aftermath of a lengthy process of re-visioning and re-direction and as well as at the crossroads of ongoing disciplinary transformation. This affirmation I should like to situate and expand within the overall framework of contemporary critical opinion. I shall do so in three respects: general perception, actual evaluation, and historical consciousness.

First, regarding such a view of the present state of affairs, all critics, I should think, would be in fundamental agreement, regardless of methodological or theoretical anchoring. Who would disagree that major discursive and material changes have affected the discipline for some time now? Second, regarding disposition toward such a state of affairs, sharp disagreement rules the day among critics. The spectrum of opinion can be readily outlined. In some quarters such developments are decried as involving a regrettable and damaging loss of scholarly rigor. From this angle of vision, criticism is urged to respond with steadfast resistance and determination. In other quarters these changes are viewed as yielding a bewildering but inescapable critical landscape. From this perspective, the call is for explicit acknowledgment and outright coping, in one way or another. In yet other quarters such developments are hailed as constituting an imperative and salutary move in academic sophistication. From this angle of vision, criticism is urged to react by way of full embrace and sustained advancement. Lastly, on a sense of beginnings for this state of affairs, all critics, I should think, would agree, regardless of attitude, that this period of transformation started in the middle 1970s.

At this point, therefore, as the discipline approaches the fifty-year mark since the irruption of this process of transformation, critics, I would repeat, find themselves both in the wake of unrelenting and multidirectional changes and in the face of ever more expansive and more complex discursive discussions. As my affirmation at the beginning testifies, such has certainly been my case: I have been and remain acutely conscious of this process as well as of the need for theorization in this regard. On my own disposition toward this process, I would readily situate myself within the ranks of the last, and welcoming, critical formation outlined. Thus, I look upon this turn of events as very much in order and as decidedly beneficial. I see it, therefore, as a process that must be addressed and mapped, weighed and critiqued, appropriated and furthered. On the question of beginnings, I would agree as well that it began in the mid-1970s. In fact, for me the Society of Biblical Literature's launching of the journal *Semeia* in 1974, described from its inception as "experimental," functions as an ideal signifier in this regard. Indeed, I would propose the appearance of the first issue and its date of publication as the symbolic point of origins for the process of transformation—taken not in isolation but within a series of events, both preceding and following, that reflected a similar quest for re-visioning and re-direction. Given such a sense of historical contextualization, I view the year 2014 as the symbolic fortieth anniversary of the process—a temporal marker whose commemoration occasioned the original version of this chapter.

I should like to acknowledge this temporal marker by addressing, in a beginning fashion, the question posed by the title, "A Theological Reading of Scripture?" against the background of the process of transformation specified in the subtitle. How, in effect, has the notion of a theological reading fared in biblical criticism during this period of re-conceptualization and re-formulation in the discipline?

1. Introduction

The problematic posed by this process of transformation in biblical studies, I would submit, is by no means unrelated to matters religious-theological in general, to Christian studies and religious studies in particular, and to theological studies in concrete. To the contrary, such a relationship is evident and operative at all levels.

Such is the case, certainly, at the level of what might be characterized as emic disciplinary relations in the study of the religion of Christianity. In the eyes of many critics, who identify themselves and carry out their work as followers of Christianity in any variation thereof, biblical studies and theological studies constitute disciplines within the field of Christian studies, alongside such other fields as historical studies, ethical studies, and practical studies of Christianity and Christian ministry. In this regard it would be most illuminating to trace, in comparative fashion, the trajectories of these two discourses from the 1970s to the present.

Within Christian studies, it is also the case at the level of theological reflection. Theological studies views Scripture as a foundational source for its work and reveals a long-standing tradition of activating and deploying the biblical texts in such work. Here, too, it would prove most insightful to study the appeal to and application of the Bible in theological construction.

Within Christian studies as well, it is further the case at the level of critical interpretation. Biblical studies encounters and addresses religious-theological terms and concepts in the analysis of the biblical texts and possesses a long-standing tradition of theological reading as part of its critical repertoire. Here, it would also prove most revealing to examine the concept and practice of theological reading in biblical interpretation.

Such is also the case at the level of what might be described as etic disciplinary relations in the study of Christianity as an ancient religion. For many critics, whether actual adherents of Christianity or followers of other religions or scholars with secular or non-religious commitments, biblical studies is approached as a discipline within the field of religious studies. As such, it is pursued, on the one hand, without reference to Christian studies and its set of constitutive disciplines (such as theological studies) and, thus, on the other hand, as a discipline engaged in the study of the texts and contexts of ancient religions of the circum-Mediterranean. In this regard it would be most interesting to trace, in comparative fashion, the trajectories of such discourses from the 1970s through today.

A Theological Reading of Scripture? 105

The religious-theological element is thus, again, present and active at all levels of biblical criticism. What I mean by this should be clear: that ideological dimension of society and culture involving differential relations of power—a dialectics of domination and subordination—in terms of religious-theological formations and relations.

Such is the case, therefore, whether this ideological element is acknowledged or not. If affirmed, such a move is openly on the table, to some degree or another, from simple mention to careful unpacking. If denied, often on the basis of a proposed bracketing by way of claims to scientific impartiality and objectivity and hence to universality and non-confessionality, such a move remains, ultimately and irretrievably so, no less ideological and just as religious-theological in character. Either way, whether surfaced or erased, any such move in criticism is subject to analysis and critique, in terms of context and agenda as well as grounding and ramifications.

The possibilities for analysis, as suggested under the various levels, are multiple and attractive. My aim in this study lies along the lines of the third direction noted. I should like to foreground and analyze the connection between biblical interpretation and theological construction through a focus on the concept and practice of theological reading within criticism. This task I should like to pursue, as anticipated by the subtitle, in two ways. First, I shall cast a look backward: tracing past developments on the way toward the critical problematic presently before us. Then, I shall cast a look forward: discerning future possibilities, in the light of such a crossroads, toward a critical vision for the discipline. This I shall do by unfolding a narrative of the discipline's path from the early 1970s and before, through the middle 1970s, to the late 1970s and beyond.

Toward this end, I shall outline, in grand strokes, the various phases of the transformation, while exposing in the process the operative conceptions of theological reading—the representations and ramifications of such models—present in the course of these stages. On the one hand, the task of interpretive unpacking demands close reflection on matters of method and theory. On the other hand, the task of theological surfacing calls for close attention to the question of the religious-theological in method and theory. The result is a sense of the discursive terrain that has come about from this process of transformation. From within this crossroads, then, I shall go on to offer a vision of desiderata for the future, with matters of method and theory as well as the question of the religious-theological in mind.[1] A number of comments regarding *modus operandi* in this endeavor are in order at this point.

First, in identifying the major stages in the process of transformation, the narrative that I shall unfold is one that I have already laid out in detail in a series of previous works.[2] It involves a number of shifts in critical movements, what I have called paradigms or grand models of interpretation. This schema is presented here in summary fashion; it is also presented in revised fashion, as the section on looking forward will show, in the light of more recent work.

Second, in addressing the problematic of theological reading in criticism, I shall draw on two recent reflections on the discipline by Wayne Meeks and Carolyn Osiek. As presidential addresses to learned societies in the field, both pieces cast a broad look at its recent trajectory and present crucible.[3] Further, both raise the religious-theological

---

[1] At the center of any academic discipline or subject, any field of study and research, lies the twofold question of method and theory—the interrelated and interdependent questions of procedure and rationale. With regard to procedure or strategy, the question is how to go about doing whatever it is that one does or wishes to do. With respect to rationale or framework, the question becomes why go about doing what one does or wishes to do. Biblical studies is no different in this regard: to enter the world of biblical criticism, the world of the academic reading of biblical and related texts, is perforce to enter the world of method and theory. Such has been the case since the formation of the discipline in the early nineteenth century, and it is even more true today, in the early twenty-first century, as the discipline continues to ponder, in intensive and expansive fashion, the fundamental questions of why and how and indeed what and who. In the world of biblical criticism, moreover, a core dimension at work in method and theory, and hence present across the range of such fundamental questions, is the religious-theological one—the role and parameters allowed for this problematic in the various stages and models. Consequently, I find it imperative to trace the notion and practice of theological reading, its representations and ramifications, in the discipline with reference to the methodological and theoretical frameworks in place.

[2] See my introduction to Fernando F. Segovia and Mary Ann Tolbert, eds., *Reading from This Place*, 2 vols. (Philadelphia: Fortress Press, 1995). Also see recast versions in Segovia, *Decolonizing Biblical Studies: A View from the Margins* (Maryknoll, NY: Orbis Books, 2000); Segovia, "Methods for Studying the New Testament," in *Reading the New Testament Today*, ed. Mark Allan Powell (Louisville, KY: Westminster/John Knox Press, 1999), 1–9.

[3] See Wayne R. Meeks, "Why Study the New Testament?," *New Testament Studies* 51 (2005): 155–70 (given at the 2004 Annual Congress of the Society for the Study

problematic: Meeks, with regard to Protestantism; Osiek, with respect to Catholicism. Finally, both are penned by long-active and much-respected scholars, at the center of the discipline: scholars who have witnessed the transformation of the field from its origins to the present, who have espoused throughout a similar approach in criticism (historicism by way of recourse to the social sciences),[4] who are aware of the convoluted and contested character of the crossroads at hand and who, in the face of such a quandary, feel the need, even duty, to come forward and offer suggestions for the future.

Third, in dealing with this problematic, I am keenly aware of the enormous body of literature as well as the significant discussions that exist on the conceptualization and execution of theological reading. Such conversations and publications, I am very much aware as well, pursue the problematic in multidimensional character: in general fashion;[5] in book-by-book summary;[6] with emphasis on method;[7] with reference to canonical criticism;[8] or in terms of specific ecclesial

---

of the New Testament); Carolyn Osiek, "Catholic or catholic? Biblical Scholarship at the Center," *Journal of Biblical Literature* 125 (2006): 5–22 (given at the 2005 Annual Meeting of the Society of Biblical Literature).

[4] Meeks notes his own turn toward the social sciences in his address: Meeks, "Why Study the New Testament?," 161. Osiek, however, does not, yet her involvement in this regard has been long active: see Carolyn Osiek, *What Are They Saying about the Social Setting of the New Testament?* (New York: Paulist Press, 1984).

[5] See Daniel J. Treier, *Introducing Theological Interpretation of Scripture: Recovering a Christian Praxis* (Grand Rapids, MI: Baker Academic, 2008); and Stephen E. Fowl, *Theological Interpretation of Scripture* (Eugene, OR: Cascade Books, 2009).

[6] See Kevin J. Vanhoozer, *Theological Interpretation of the New Testament: A Book-by-Book Survey* (Grand Rapids, MI; London, UK: Baker Academic; SPCK, 2008).

[7] See Robert Morgan, "The Bible and Christian Theology," in *The Cambridge Companion to Biblical Interpretation*, ed. John Barton (Cambridge: Cambridge University Press, 1998), 114–28; and Stephen E. Fowl, "The New Testament, Theology, and Ethics," in *Hearing in the New Testament: Strategies for Interpretation*, ed. Joel B. Green, 2nd ed. (Grand Rapids, MI: Eerdmans, 2010), 397–413.

[8] See Kent D. Clarke, "Canonical Criticism: An Integrated Reading of Biblical Texts for the Community of Faith," in *The Cambridge Companion to Biblical Interpretation*, ed. John Barton (Cambridge: Cambridge University Press, 1995), 170–221; and Mary C. Callaway, "Canonical Criticism," in *To Each Its Own Meaning: Biblical Criticism and Their Application*, ed. Steven L. McKenzie and Stephen R. Haynes (Louisville, KY: Westminster/John Knox Press, 1999), 142–55.

contexts.[9] I see the present study, therefore, as but an initial effort on my part—a foundational proposal, as it were—to come to terms with the problematic from within my own theoretical and methodological framework. As such, it is clearly an exercise that will demand, in the future, much interchange with such scholarship as well as much additional, no doubt even revisionary, work regarding this initial analysis of mine.

Finally, in pursuing this study, I speak often of biblical studies. However, given my area of expertise, my point of reference in what follows will be early Christian or New Testament studies, although my remarks would be readily applicable to Hebrew or Old Testament studies as well.

2. Casting a Look Back: A Vision of the Transformation

The narrative that I have constructed, and deployed for some time now, for mapping and explaining the path of the discipline exhibits the following set of constitutive features: it encompasses four critical movements, now expanded into five; it presents a plot with three major stages of development, driven by conflict; and it reflects a tale of progress, leading to greater diversity throughout, materially as well as discursively. It is also a story told from the point of view of a critic who has lived through and has engaged in the various tectonic shifts in question from within and who thus functions along the lines of an observing participant, though from the margins.

The three stages in question proceed as follows. The first, lasting from the nineteenth century through the early 1970s, is marked by stability and involves the presence of an initial interpretive paradigm—historical criticism. This movement is long-established, deeply entrenched, and decidedly exclusive (i.e., without any sense of critical alternatives). The second stage, erupting around the middle 1970s, signals a period of crisis and involves the emergence of two other paradigms—literary criticism and sociocultural criticism. These movements problematize the claims of the existing grand model, displace it in principle but not in practice from its position of hegemony, and

---

[9] See Luke Timothy Johnson and William S. Kurz, *The Future of Catholic Biblical Scholarship: A Constructive Conversation* (Grand Rapids, MI: Eerdmans, 2002).

begin to turn the discipline into a diverse and competitive arena. The third stage, extending from the late 1970s through the present, marks a period of resolution, by way of unstable stability, and a further paradigm: ideological criticism. This movement problematizes the claims of the previous grand models, offers a full-fledged explanation for the process of diversification as such, and renders the discipline into an even more diverse and competitive arena.

Since these critical movements constitute highly complex discursive frameworks, the actual unfolding of the plot can be unpacked in various ways. I have done so by foregrounding their respective conceptualizations and formulations of the relationship between subject and object.[10] I have thus explained the rise of conflict and the advent of diversity in the discipline by way of the varying notions at work regarding the relationship between practitioner and field of study—critics and texts; historians and history; inquirers and inquired. In so doing, I have characterized the stages at work in the plot as follows: Diversity Bound; Diversity Unbinding; Diversity Unbound.

In what follows, then, I shall proceed in three steps. I shall begin by summarizing the interpretive visions operative in the various critical movements. I shall continue by bringing to the fore their theological visions, their representations of and attitudes toward theological reading. From this perspective, I would propose, the three phases may be further labeled as follows: the Theological Historicized; the Theological Historicized and Modulated; and the Theological Integrated but Unpursued. I shall conclude with a dialogical reflection involving, from within their own frameworks and in their own words, the positions of Meeks and Osiek regarding such proposed stages of development in the discipline and the corresponding critical movements in question, with attention to both interpretive and theological vision.

---

[10] For a different explanation, see Janice Capel Anderson and S. D. Moore, "Introduction: The Lives of Mark," in *Mark & Method: New Approaches in Biblical Studies*, ed. Janice Capel Anderson and S. D. Moore, 2nd ed. (Minneapolis: Fortress Press, 2008), 1–28. Here the transformation is traced through changing perceptions regarding the figure and role of an evangelist, Mark, as author, with five phases identified in the course of such changing fortunes: becoming an author; becoming a narrator; losing the grip on the text; becoming increasingly distant; and addressing the Empire.

The Theological Historicized: Historical Criticism

Through the early 1970s, historical criticism functioned as the dominant grand model of interpretation in the discipline. A historical approach to the world of early Christianity, its texts and contexts, had reigned supreme for a hundred and fifty years, from the formation of the discipline in the first half of the nineteenth century, following upon the period of intellectual ferment in the wake of the French Revolution. The study of Christian beginnings turned to the similarly nascent academic discipline of historical studies for grounding. This was a phase of remarkable stability, although not without flux, for within the model a variety of different practices emerged over time.

Interpretive Vision

Historical criticism sought to study the writings of early Christianity in the light of their context, broadly understood—historical, literary, social, religious. This it did from a variety of perspectives, depending on the focus of study in the project of contextualization at any one point over its long duration: text criticism, source criticism, comparative criticism involving matters social and cultural, form criticism, redaction criticism, composition criticism. Underlying these different approaches lay a specific view of the relationship between the practitioner and the field of studies—the ideal of exegesis.

For historical criticism, a wide historical and cultural gulf separated text and critic: the text was "out there"; the critic was "over here." The text represented historical evidence from and for the time of composition and called for contextualization. As such, it was to be read in its own terms, within its own context and as evidence for the reconstruction of that context. Its meaning was treated, if not viewed, as univocal and objective, as was the path of history itself. It was thus possible to re-create meaning and to reconstruct history. To do so, however, the decontextualization of the critic was essential. Such re-creation and reconstruction could be achieved only by means of a scientific method that guaranteed impartiality and objectivity on the part of the critic. For anyone to attain such a level of reading, a process of divestiture was in order: putting aside all biases and taking on the mantle of universality.

The result was clear: historical criticism pursued with relish the diversity of Christian beginnings as reflected in the early Christian writings, yet it frowned severely on diversity at the level of interpretation. With regard to critics, therefore, diversity remained bound: all would-be practitioners were to become alike—informed, neutral and objective, universal readers.

THEOLOGICAL VISION

The project of contextualization captures the modernist spirit of historical criticism. This movement sought freedom from the perceived restraints imposed by dogma and tradition on interpretation: the freedom to wrest the Bible away from the constrictive and distorting optic of the church and to bring it under the corrective and liberating lens of the academy. At the same time, behind the ideal of exegesis in contextualization, a specific view of theological reading can be discerned: its objective was historical appropriateness and accuracy, not confessional relevance and concordance. The past was the past, and the present was the present. Here, moreover, a bifurcation between texts and critics applied.

With regard to early Christianity, its texts and contexts, the focus of historical criticism could be described as intensely religious-theological in character and its prevailing model of analysis in this regard as one of conflict. Critics were interested in establishing the religious-theological positions of the texts at all levels of inquiry: from the earliest strata of oral tradition, through the various literary layers identifiable, to the final and present lay-out. Such positions were invariably represented in terms of controversies within and among the early communities, so that vigorous debates and disputes were perceived and delineated as present throughout. These stances and conflicts were often cast against the broader social and cultural background and/or in interaction with concrete religious-theological formations within it, whether with the microcontext of Judaism or the macrocontext of the Greco-Roman world in view.

With regard to the study of early Christianity, its discursive production, and its material matrix, the emphasis of historicism was on transcendence of context and perspective. Critics viewed themselves as scientific scholars—beyond confessional moorings or inclinations in their research. As such, it did not matter what ecclesial tradition they came from or belonged to, nor, for that matter, whether they were believers or not. Analyzing the positions and disputes of early Christianity was thus possible without influence from or reference to the religious-theological stances and conflicts of critics. The objective was to lay out the facts, discursive or material, of early Christianity, not to pass judgment on them or, much less, to engage them critically in terms of the present. If anything, critics saw their work as seeking to provide a secure foundation for the constructive religious-theological work incumbent on the other disciplines of Christian studies.

The result was evident: historical criticism pursued without reserve the religious-theological terrain of Christian beginnings, with full awareness of its complex and conflicted character, but refrained altogether from examining the contemporary religious-theological terrain, whether by way of influence on them or by way of engagement with the texts. With regard to critics, therefore, the religious-theological dimension was thoroughly historicized—of driving interest in the past but of no concern in the present. Critics functioned, in principle, as a-religious and a-theological readers.

Dialogical Reflection

As critics originally trained and subsequently steeped in the élan and practice of historicism, both Meeks and Osiek are very much aware of its spirit and claims. With the advantage of distance, they both approach such spirit and such principles in highly sympathetic and commendatory fashion. Their angles of vision, in so doing, prove quite different. Meeks moves within the orbit of religious studies, following an autonomous academic model of research in early Christian studies. The New Testament represents a set of texts to be read alongside other texts of the period and without reference to any anachronistic concept of canon.[11] Osiek is at home in the realm of Christian studies, opting for a collaborative academic-ecclesial model of research in biblical studies. The Bible, and hence the New Testament, constitutes a set of texts that belongs "not to theologians, denominations, national committees, bishops, or biblical scholars" but to the "church,"[12] and that thus has to be read contextually and ecclesially at once.

---

[11] Meeks, "Why Study the New Testament?," 158.
[12] Osiek, "Catholic or catholic? Biblical Scholarship at the Center," 21.

Meeks speaks from the perspective of what has been characterized as the "heroic model of science,"[13] as applied to historiography in general and hence to the historiography of the early Christian movement in particular. The model is variously described as follows: grounded in philosophical realism (a view of history as empirical and unilinear and of research as securing a correspondence between history and reason); propelled by a sense of liberation (freedom from the clutches of tradition and authority); and guided by the ideals of impartiality and objectivity (a commitment to scientific inquiry). In his description of the "practice" of historical criticism,[14] Meeks recalls and retells all of these features in his own words: its sense of history as "science," aspiring after the natural sciences, as a "weapon of liberation," as having "objectivity" as its "ideal."[15] Indeed, Meeks's recollection of this now-lost world captures its spirit in glorious fashion: "We saw ourselves, our students, sometimes even our churches, being set free from lazy credulity, from dogmatic abstractions, from venomous prejudices, from authoritarian structures—all just by telling the truth about the past, especially about the *beginnings*."[16] Such freedom, he affirms, was inherited from the Reformation and the Enlightenment and defended through the struggle between modernism and fundamentalism—"a temporary triumph," he exults, "but a brilliant one."[17]

Osiek speaks from the perspective of what might be described as the "alliance model of science and church," bringing together the scientific ideals of historical criticism and the ecclesial commitments of Roman Catholic criticism. Such criticism does include the heroic model of science and its constitutive features: a foundation in realism (history as empirical and unilinear, the locus of revelation of the Word of God, and research as the recovery of this revelation as incarnated in history); a story of liberation (the commitment to scientific research as a long and arduous struggle within the Church); and adherence to scientific principles of impartiality and objectivity (recourse to all tools of human research, under the conviction of no ultimate discrepancy between the

---

[13] Joyce Appleby, Lynn Avery Hunt, and Margaret C. Jacob, *Telling the Truth about History* (New York: Norton, 1994), 15.
[14] Meeks, "Why Study the New Testament?," 159.
[15] Ibid., 157.
[16] Ibid.
[17] Ibid.

truth of science and the truth of theology).[18] Such criticism also includes the ecclesial ideals of Catholic criticism and a corresponding set of constitutive principles: a foundation in a view of Scripture as the Word of God in human language, involving the triad of Scripture, tradition, and the magisterium; a need for a sense of affinity between text and interpreter, with "one eye" always on "the good of the community";[19] and a call for adherence to a multilayered view of meaning in Scripture as the Word of God in human language. Osiek's description of this grand alliance proves just as glorious: "Therefore, biblical scholarship and interpretation must be in some way oriented to the nourishment and growth of the community. This is not in any way to impede the necessary freedom, integrity, and autonomy that scholars must have to engage in research for its own sake."[20]

While Osiek is explicit about the religious-theological framework of criticism, situating herself squarely within the context of the Roman Catholic tradition of interpretation, in the end Meeks does peek beyond the veil of scientism and exposes the religious-theological character of criticism. Its social-cultural setting was the "western Christendom" of "northern Europe, Britain, and their American diasporas" in the "high modern period."[21] Its implied audience was thus "genetically protestant" and its point of reference was the "centrality of preaching."[22] Its goal therefore was to have the results of criticism reach the people through the "sermon." "We wrote," Meeks states, "if for anybody outside our own charmed circle, for theologians, and theologians were instructors of preachers."[23]

A Concluding Comment

Both Meeks and Osiek look back on historical criticism as embodying the ideal of exegesis, of bringing research in tune with history, through analysis of the early Christian texts and contexts. Behind such espousals, moreover, clearly lie religious-theological concerns

---

[18] Osiek, "Catholic or catholic?," 21.
[19] Ibid.
[20] Ibid.
[21] Meeks, "Why Study the New Testament?," 158.
[22] Ibid.
[23] Ibid.

and interests—explicit in Osiek; implicit in Meeks. Yet, neither sees such concerns and interests, in principle, as upsetting or influencing the task of scientific research. Within historical criticism, critics did presume to function as a-religious and a-theological readers, even in the presence of religious and theological sensibilities and agendas. Meeks and Osiek would not disagree in this regard. I would argue, however, that any historical reading today should be accompanied by critical analysis of the religious-theological framework of critics and their work.

Theology Historicized and Modulated: Literary and Sociocultural Criticisms

Toward the middle of the 1970s, two other grand models of interpretation began to emerge: literary criticism and sociocultural criticism. These evolved into major critical movements through the late 1970s and into the 1980s and, since then, have continued to expand in diversity and sophistication. The voices of dissatisfaction that drove these movements came from different quarters, addressed different perceived shortcomings of historicism, and remained largely independent of one another. On the one hand, there was dissatisfaction with the way in which texts had been approached. Various tendencies of historical criticism were now viewed as bypassing the text as such: its emphasis on textual ruptures (fracturing), its concern for pre-existing stages of texts (excavative), and its focus on verse-by-verse analysis (atomistic). The text, it was argued, was worthy of analysis in and of itself—as text, with a focus on its formal features. On the other hand, there was also dissatisfaction with the way in which contexts had been approached. Certain tendencies of historical criticism were now similarly perceived as simplifying the context as such: its lack of models (impressionistic), its pointillistic attention to detail (unstructured), and its lack of theorized distance (ethnocentric). The context, it was argued, was worthy of analysis in and of itself—as context, with a focus on its social features. Both sets of voices looked elsewhere for grounding and direction: the former, to the human sciences (literary, rhetorical, psychological studies); the latter, to the social sciences (sociological and anthropological studies). The result was a period of crisis, in which the long-standing and near-exclusive association between early Christian studies and historical studies was severely called into question.

The Theological Historicized: Historical Criticism

Depending on the particular focus of study in question, a broad set of approaches gradually came into being within each model. From the point of view of literary criticism, one finds structuralist criticism, psychoanalytic criticism, narrative criticism, rhetorical criticism, reader-response criticism, and deconstructive criticism. From the point of view of sociocultural criticism, one finds sociological criticism and anthropological criticism. With regard to the ideal of exegesis, a distinction is imperative in both models.

For the most part, this ideal remained unquestioned. In fact, both literary and sociocultural criticism set out to outdo historical criticism by seeking to advance, from a methodological and theoretical point of view, a more secure foundation and strategy for dealing with the text as text and the context as context. The basic perception was that the task of contextualization had not been properly executed. At the same time, certain developments within both movements pointed to the first signs of cracks in this ideal. From the perspective of literary criticism, the concepts of univocality and objectivity did yield some ground, given the increasing emphasis on the plurality of interpretations, whether due to the polysemy of texts and the agency of readers. From the perspective of sociocultural criticism, these same concepts yielded further ground, given the increasing focus on the sociocultural dimensions of readers. In attempting to refine the task of contextualization, therefore, the grounds for radical reconsideration had been laid as well. While the scientific goals of re-creation and reconstruction, neutrality and impartiality, prevailed, a degree of erosion was evident as well.

The result was evident: while both grand models continued to pursue unreservedly the diversity of Christian beginnings, the first hints of diversity at the level of interpretation began to surface. With respect to critics, this was a case of diversity unbinding. First, expectations regarding practitioners underwent a fundamental change from one grand model to a variety of such models—universal and informed readers, along different and contested lines of approach. Second, expectations regarding the ideal of exegesis began, ever so slightly, to be relaxed—informed readers, but not as universal as before.

THEOLOGICAL VISION

This project of constrained contextualization preserved the modernist impulse of historical criticism. Both grand models sought freedom from the perceived stranglehold that historicism had on the discipline: the freedom to approach the texts and contexts of early Christianity as literary texts and as sociocultural contexts in their own right, respectively. Behind such proposed refinement lay, again, a working view of theological reading: its aim was greater historical accuracy and reliability through modulation of the religious-theological dimension in terms of literary expression and sociocultural embodiment. The past was the past, and the present was the present, but the past called for literary and sociocultural nuancing. The existing bifurcation between texts and critics remained largely unaffected.

With respect to the texts and contexts of early Christianity, the earlier focus on religious-theological positions and controversies did not change. What did change was the adoption of a nuanced approach toward such stances and conflicts, so that the religious-theological dimension emerged as a signifier for other concomitant dimensions of meaning. Critics viewed such positions and controversies as not just revolving around issues of belief and practice—involving individuals, parties, or communities—but also as bearing broader discursive as well as material implications. Attention was centered on such implications: on the one hand, their literary-rhetorical dimension, such as matters of structuration and expression, of argumentation and strategies; on the other hand, their social and cultural dimensions, such as questions of organization and interchange, of values and customs. The religious-theological was now seen as having recourse to artistic features and as displaying material channels, which, given the previous lack of attention, now rose to the fore.

With respect to the production and matrix of early Christian studies, the earlier insistence on abstraction from context and perspective saw little change, and then only by way of surface cracks. The project of laying out the facts of early Christianity, in scientific fashion, without evaluation or engagement, did not relent, but did become more involved, given the call for a calibration of the religious-theological domain by appeal to literary as well as social theory. Securing a foundation for Christian studies continued as the main task, but with a certain sense of fragility, given the beginnings of an acknowledgment of interpretive agency and textual fluidity.

118 *Disputed Questions—Part 2*

The result was evident. Both grand models sharpened their pursuit of the religious-theological terrain of Christian beginnings, diminishing its overall importance in the process, and abstained from carrying out a similar expansion in the religious-theological terrain of early Christian studies, despite its incipient challenge to the values of textual univocity and critical objectivity. With regard to critics, therefore, the religious-theological dimension remained thoroughly historicized, though now highly modulated and hence decidedly attenuated. Critics still functioned, in principle, as a-religious and a-theological readers.

Dialogical Reflection

Given the advantage of distance, both Meeks and Osiek accompany their sympathetic and commendatory representations of historical criticism with a corresponding dose of pointed critical evaluation. Meeks points to the "crumbling pillars" that underlie such practice and its traditional sense of self-confidence,[24] while Osiek brings the charge of "inappropriate totalitarian claims" against it.[25]

The crumbling noted by Meeks is sharply outlined, both in terms of writing history and reading texts. With regard to historiography, new approaches have pointed to any number of "blind spots" in historicism, raising new questions and opening new horizons of inquiry in the field.[26] Among these lies social history, within whose ranks Meeks places himself, insofar as it calls for looking beyond the elite and beyond doctrine, toward the "typical life worlds of those unrecorded people who were the first Christians and their neighbors."[27] With regard to reading, new approaches have questioned the concept of "original meaning" in texts, in favor of a transactional view of meaning involving text and reader: "the force of a statement always contextual, all texts malleable and their functions transformable through time."[28] The totalitarianism registered by Osiek is captured just as sharply, in terms of overreaching proper boundaries. First, while scientism claimed to be a "foolproof method" for reaching the "literal level" of

---

[24] Ibid., 159.
[25] Osiek, "Catholic or catholic?," 18.
[26] Meeks, "Why Study the New Testament?," 160.
[27] Ibid., 161.
[28] Ibid., 162.

the text, this stance has been discounted by new approaches. Second, while scientism claimed "to yield convincing results that can be verified by independent researchers, and that these results are the only ones that matter," this stance takes it beyond the limits of science into the realms of theology and philosophy and should be discounted as well.[29]

In both, the religious-theological dimension of the crisis comes to the fore in no uncertain terms. In the case of Meeks, the crumbling extends to the Protestant framework that underlay the model as a whole. With the weakening of the "culture of Christendom," criticism has been left "approaching a state of complete isolation"—whether in the university, in the world, or in the public realm.[30] Whereas in Europe one finds little regard for the New Testament as a "religiously important" document, in North America the denominations that appreciated this type of scholarship have yielded in number to more conservative formations that "ignore or deplore" it, while at the same time the popular media offer an "either-or" choice involving skepticism and fundamentalism. On both sides of the Atlantic, moreover, populations have become much more diverse, more non-Christian, through the processes of globalization. In the case of Osiek, the noted totalitarianism rules out philosophical and spiritual interpretations of reality in favor of empirical and materialist interpretations. Such a stance goes against the very grain of Catholic interpretation, which not only seeks to hold together scientific culture and religious tradition but also allows for a "variety of levels of meaning" in texts.[31]

A Concluding Comment

Meeks as well as Osiek register their agreement with various critiques brought against traditional historicism from the point of view of method and theory. Behind such moves lie religious-theological concerns and interests—rather indirect in Meeks; quite direct in Osiek. For both, these concerns and interests come across as compatible with the task of historical research, as revised. In both literary and

---

[29] Osiek, "Catholic or catholic?," 18.
[30] Meeks, "Why Study the New Testament?," 163.
[31] Osiek, "Catholic or catholic?," 19.

sociocultural criticisms, despite the presence of religious-theological sensibilities and agendas, critics remain, in principle, a-religious and a-theological readers, devoted to the continued historicization, now in highly modulated fashion, of the religious-theological dimension. Neither Meeks nor Osiek, both critics with a sociocultural orientation, would disagree in this regard.

Theology Problematized yet Untheorized: Ideological Criticism

In the late 1970s another grand model of interpretation began to appear: ideological criticism. Not long after the emergence of literary and sociocultural criticisms, other voices of dissatisfaction came to the fore, now with all previous grand models in mind. These voices came from varying interests and emerged on the critical scene in gradual fashion. The first such voices, addressing the problematic of gender and economics, came to expression in the late 1970s. Then, as these became increasingly vibrant formations through the 1980s, they were joined by other voices dealing with the problematic of race and ethnicity. Subsequently, while these formations continued to grow in strength, yet other voices turned to the problematic of sexuality and geopolitics. More recently, newer voices have begun to call for attention to the problematic of disability and ecology, among others. Such dissatisfaction came from both inside and outside the earlier critical movements. From the inside, the initial cracks regarding the ideal of exegesis widened and deepened. From the outside, momentous demographic changes were taking place in a discipline that up to this point had been male, clerical, and Western. These two developments coincided with and reinforced one another, yielding in the process a further grand model, which was able to account for the plurality of grand models as such. The result was a sense of resolution, marked by stability, though of a peculiar sort—a stability of intractable pluralism in method and theory, and hence inherently unstable.

Dissatisfaction from the inside was inevitable, as the focus on the plurality of interpretations and the agency of interpretive readers intensified. A number of voices began to argue that behind all re-creations of meaning and reconstructions of history, behind all methods and models, stood real readers and that such flesh-and-blood readers were always and inescapably contextualized and perspectival. Dissatisfaction from the outside became inevitable as well, as more and more outsiders to the discipline joined its ranks: from Western women, to men and women from the non-Western world, to women and men from non-Western minority groups in the West. These insisted on interpretive plurality and readerly agency as well as on the contextualization and perspective of real readers in interpretation. In both regards these rumblings were paralleled and aided by similar discussions across the disciplinary spectrum of the human and social sciences. On all fronts, therefore, critical emphasis turned to the problematic of representation and the ideological analysis of differential relations of power with regard to texts and critics alike.

INTERPRETIVE VISION

Within this model, a variety of formations developed over time, depending on the particular factor of critical identity under consideration and the resultant constructions and relations in question. The following were most prominent: feminist criticism, materialist criticism, ethnic-racial criticism, queer criticism, and postcolonial criticism. For the ideal of exegesis, this model proved shattering.

Given the emphasis on agency on the part of contextualized and perspectival readers, the sense of a wide divide between critic and text is cast aside. The basic perception now arises that the task of contextualization is fundamentally defective as formulated, since behind such contextualization lies not, as required, a neutral and impartial reader but rather a reader who is very much at work, in any number of ways, in the task of re-creation and reconstruction. For ideological criticism, the reader is ultimately engaged in construction—the re-creation of meaning in texts and the reconstruction of history in contexts. Given the enormous variety of real readers engaged in such a task, such constructions will of necessity exhibit widespread and conflictive diversity. As a result, the phenomenon of diversity is explained and justified at a foundational level. In the end, contextualization for ideological criticism becomes a far more demanding and complex task, equally applicable to texts and critics; in fact, exegesis and eisegesis now go hand in hand.

The result was evident: with this grand model of interpretation, diversity at the level of interpretation becomes an established critical principle. With regard to critics, therefore, this is a case of diversity unbound. First, expectations regarding critics now included a further grand model within the repertoire of the discipline: readers, informed along even more different and contested lines of approach. Second, expectations regarding exegesis underwent a profound reversal: readers radically contextualized and perspectival, as well as thoroughly at work in constructing texts and contexts.

Theological Vision

This project of overarching contextualization, encompassing both the axis of texts and the axis of readers, maintained the modernist impulse of literary and sociocultural criticism. This model sought freedom from the perceived stranglehold of objectivism on the discipline, as conveyed by the concepts of texts as independent entities and of critics as abstracted decipherers. This was the freedom to approach interpretations of early Christian texts and contexts as exercises in construction on the part of interpreters and to approach interpreters as contextualized and perspectival agents. Behind this proposed expansion, a working view of theological reading was once again at play: its aim was calibration of the religious-theological dimension by attention to unequal relations of power in society and culture throughout. The past was now in the present, and the present in the past, and both called for discursive and material nuancing of all sorts. In the process, the bifurcation between texts and critics was distinctly affected, but more in principle than in practice.

With regard to the texts and contexts of Christian beginnings, the sustained focus on religious-theological positions and debates underwent significant change. On the one hand, the religious-theological dimension became an even broader signifier for other dimensions of inquiry, beyond the literary and the sociocultural, through the integration of the problematic of power, of domination and subordination, in society and culture. Alongside matters of belief and practice, and in addition to implications of literary expression and sociocultural embodiment, critics viewed these stances and controversies as involving questions of identity and representation (gender, economy, race-ethnicity, sexuality, geopolitics, and so on). The religious-theological dimension was thus approached as reflecting and conveying differential constructions and relations of power, which, given their previous lack of attention, now became primary. On the other hand, attention to power relations and constructions tended to become the main object of inquiry, displacing the religious-theological dimension as such. In both regards, a peculiar situation obtained: while this dimension constitutes an axis within the problematic of power, analysis of its relations and constructions was deflected and unproblematized.

With respect to the production and matrix of early Christian studies, the sustained emphasis on abstraction from context and perspective witnessed even more radical change. The project of unearthing the discursive and material facts of early Christianity—already showing signs of fragility—collapsed, yielding two important results: on the one hand, the awareness of agency and construction in any project of interpretation; on the other hand, an alternative project of examining the dynamics and mechanics of such agency and such constructions. As a result, the realm of interpreters and interpretations was now viewed as thoroughly crisscrossed by unequal relations of power across all axes of human identity with consequences for the task of criticism. Again, however, the analysis of the religious-theological axis of power among critics failed to be pursued as such.

The result was evident. Ideological criticism expanded the pursuit of the religious-theological terrain of Christian beginnings, further reducing in the process its overall importance in the face of power, and carried such expansion to the religious-theological terrain of early Christian studies, though in neither case was the religious-theological foregrounded as an axis of power in its own right. With regard to critics, therefore, the religious-theological dimension was now no longer historicized but universalized, more highly calibrated in its implications but largely unproblematized in and of itself. Critics now functioned, in principle, as religious-theological readers, but without analysis of such a web of constructions and relations.

Dialogical Reflection

In their pointed critiques of historical criticism, Meeks and Osiek both raise the question of ideology and the dynamics of power in society and culture. Immediately following his eloquent recollection of historicism as a weapon in the struggle for liberation, Meeks advances a devastating deconstructionist exposé of the movement. As a practice, he admits, historical criticism was by no means "innocent" but rather a "means of power." Its practitioners, furthermore, were by no means disinterested but self-serving: through their claim as "knowers and purveyors of the truth," they secured "commanding positions" in the "establishment constituting academic theology."[32] Similarly, following up on her accusation of inappropriate totalitarian tendencies in historicism, and citing Meeks's exposé of innocence and disinterest in the process, Osiek issues a call for attention to power. It is imperative for criticism, she argues, to integrate new approaches, such as "liberation, feminist/womanist/mujerista, and postcolonial interpretation," that embody a "hermeneutic of suspicion" and that foreground the question of "how power is used." In challenging "established power bases"—and they do indeed—these new approaches stand as "new manifestations" of the traditional and inspiring critical principle.[33]

For Meeks, the crumbling of the pillars refers to the demise of the ways that writing history and reading texts embraced the claims of impartiality and objectivity. New approaches are portrayed as not only bringing out "blind spots" in lines of research but also unmasking the "ideological dimensions" of historical criticism. After an initial "shock" in terms of the problematic of religious othering by way of anti-Semitism, in the aftermath of the Second World War, a variety of new "attacks" have been mounted in more recent times as well—"by feminists, by liberationists, by post-colonialists interpreters—to name only the most prominent." Such ideological "blind spots," Meeks concedes, represent "very serious holes in our armor of objectivity" and reveal how privilege, its enjoyment and pursuit, need not be at all self-conscious in character.[34] For Osiek, the totalitarian impulse of historical criticism extends to any assumption "that the text can have only one meaning." All texts are described as having "many possible levels of meaning," yielding a situation of enormous complexity in interpretation, and Scripture is no exception in this regard. In fact, a traditional threefold set of meanings is acknowledged for the biblical texts: the literal, the spiritual, and "the so-called fuller sense"—the *sensus plenior*. On the one hand, therefore, any insistence on one meaning, or any undeviating focus on the literal level, on the part of historical criticism represents an exclusivistic move. On the other hand, it is under the umbrella of the spiritual level of meaning that

---

[32] Meeks, "Why Study the New Testament?," 157.
[33] Osiek, "Catholic or catholic?," 20.
[34] Meeks, "Why Study the New Testament?," 160.

"we bring our new understandings to the task, out of our own new questions, and discover new levels of meaning as participants in the ongoing flow of tradition." It is here, therefore, that Osiek situates the new approaches focusing on suspicion and power, welcoming them as expressions of new understandings and new questions of "today's preunderstandings."[35]

In both Meeks and Osiek, the raising of ideology and power as part of the crisis and critique of historicism reveals a clear religious-theological dimension as well. This comes across subtly in Meeks and overtly in Osiek.

In Meeks this dimension is at work in two respects. It is so, first of all, as part of his representation of critics as interested: in their claim as possessors and dispensers of truth, historical critics, he states, were engaged in enhancing their own "professional positions" in the academy and the church,[36] setting themselves up as unassailable and path-setting. It does so as well in his description of the vision and mission of the *Studiorum Novi Testamenti Societas*: from inception to the present, he argues, the sense that such study of the New Testament might "have consequences in the 'real world' outside academia" has ruled.[37] This was certainly so at the beginning, in the 1930s and 1940s, a time "when the international scene seemed very bleak indeed," when such joint study was perceived as an endeavor "that would cross hostile political boundaries, that would search for truth, for hope, and for life in a time of propaganda." It also remains so today, he adds, when such study is cast as "internationalist" in aspirations, extending beyond "the boundaries of our world" in the light of global developments.[38]

In Osiek this dimension is linked to the concept of the spiritual layer of meaning in Scripture. What the Church brings by way of pre-understanding to the spiritual sense is set forth as threefold, yielding a reading that is "under the influence of the Holy Spirit," "within the context of the paschal mystery of Christ," and within the context "of the new life that flows" from the paschal mystery.[39] For Osiek, the

---

[35] Osiek, "Catholic or catholic?," 19–20.
[36] Meeks, "Why Study the New Testament?," 157.
[37] Ibid., 156.
[38] Ibid.
[39] Osiek, "Catholic or catholic?," 20. Here Osiek appropriates and cites the official position on interpretation set forth by the document *Interpretation of the Bible in the*

understanding of how new life flows from the paschal mystery should be seen as changing from epoch to epoch, and today, she declares, such new life revolves around the problematic of power, as brought to the fore by the new approaches of suspicion. Indeed, these new approaches are described as informed by "the desire to have us live more authentically the new life that flows from the paschal mystery" and must, therefore, be seen as integral to the exercise of "spiritual reading."[40] They function no differently in this regard than earlier methods had, such as historical criticism, but they do show how earlier approaches "are not yet open to a wider and more inclusive way of living and loving."[41]

A Concluding Comment

Both Meeks and Osiek signal their agreement with the critique lodged against traditional historicism from the point of view of ideology and axes of power in society and culture. Behind such moves lie religious-theological concerns and interests—more muted in Meeks, quite pronounced in Osiek. For both, such concerns and interests can be properly integrated in the task of historical research. In ideological criticism, critics do become, in principle, religious and theological readers, given the attention to be paid to all axes of power in society and culture, yet remain functionally a-theological and a-religious, given the failure to pursue the web of formations and relations at work in such an axis. Meeks and Osiek would follow suit in this regard.

3. Casting a Look Forward: A Vision for the Future

The preceding charting of the process of transformation, of re-visioning and re-direction, yields a distinct sense of the discursive terrain in the discipline at present. What emerges is a crossroads marked by increasing multiplicity of critical approaches, expanding integration

---

Church, issued by the Pontifical Biblical Commission in 1993, which designated historical criticism as the indispensable method for the scientific study of the Scriptures. See Dean P. Béchard, ed. and trans., *The Scripture Documents: An Anthology of Official Catholic Teachings* (Collegeville, MN: Liturgical Press, 2002).

[40] Osiek, "Catholic or catholic?," 20.
[41] Ibid.

of reading traditions, and a growing repertoire of academic interlocutors. It is from within such a crossroads that I should like to venture a vision for the future, with matters of method and theory as well as the question of the religious-theological in mind. It is a vision offered in dialogical interaction with those advanced by Meeks and Osiek, toward which I turn as point of departure.

DIALOGICAL REFLECTION

Meeks's vision, advanced in the face of a perceived crumbling of the pillars underlying the practice of historical criticism, is more expansive, insofar as it touches on the various foundations in question. It is, by and large, a call for discussion and action by way of "propositions to be debated" by the guild.[42] These propositions are formulated in broad terms, emphasizing general lines of direction rather than outlining an inventory of specific measures to be adopted or specific roads to be traversed. Osiek's vision, offered in the face of perceived tendencies toward totalitarianism lurking within the method of historical criticism, is more focused, insofar as it insists on the need for proper boundaries, with respect for and collaboration across such boundaries, between scientific inquiry and religious tradition. It too is, by and large, a call for discussion and action, by way of a guild that is open to a diversity of methods. Such openness is also formulated in broad terms, stressing a general sense of ethos instead of delineating actual lines of rapprochement.

Meeks's vision is threefold: writing history; reading texts; addressing audiences. First, it calls on criticism "to do better history,"[43] for, as he puts it, "The task of reconstructing a more fair and honest picture of the past never ends."[44] Toward this end, various recommendations are offered, the first two of which reveal his commitment to social history: emphasizing the history of communities rather than the history of doctrine; pursuing the history of interpretation, including the social character of modern early Christian historiography; and wrestling with the character of history as both fiction and science, a "fiction about the

---

[42] Meeks, "Why Study the New Testament?," 164.
[43] Ibid., 161.
[44] Ibid., 164.

past that is corrigible," insofar as it involves both interpretation and facts.⁴⁵ Second, the vision calls on criticism "to stand as the defender of the text's integrity."⁴⁶ Its primary aim should continue to be addressing the meaning of the text in its historical context. At the same time, however, from a hermeneutical point of view, attention should be paid not only to the normative or doctrinal uses of the text, as in the past, but also to its whole range of formative uses. Lastly, it calls on criticism "in the world after Christendom" to engage a broader public arena, "at once wildly diverse and very small."⁴⁷ To be sure, the communities of faith are to remain the primary audience. Yet, it is imperative to ponder and express why believers of today should learn about early Christianity, its texts and contexts. In this regard Meeks offers a piece of concrete advice: the project of biblical theology has run its course and should be abandoned. At the same time, two other audiences must be addressed. On the one hand, there is the intellectual community with the university as base, since matters of religion and Bible are now discussed from any number of critical angles other than its original theological parameters. Here, dialogue is essential, for the sake of mutual learning. On the other hand, there is the non-Christian population at large, since they now constitute the majority in the world and have become our own neighbors. Here, dialogue is imperative as well, for the sake of mutual learning about traditions and cultures as well as mutual reflection on the phenomenon of globalization.

Osiek's vision is concentrated: following the model of reading Scripture as encompassing a variety of levels of meaning (literal, spiritual, fuller sense), the call is for criticism to be open to a variety of methods. Thus, under the umbrella of spiritual reading, all approaches foregrounding power and suspicion can and should be readily integrated. Further, under the category of fuller-sense reading, represented as that meaning that is "comprehensible at a later point in the unfolding of tradition,"⁴⁸ other approaches can and should be integrated, such as canonical criticism and psychological criticism. This is a vision that seeks to hold together "ancient text, ongoing history of interpre-

---

⁴⁵ Ibid., 166.
⁴⁶ Ibid.
⁴⁷ Ibid., 167.
⁴⁸ Osiek, "Catholic or catholic?," 21.

tation, modern science, and postmodern insights," all with a sense of belonging within a living religious tradition. It calls not simply for "toleration" of other methods but for "inter-understanding" among methods, not just for a view of diversity as "cacophony" but rather as "symphony"—a vision that attends to "how they complement each other, can be integrated with each other, and can together form a rich network of interpretations."[49]

Both visions of the future bear a definite religious-theological tinge. Indeed, both remarkably conclude with a reference to Paul, by way of blessing, as it were, upon the whole enterprise. In Meeks, this tinge is lighter. It comes across in various respects. It can be discerned, first of all, in his designation of believers as the audience par excellence of New Testament studies, for it is belief that accounts for the prominence of these texts. It can also be discerned in the key role assigned to biblical critics as ideal brokers in the proposed dialogue between Christians and non-Christians, given their long-standing rejection of a fideist hermeneutics bent on conversion and emic reading. It can be further discerned in the insistence on criticism as a bulwark against the forces of fundamentalism, for only such study can prevent abuses of the texts in both the religious and the public sphere. In the end, Meeks draws on the model of Paul in 1 Corinthians 13:1 to argue that criticism must look to the future, "openly" as well as "humbly," for it does not and cannot possess "the final word" now, but only eschatologically.[50] In Osiek, the tinge is darker. It comes across in her combined view of meaning as multidimensional and of criticism as open. Such positions are offered, first, as a proper unfolding of the paschal mystery in the contemporary world, as an option for life. They are also offered as the particular contribution that Roman Catholic criticism can make to the "common catholic (small c) tradition of biblical interpretation."[51] In concluding, Osiek draws on the model of Paul in Philippians (3:13-14) to argue that criticism must press on toward the future. Both visions, I would submit, end, through their invocation of Paul, with a profoundly religious-theological sense of interpretation as on the way to fulfillment.

---

[49] Ibid., 22.
[50] Meeks, "Why Study the New Testament?," 170.
[51] Osiek, "Catholic or catholic?," 22.

130 *Disputed Questions—Part 2*

DIALOGICAL ENCOUNTER

These visions offer much material for critical interchange. I shall focus on three elements in particular: first, the historiographical project at the core of such programs; second, the call to examine uses of the Bible outside scholarship; finally, the attention paid to discursive frameworks outside biblical criticism.

To begin with, Meeks and Osiek both call for a revised approach to the study of early Christianity. To my mind, such a revision is too guarded. Despite the serious shortcomings exposed in the theory and method of traditional historicism, whether in terms of crumbling foundations or totalitarian usurpations, these visions of the future remain much too tied to the heroic model of scientific historiography. Although the critiques advanced by way of literary and sociocultural expansion as well as by way of ideological awareness and scrutiny are acknowledged and appropriated, to one degree or another, such admission fails to bring about proper modifications in the underlying model of analysis. The result is clear: a view of early Christian history as empirical and unilinear, of early Christian texts as bearing meaning in the light of their context, and of early Christian criticism as the attempt to reconstruct such history and re-create such meaning as accurately as possible. To be sure, the ideals of objectivity and impartiality are expressly challenged and cast aside, yet what emerges in the process is a vision that fails to integrate sufficiently what the loss of such ideals implies and entails for criticism.

This can be shown in two ways. On the one hand, what emerges is a vision of the new approaches as broadening and correcting the view of the dynamics and mechanics at work in early Christian texts and history. The visions advanced come across as embodying a better historiography, substantially expanded and ever expendable, through ever greater inclusion of diverse angles of inquiry. Consequently, such visions bring about visions of a more inclusive history of early Christianity, more accurate and more detailed. The eschatological dimensions bestowed on such visions only reinforce such impression: in the end, we shall see face to face (à la Meeks) or make it our own (à la Osiek). On the other hand, what emerges as well is a vision of the new critics as ultimately unaffected in their work—in their reconstructions of early Christian history and re-creation of early Christian texts—by their own contextuality and ideology, and their locations and agendas within the various formations and relations of differential power in society and culture, including the religious-theological axis. As a result, such visions come across as visions tied, indirectly (à la Meeks) or directly (à la Osiek), to ecclesial traditions, projects, and agendas, yet curiously independent of such ties in the actual modes and results of application. In sum, while history and historiography undergo significant expansion, they fail to undergo a crucial transformation, as they should if the critiques of traditional criticism are taken to heart. I believe that such critiques must be addressed much more pointedly and constructively.

Second, Meeks calls for critical attention both to the history of interpretation, through contemporary times, and to uses of the Bible in other areas of ecclesial life and other venues of society and culture. I could not agree more. In fact, I believe that such a course of action needs to be far more ambitious. I would posit, as anticipated earlier, a fifth grand model of interpretation, cultural biblical criticism, which would bring together biblical studies and cultural studies. Such a paradigm would analyze the invocation and deployment of the biblical texts and contexts across a wide number of traditions of reading besides the academic-scholarly one. Third, Meeks also calls for greater interaction with other fields of study, a call that I also infer from Osiek in light of her arguments and recommendations regarding the optics of suspicion. Again, I could not agree more. I believe however that such interdisciplinary resolve needs to be far more thorough and encompassing.

ENVISIONING THE FUTURE

What follows, I reiterate, is but an initial attempt on my part to conceptualize and formulate a way forward. I shall do so in terms of the crossroads as delineated above: increasing multiplicity of critical approaches, expanding integration of reading traditions, and a growing repertoire of academic interlocutors.

1. Multiplicity of Critical Approaches. The fundamental shifts in method and theory have brought about a drastically altered state of affairs in the conception and exercise of the discipline. This is true in terms of both critical diversity in general and ideological focalization in particular.

To begin, the impact of critical diversity has been enormous. What should be expected of critics today differs radically from what was expected through the early 1970s. Up until then, the field required expertise in one grand model of interpretation. Such training entailed one's mastery of and dexterity in a variety of reading strategies and theoretical frameworks. However, these presupposed a fairly distinctive and rather homogeneous mode of discourse—though, to be sure, with variations across the different methods and models. Since then, the field demands expertise in an increasing number of such grand models. This training calls for familiarity with and facility in various reading strategies and theoretical frameworks within each model. While each involves a fairly related and recognizable mode of discourse across strategies and frameworks, the variations in question now prove far more complex and demanding. It was one thing to go from, say, form criticism to redaction criticism. It is quite another to move from, say, literary criticism to postcolonial criticism, or from feminist criticism to materialist criticism.

In addition, the impact of ideological focalization has proved similarly far-reaching. On the one hand, the search for Christian antiquity (the securing of the foundations) has given way to a search for the construction of Christian antiquity (the exposé of the foundations). Rather than a sense of progressive research toward an ever-fuller portrayal of early Christianity, what prevails now is a sense that the constructions of early Christianity differ according to the particular discursive frameworks brought to bear upon the texts and contexts. On the other hand, the search for universality and neutrality in interpretation (the ideal of exegesis) has yielded to a search for the location and agenda of interpretation (the exposé of eisegesis). Instead of a sense of dispassionate observation in re-creation and reconstruction, what now prevails is a sense that critical context and perspective are inextricably involved in all interpretation as well as in the interpreters behind them.

Such developments cannot but have a significant effect on the concept of a theological reading in criticism. Several come readily to mind:

(1) The traditional historicization of the religious-theological dimension must be set aside altogether. My vision calls for a pursuit of this angle of inquiry across all interpretation as well: not only with respect to critics and their production in the contemporary postmodernist era, but also by revisiting and re-reading critics and their production from the modernist era.

(2) The religious-theological dimension as a central factor of human identity and as a problematic of power yielding unequal constructions and relations in society and culture must be foregrounded and analyzed in both the world of Christian antiquity and the world of early Christian studies. My vision calls for a pursuit of this problematic with the same intensity and rigor as the pursuit of other such problematics in recent decades. Just as critics must acquire expertise in such fields as gender studies and postcolonial studies, so they cannot do without expertise in constructive theological studies.

(3) Any sense of critics as a-religious and as a-theological must be abandoned, along with any dreams of establishing the foundations for constructive work in other theological disciplines. My vision calls for an approach to early Christian studies as an exercise in religious-theological construction of its own and for a view of critics as religious-theological agents in their own right, producing competing representations of early Christianity.

This aspect of the vision can generate many projects for the future. For example, in her evaluation of the project on minority criticism titled *They Were All Together in One Place? Toward Minority Criticism*, Mayra Rivera Rivera presses the project on the underlying conception of God at work in the project, at once noting the absence of such reflection on the part of contributors and urging attention to religious-theological issues.[52] Similarly, the concept of the role and task of criticism must be addressed as a problematic. What exactly is it that we do and why do we do it? This is precisely what a project on Latino/a criticism has undertaken to investigate.[53]

2. Integration of Reading Traditions. The shifts in method and theory have also brought about a reshuffling in the conception and practice of the discipline in terms of reading traditions, with academic or professional criticism viewed as one among several such traditions.

---

[52] See Mayra Rivera Rivera, "Incarnate Words: Images of God and Reading Practices," in *They Were All Together in One Place? Toward Minority Biblical Criticism*, ed. Randall C. Bailey, Tat-siong Benny Liew, and Fernando F. Segovia, Semeia Studies 57 (Atlanta: SBL Press, 2009), 313–29.

[53] See Francisco Lozada and Fernando F. Segovia, eds., *Latino/a Biblical Hermeneutics: Problematic, Objectives, Strategies*, Semcia Studies 68 (Atlanta: SBL Press, 2014).

Up to the early 1970s, among critics it was consensus opinion, if not an article of faith, that the scholarly reading of the Bible was inherently superior and hermeneutically privileged, providing the one proper and correct reading of the texts. This view of criticism was certainly elitist but by no means gnostic. First, it was a reading that called for systematic and arduous training but that was also open to anyone able and willing to undergo such training. Second, it was also a reading that called for dissemination from top to bottom—from graduate venues, to academic and ministerial venues, to ecclesial venues. Nowadays, given the view of the discipline as a crossroads involving a variety of grand models of interpretation, this sense of scholarly reading as unique has been displaced. On the one hand, professional criticism has emerged as a reading tradition based in the academy, subject to critical analysis regarding origins and principles, strategies and findings, context and agenda. On the other hand, professional criticism is further placed as one among several such traditions, all long-standing and wide-ranging and all subject to similar intensive scrutiny. Consequently, claims of hermeneutical privilege and inherent superiority no longer constitute a critical given but become instead features of a particular ideological project subject to critique.

To be sure, academic criticism is by no means abandoned as a result; the study of disciplinary history does remain a must, but attention to other reading traditions becomes a must as well. This is the move that I propose as cultural biblical criticism. Such study would include all other traditions of reading:

(1) The religious-theological tradition, which would encompass any number of different modes, such as the academic-scholarly (the constitutive disciplines of Christian studies and the tradition of religious studies), the institutional-ecclesial (liturgical and homiletical, denominational and official, catechetical and pastoral) and the popular-devotional (the many beloved and enduring practices observed in the daily lives of believers).

(2) The social and cultural tradition, which would bring together the appropriation and use of biblical motifs and themes, scenes and situations, in cultural production and social framework at large.

The ramifications of this development for theological reading in criticism are immense. This is a move that brings criticism into the full arena of Christian studies, no longer as a foundational discipline for the others but as a scrutinizing discipline of them, seeking to surface and analyze the dynamics and consequences of their use of the Bible, direct or indirect. This is also a move that brings criticism into the whole arena of Christian practices, no longer as imparting the truth but as analyzing the practices and results of reading the Bible wherever such activity takes place. Such a vision foresees the generation of any number of projects as well.

For example, within the American Academy of Religion my colleague Francisco Lozada and I have launched a multi-year project examining the use of the Bible in Latino/a constructive theology. In addition, within the Society of Biblical Literature, we have launched another multi-year project looking at the use of the Bible in Latin American theology. Similarly, the Free University of Amsterdam, under the leadership of the Dom Helder Camera Program and Professor Hans de Wit, has been pursuing a global project on intercultural criticism, with a focus on comparative reading of texts between and among concrete Christian communities throughout all continents.[54]

3. Broadening of Academic Interlocutors. The shifts in method and theory have further created a revamping in the conception and practice of the discipline in terms of interdisciplinary conversations. To be sure, the discipline has always been interdisciplinary in character, but the process of transformation has rendered it far more explicitly and broadly so.

Up to the early 1970s, introductions to the method and theory behind the established grand model of interpretation were uncommon. Introductions to the field focused briefly, if at all, on questions of method and theory and did not seek to connect with ongoing trajectories and debates in historical studies. Nowadays, given the recourse to literary and social studies as well as the appeal to the spectrum of ideological studies, it is indispensable, with regard to any major movement or grand model, to become conversant with the origins and parameters, the development and reception, of such methods and models within their respective fields of study. This means more than just a simple nod to a theory or theorist; it means critical appropriation of a body of literature and of any theory or theorist within such a corpus.

---

[54] See Daniel Schipani et al., eds., *Through the Eyes of Another: Intercultural Reading of the Bible* (Amsterdam: The Institute of Mennonite Studies and the Free University, 2004).

The consequences for theological reading in criticism are boundless. Intrinsic to any religious-theological reading, whether in the ancient world or in the modern and postmodern worlds, is the realization that this dimension cannot do without pursuit of what it presupposes and implies in terms of relations of power in society and culture. It is impossible to do theology in universal and innocent fashion. At the same time, such a reading cannot be occluded by such power constructions and relations but must be pursued in the light of them and with all of them in mind. It is impossible to reduce the religious-theological dimension to other levels of inquiry.

Examples of needed projects abound. In the conjunction between postcolonial studies and biblical studies, there is the theoretical mapping provided by *Postcolonial Biblical Criticism: Interdisciplinary Interventions* and the *Postcolonial Commentary on the New Testament Writings*.[55] Much needed are similar works pursuing the juncture between biblical studies and racial-ethnic studies as well as materialist studies, respectively. There is also an evident need for a sense of the biblical texts as an intersectional document, along with a sense of biblical critics as intersectional human beings.

4. Conclusion

I should like to conclude with a budding reflection about approaching the Bible as theory. I do so with two recollections in mind: the call by Meeks for biblical critics to address a variety of publics, beyond Christian communities and the academy, and the call by Osiek for biblical critics to address the critical questions of our time, beyond ecclesial communities. Both calls presuppose and activate a view of criticism as a public and engaged force in the world. Thus, for Meeks, critics have a key role to play in the dialogue between Christians and non-Christians, which includes not only matters religious and theological but also matters social and cultural, including the phenomenon of globalization. Similarly, for Osiek, critics have a role to play in the

---

[55] See, respectively, Stephen D. Moore and Fernando F. Segovia, eds., *Postcolonial Biblical Criticism: Interdisciplinary Intersections*, The Bible and Postcolonialism (London; New York: T&T Clark, 2005); and Fernando F. Segovia and R. S. Sugirtharajah, eds., *A Postcolonial Commentary on the New Testament Writings*, The Bible and Postcolonialism (London; New York: T. & T. Clark, 2007).

advancement of life over death in society and culture. My concept of the Bible as theory also presupposes and activates a public and engaged role for the critic in the world.

I do not have in mind the project of outlining, say, a theology of the New Testament which can then serve as a sort of charter for proper theological construction and praxis. I also do not have in mind a project involving a sense of Scripture as divinely revealed and uniquely normative. I have in mind, rather, an approach to early Christian production as an overall field of vision for reading and addressing the world, the other-world, and the relationship between the two worlds—all within a specific material matrix.

This field of vision I imagine as highly complex and conflicted, where convoluted and conflictive views of the world, the other-world, and their interaction are advanced. Such a field critics would address and critique from their own views of the world, the other-world, and their relation—from within their own specific material matrices. This would be done with a sense of the early Christian tradition as a way of thinking and acting in the world and of dealing with the problematic of society and culture as a whole. This would also be done with a sense of this tradition not as setting constricting parameters but rather as providing dialogical models. This would be further done with an eschatological vision of a world gone deeply awry in so many ways and of a world in which freedom and liberation, justice and peace, dignity and well-being, are desperately and relentlessly sought. It is such vision, decidedly incipient at this point, that I have in mind for doing biblical theory, as a theological reading of Scripture in and for our times.

CHAPTER 7

Negative Dialectics and Doxological Hope
Elements of a Critical Catholic Theology

Andrew Prevot

The claim that Catholic theology is a hermeneutical practice is not particularly controversial today. Disagreements remain about how exactly the self-implicating interpretation of Scripture, tradition, and experience should be carried out, but the interpretive task itself provides some common ground as a widely accepted alternative to manualist neoscholasticism.[1] By contrast, the claim that Catholic theology is a critical-theoretical practice is more fraught. Catholic theology and critical theory may be seen as rival, and perhaps even incompatible, pursuits.[2] To be sure, a large number of Catholic theologians have

---

[1] For example, the hermeneutical status of Catholic theology is affirmed and variously inflected in David Tracy, *The Analogical Imagination: Christian Theology and the Culture of Pluralism* (New York: Crossroad, 1998); Sandra Schneiders, *The Revelatory Text: Interpreting the New Testament as Sacred Scripture*, 2nd ed. (Collegeville, MN: Liturgical Press, 1999); and Joseph Ratzinger/Pope Benedict XVI, *Jesus of Nazareth* (New York: Doubleday, 2007).

[2] See, e.g., the evident tension between Catholic theology and critical theory in Paul Griffiths's article "Christ and Critical Theory," *First Things* (Aug./Sept. 2004): 46–55. Although Griffiths recognizes a certain "yearning" among secular critical theorists (such as Terry Eagleton, Jean-François Lyotard, Alain Badiou, and Slavoj Žižek) for the riches already contained in Catholic theology, he does not clarify the conditions under which Catholic theology could benefit from or enact some sort of critical theory. As a result, he gives the impression that Catholic theology and critical theory are on opposite sides of a major cultural and intellectual divide.

resisted this assumption by attempting to integrate some variety of critical theory into their theology (for example, calling their work political, liberation, black, feminist, queer, postcolonial, ecological, etc.).[3] But whether this highly pluralized integration of critical theory into Catholic theology is a coherent possibility and, if so, under what conditions, remain contested issues in need of further clarification.

Since hermeneutics and critical theory have a tense historical relationship of their own (reflected in the classic debate between Hans-Georg Gadamer and Jürgen Habermas),[4] the effort to clarify the idea of such a critical Catholic theology introduces unavoidable questions regarding the value of Catholic theology's now fairly standard hermeneutical self-definition. Has the Catholic theological alliance with hermeneutics sometimes functioned problematically as a self-protective shield against the full force of ideology critique? In other words, has the regnant understanding of Catholic theology as an act of interpretation within pre-given horizons of meaning reinforced a condition of blinkered complicity with certain pervasive (if often concealed) structures of violence and negativity in the world? Another sort of question arises from the other side: Would a more concerted effort to do critical theory within Catholic theology jeopardize the most welcome gains of the hermeneutical approach, such as the rewarding sense of belonging to a symbolically rich and normative faith tradition that calls for endless interpretation and retrieval?

In this discussion, it will also be important to consider to what extent the general models of hermeneutics and critical theory emerging from post-Enlightenment traditions of modern philosophy need to be challenged and corrected by Catholic theology. Surely Catholic

---

[3] In addition to the critical Catholic theologians featured in this essay below, one might consider other prominent examples of this trend such as Gustavo Gutiérrez, *A Theology of Liberation: History, Politics, and Salvation*, trans. Sister Caridad Inda and John Eagleson (Maryknoll, NY: Orbis Books, 2005); M. Shawn Copeland, *Enfleshing Freedom: Body, Race, and Being* (Minneapolis: Fortress Press, 2009); Paul Lakeland, *Theology and Critical Theory: The Discourse of the Church* (Nashville: Abingdon, 1990); and Susan Abraham, *Identity, Ethics, and Nonviolence in Postcolonial Theory: A Rahnerian Theological Assessment* (New York: Palgrave Macmillan, 2007).

[4] For a summary and analysis of this debate, see Paul Ricoeur, "Hermeneutics and the Critique of Ideology," in *From Text to Action: Essays in Hermeneutics, II*, trans. Kathleen Blamey and John Thompson (Evanston, IL: Northwestern University Press, 2007), 270–307, esp. 345n1.

theology cannot receive its fundamental identity and method entirely from traditions that, in their anthropocentrism, implicitly or explicitly contest it. But what then is the distinctively Catholic—and therefore ultimately theocentric—contribution to hermeneutics and critical theory? What is the Catholic theological mode of these contemporary intellectual practices, and what difference does it make? Any Catholic theology of the present or future that aspires to maintain a significant relationship with hermeneutics and critical theory will have to address these questions, namely, about the relative strengths and hazards of hermeneutics and critical theory and about their distinct modes of appearance inside and outside of Catholic theology.

Without pretending to resolve all of these issues here, I shall advance three interrelated theses that start to address them. First, I shall argue that certain characteristic features of Catholic theology (namely, its prophetic, apocalyptic, ascetical, and mystical aspects) demonstrate that it has an intrinsic capacity for the sort of *negative dialectics* that is definitive of critical theory. Catholic theology, therefore, does not need to acquire the *idea* of critical theory exclusively from the outside; it can and must develop this idea, along with its concrete historical and practical implications, from within. To be sure, critical theories formed outside the Catholic theological tradition may make significant and even somewhat disruptive challenges to the Catholic Church and to structures and societies in which it has been inculturated. These critical provocations may very well be worth receiving into the Catholic theological tradition as spurs toward needed transformation or development. But this reception will only be recognizable as a coherent possibility in the eyes of both Catholics and non-Catholics if the very idea of critical theory can be shown to have a valid place within the fundamental structure of Catholic theology or at least to be compatible with what is essential to this tradition. Otherwise any appearance of externally prompted changes will seem to imply some degree of self-contradiction, capitulation, or insincerity on the part of the Catholic Church.

This is why, in addition to studying concrete cases, it is important to investigate whether the very idea of critical theory is in any respects immanent to the constitution of Catholic theology, as I claim it is. Against any thinker (whether secular or theological) who suggests that Catholic theology lacks an internally consistent capacity to receive and engage in critical theory, I shall contend on the contrary that negative dialectics is an inherent and crucially important element of the Catholic theological tradition; it appears with various prophetic, apocalyptic, ascetical, and mystical accents but in all such cases remains absolutely essential. The works of Catholic theologians such as Edward Schillebeeckx, Ignacio Ellacuría, Johann Baptist Metz, Leonardo Boff, Jean-Luc Marion, and Maria Clara Bingemer support my contention in this regard.

As a second thesis, I shall argue that within Catholic theology negative dialectics is never separable from the equally constitutive element of *doxological hope*—that is, expectant longing for the divine savior who has already been shown (through the *doxa* and *logos* of divine revelation) to be worthy of infinite praise. The prophetic, apocalyptic, ascetical, and mystical features of Catholic theology illustrate in various ways the profound unity of negative dialectics and doxological hope. Moreover, these features thereby clarify the meaning and benefits of a theocentric (as opposed to anthropocentric) mode of critical theory. To sharpen the latter point, I shall examine Theodor Adorno's *Negative Dialectics* as a major source of contemporary critical theory in both secular and theological circles. On the one hand, I shall specify the considerable extent to which a critical Catholic theology can, from its own premises, endorse Adorno's negative dialectical method. On the other hand, I shall seek to demonstrate in what ways doxological hope distinguishes critical Catholic theology from the secular critical theory of Adorno and others.

The difference that emerges here is not inconsequential. Whereas Adorno suggests that theological commitment compromises negative dialectics, I shall argue on the contrary that such commitment (in the form of doxological hope) supports and strengthens it. Doxological hope does this not least by distancing negative dialectics more convincingly than Adorno does from the nihilism of an endless, insatiable critique (which I shall call an "interminable practice of negativity"). Moreover, insofar as doxological hope demands and brings about a rigorous negative dialectics of its own, it also avoids the no-less-threatening nihilism of blithe conformity to the structurally violent status quo (or "permanently tolerated negativity"), which is Adorno's very legitimate worry. Doxological hope thus seems to provide the only promising path beyond a *de facto* (if not strictly *de jure*) absolutization of the negative.

The third and final thesis that I shall argue is that a critical Catholic theology challenges the interpreting subject of hermeneutical philosophy and theology in two important ways. First, such a theology confronts this hermeneutical subject with a more pervasive awareness of negativity. It does not limit this unsettling consciousness of ideological distortion and destructive social forces to a mediating phase of "distanciation" within a more comprehensive fusion of cultural and personal horizons, but rather lets its interruptive power constantly provoke the question of the adequacy of any given horizon. Second, such a critical Catholic theology confronts the hermeneutical subject with a more serious theocentrism. It sets the self-constituting and meaning-making attempts of this subject over against the disconcerting background of an incomprehensible God whose glory and word will alone be decisive. To develop this third line of argument, I shall take up Paul Ricoeur's work (particularly *From Text to Action*) as a paradigmatic case of contemporary hermeneutical theory. Ricoeur's project has been welcomed without much criticism into the hermeneutically situated mainstream of Catholic theology. I see no reason why the key concepts of his theory of interpretation should not continue to inform and assist theologians who are striving to make sense of the symbols and texts in the Catholic faith tradition. Nonetheless, my critical intervention here is to claim that Ricoeur's hermeneutical theory and others comparable to it should be situated *within*—and thus not be allowed to over-determine, moderate, or in any other way significantly diminish—the unified practice of negative dialectics and doxological hope that is constitutive of critical Catholic theology. The interpretive decisions that "I" as hermeneutical subject make are dangerous if they are not constantly held in question both by a critical exposure of the worldly contradictions in which they may be implicated, and by the humble awareness that God's hidden ways are finally definitive. In these crucial respects, the best sort of Catholic theology may (surprisingly or not) be more closely aligned with the critical-theory side of the critical theory–hermeneutics debate than with the hermeneutics side. As the confrontation with Adorno demonstrates, such a critical Catholic theology simply needs to rethink the critical-theory side theocentrically.

Definitions of Negative Dialectics, Nihilism, and Doxological Hope

First, some definitions are in order.[5] With the term "negative dialectics," I mean to refer to any instance of thought, discourse, or practice that seeks to negate a negation or that at least has the somewhat intended possibility of doing so. In general, the idea here is that something is not true, is not just, is not good, and so on. Therefore, this first negation of truth, justice, goodness, or some similarly desirable condition (which may or may not be glimpsed exclusively in such cases of negative contrast or nonidentity) needs to be opposed by a second negation that helps us overcome it (a *negatio negationis*, in classical parlance). In more sophisticated modes of such negative dialectics, this second negation is achieved by a deeper analysis that exposes a primary negation that would otherwise have remained hidden beneath superficial positive values operating in culture and society. These obfuscating values, masquerading as the real thing and imbibed unthinkingly by participants in the cultural and social realities that they produce, can be called "ideologies" (with the strong pejorative connotation intended). "Critical theory," in the broad sense presupposed by the present argument, is nothing other than such an intellectually sophisticated, negative dialectical exposition of ideologies; this is why it may also be called "ideology critique." Such critical theory is most persuasive when it does not settle for mere polemic (a "No!" shouted angrily from the rooftops) but rather offers a well-researched negative disclosure of justice, truth, or goodness in the midst of certain justice-, truth-, or goodness-concealing circumstances.

Because the primary negations found in experience are not merely of a theoretical nature, they often require a secondary negation that is more than theoretical in order to address them. At its best, critical theory is thus cooperative with and "organically" connected to critical practices of active resistance against this or that structure of violence or harmful ideology. Whether more theoretically or practically oriented in

---

[5] Because this section is definitional, I have decided not to complicate it with numerous textual references. For a more thorough, textually mediated treatment of the relationship between critical theory and doxological hope, see Andrew Prevot, *Thinking Prayer: Theology and Spirituality amid the Crises of Modernity* (Notre Dame, IN: University of Notre Dame Press, 2015), esp. part 2. See also the discussion of particular Catholic theologians below.

any given instance, negative dialectics is supposed to have a purifying, enlightening, and liberating function. It is supposed to fight against idolatry, distortion, and complicity with evil wherever they appear. This is the reason for its widespread positive appeal. It represents the possibility of *freedom from*.

However, it is unfortunately very likely (perhaps even inevitable) that the supposedly liberating secondary act of negation which is the business of any critical theory or critical practice will have its own adverse characteristics that mirror the first and that will need to be met by another negation. What in this corrupt world has escaped every trace of some discoverable corruption? There is thus real potential for an endless repetition of the *negatio negationis* operation. Total purity is so elusive as to seem fantastical (i.e., "utopian," present nowhere). To be sure, this raises legitimate doubts about an encroaching nihilism. Can anything be wholeheartedly affirmed once critical theory has begun calling everything concrete into question? Let us call this the threat of an "interminable practice of negativity." And yet, any effort to avoid such a nihilistic fate by striving to halt the process of negative dialectics opens itself up to the equally odious danger of collaborating with deception and evil. This is another species of encroaching nihilism, which we might call the threat of a "permanently tolerated negativity." In either case, we have a negation or nonidentity that is rendered irremovable and in this sense absolutized. It is reasonable to ask what hope there can be in such an inescapably perilous situation. The very definition of negative dialectics as *negatio negationis* confronts us with the question (much more challenging than it may first appear) about how to escape some sort of at least *de facto* (i.e., not explicitly asserted) nihilism.

To the extent that the Catholic theological tradition answers this question, it does so hopefully and doxologically. In the midst of the world's ceaseless negations, uncertainties, and desperate struggles, hope comes in the forms of God's glory (*doxa*) and word (*logos*), which are transmitted through creation and history and especially through the pneumatologically saturated mysteries of the total Christ—that is, through his Spirit-filled life and Spirit-led church. The gifts of divine radiance and speech that we receive in these ways, and offer up to God in return, are mysterious signs pointing toward a promised eschatological fulfillment. Although it is possible and necessary to praise the triune God in thanksgiving for the magnificent gifts that we have already received, it is also incumbent on us to hope for a still more definitive arrival of this very God, which would embrace and transfigure all of creation through love. This eagerly anticipated divine advent would overcome the disconcerting negativities that continue to beset us and thereby usher in a purer doxological experience of mutual praise and self-giving, unalloyed by worldly antinomies and horrors.

This sort of doxological hope has a complex relationship with negative dialectics. On the one hand, doxological hope depends on negative dialectics to prepare the mind and the world—to purify them both—for God's promised reign of unforeseeable, comprehensive freedom. Doxological hope thus decidedly does not endorse the highly compromised *status quo* of our fallen world; rather, it demands a rigorous self-critical and socially critical preparation for a transcendently better situation. On the other hand, this hoped-for doxological fullness is the guiding light and animating goal of negative dialectics in its Catholic theological mode, which prevents negative dialectics from speaking a disheartening last word of ceaseless negation. Hence, if it is fair to assert that doxological hope needs negative dialectics (as a means), it is also fair to assert that negative dialectics needs doxological hope (as an end). This complex relationship is the key to Catholic theological resistance against the two nihilistic threats disclosed by the very idea of critical theory, namely, the permanent tolerance and interminable practice of negativity.

Accents in Critical Catholic Theology: The Prophetic, Apocalyptic, Ascetical, and Mystical

Edward Schillebeeckx describes the Catholic theological unity of negative dialectics and doxological hope well in *God the Future of Man*. He argues that Christian hope in the "God who is to come" critically negates left-wing totalitarian ideologies, right-wing conservations of the *status quo*, hubristic technological utopias, and "all 'negative dialectics' whose critical negativity is sterile"—by which he means devoid of life-giving possibility.[6] Schillebeeckx is renowned for his effort to establish a universal, *humanum*-respecting ethics in "negative contrast experience," that is, in the primordial experience of injustice which gives rise to negative dialectics of any sort. But in this passage we see

---

[6] Edward Schillebeeckx, *God, the Future of Man*, trans. N. D. Smith (London: Bloomsbury, 2014), 117.

that his revelation-informed hope in the God who will save offers a more comprehensive basis for critical negativity and rescues it from any nihilistic sterility to which it might otherwise succumb. It is time, I suggest, to retrieve Schillebeeckx not merely as a theorist of negative contrast experience but also as a critical Catholic theologian working in a state of (Christologically shaped) expectant praise.

However, rather than devote the remainder of this chapter to the detailed analysis that Schillebeeckx's synthesis of negative dialectics and doxological hope indeed deserves,[7] I wish to broaden the discussion by indicating a variety of formal ways in which negative dialectics and doxological hope come together in the Catholic theological tradition. In particular, it seems possible to distinguish certain prophetic, apocalyptic, ascetical, and mystical accents in the shared, two-element structure of negative dialectics and doxological hope which constitutes the model of critical Catholic theology that I have been highlighting here. The work of any given critical Catholic theologian may exhibit one of these accents more than another. This variety does not erode the most fundamental point of the present argument, namely, the underlying consensus that there is a doxologically conditioned capacity for critical theory within Catholic theology. Rather, this variety supports the idea of such a critical Catholic theology by illustrating its adaptability to and operative power within distinct strands of the Catholic tradition and distinct historical circumstances.

For Ignacio Ellacuría, for instance, the most salient feature is arguably the prophetic. In his last major article, he defines "propheticism" (*profetismo*) as "the critical contrasting of the proclamation of the fullness of the reign of God with a specific historical situation."[8] He also argues that propheticism "makes manifest the limitations (lack of divinization or of grace) and above all the evils (personal, social, and structural sins) of a specific historical situation."[9] Here we have precisely the *negatio negationis* operation of critical theory but also a clear

---

[7] The enduring fruitfulness of Schillebeeckx's work is evident in Lieven Boeve, Frederiek Depoortere, and Stephan van Erp, eds., *Edward Schillebeeckx and Contemporary Theology* (New York: T&T Clark, 2010).

[8] Ignacio Ellacuría, "Utopia and Propheticism from Latin America," in *A Grammar of Justice: The Legacy of Ignacio Ellacuría*, ed. J. Matthew Ashley, Kevin F. Burke, and Rodolfo Cardenal (Maryknoll, NY: Orbis Books, 2014), 7–55, at 11.

[9] Ibid., 12.

sense that it is illuminated by and oriented toward the glorious fullness of God's reign. Ellacuría demonstrates the prophetic character of his work in other texts as well by connecting the present-day struggles of the poor with the prophetic self-understanding of Jesus and the prophetic writings of the Hebrew Bible, particularly Isaiah's suffering servant songs.[10]

In the work of Johann Baptist Metz, by contrast, the predominant accent falls on apocalyptic. Throughout his writings, he often invokes the haunting prayer at the end of the book of Revelation, "Come, Lord Jesus!"[11] He protests modern culture's progressive evolutionary logic, arguing that it is "a way of thinking in which death's dominion over history has already been established" and in which "the God of the living and of the dead" becomes inconceivable.[12] The imminent expectation of this God's interruptive and resurrecting apocalypse forms the basis of Metz's negative dialectical engagement with such a blithe, apathetic culture. His apocalyptic hope shapes his response to the theodicy question—namely, his belief that one should preserve it as a question and ask it back to God, whose justification in the face of worldly anguish awaits the end of time. Moreover, it crowns his treatment of discipleship as a socially critical practice.[13]

A certain ascetical emphasis can be discerned in Leonardo Boff's work, particularly in his effort to retrieve Saint Francis of Assisi as a model for ecoliberationist theology. The central kind of asceticism that he, along with Francis, recommends is poverty. Although Boff denounces the present material impoverishment of much of the world's population as a dehumanizing injustice, he also endorses Francis's practice of voluntary poverty as a spiritual and ethical virtue that may help free the world from such dehumanizing impoverishment. Boff

---

[10] See Ignacio Ellacuría, "The Crucified People: An Essay in Historical Soteriology," trans. Phillip Berryman and Robert Barr, in *Ignacio Ellacuría: Essays on History, Liberation, and Salvation*, ed. Michael Lee (Maryknoll, NY: Orbis Books, 2013), 195–224.

[11] E.g., Johann Baptist Metz, *The Advent of God*, trans. John Drury (New York: Newman Press, 1970), 9 and 14.

[12] Johann Baptist Metz, *Faith in History and Society: Toward a Practical Fundamental Theology*, trans. J. Matthew Ashley (New York: Crossroad, 2007), 160.

[13] See Johann Baptist Metz, "Theology as Theodicy?," in *A Passion for God: The Mystical-Political Dimension of Christianity*, trans. J. Matthew Ashley (Mahwah, NJ: Paulist Press, 1998) and Metz, *Followers of Christ: The Religious Life and the Church*, trans. Thomas Linton (Mahwah, NJ: Paulist Press, 1978).

interprets Franciscan poverty as an embodied "freedom of spirit" that empowers one to use the goods of nature and culture in a responsibly detached, ecological, solidaristic, and anticonsumerist manner.[14] In this virtuous-ascetical sense, poverty critically negates the excesses of global capitalism, liberates the human being from disordered attachments, and cultivates a deep availability to God's loving will.

Finally, I want to mention two theological proponents of the mystical: Jean-Luc Marion and Maria Clara Bingemer. Marion may seem a strange choice here, since he is not typically read as a critical theorist. Nevertheless, his way of using Dionysius the Areopagite to resist the conceptual idolatry that he perceives in Western metaphysics and in certain postmodern offshoots (Martin Heidegger, Emmanuel Levinas, and Jacques Derrida) makes him a very valuable example of the theological unity of critical negativity and doxological anticipation. Marion argues that Dionysius is best understood not merely as a negative theologian, but as one who negates even the distinction between affirmation and negation in order to make room for a predication-transcending discourse of praise.[15] Marion's reading of this founding figure of Christian mysticism is important in the present argument mainly insofar as it shows the functioning of a Catholic *negatio negationis* in the realms of epistemology and ontology in addition to the areas of sociology, economics, and politics that we have mainly been considering.

To be sure, Bingemer does more than Marion to address these latter, more practically focused areas from a mystical perspective. Drawing on Metz's understanding of a "mysticism with open eyes," she develops it further by arguing that mystics of today are able to "see with transfigured eyes the conflictive reality of humanity, their vision purified of prejudice and discrimination."[16] The contemplative intimacy with God sought and enjoyed by contemporary mystics enables them to expose the negations in worldly life that need to be resisted and, moreover, gives them the courage to put this resistance to work through their

---

[14] Leonardo Boff, *Francis of Assisi: A Model for Human Liberation*, trans. John Diercksmeier (Maryknoll, NY: Orbis Books, 2006), 56.

[15] Jean-Luc Marion, *The Idol and Distance: Five Studies*, trans. Thomas Carlson (New York: Fordham University Press, 2001), 139–95.

[16] Maria Clara Lucchetti Bingemer, "Testimony: Mysticism with Open Eyes," in *Witnessing: Prophecy, Politics, and Wisdom*, ed. Maria Clara Bingemer and Peter Casarella (Maryknoll, NY: Orbis Books, 2014), 1–12, at 11.

embodied actions, even to the point of embracing suffering and death.[17] For Bingemer, then, mysticism is not a flight from the world but rather an empowering, divinely originated source of negative-dialectical engagements with the world, which are meant to transform it.

Agreeing and Disagreeing with Theodor Adorno

Let us turn now to Theodor Adorno. Catholic theologians can agree with many of the arguments in his masterwork of critical theory, *Negative Dialectics*. Without compromising their Catholicism, they can accept his devastating critical readings of Immanuel Kant, G. W. F. Hegel, Edmund Husserl, and Martin Heidegger—and, moreover, embrace the guiding thread that ties all of these readings together. Adorno exposes the ideologically implicated doctrines of identity that reign in different ways in each of these modern philosophies.[18] Although he appreciates Kant's three *Critiques*, he argues that their critical potential is compromised by an overarching transcendental idealism and an abstractive deontological morality, which obscure the concrete conditions of freedom. Although he values Hegel's dialecticism and anti-Kantian interweaving of philosophy and sociohistorical reality, he resists Hegel's absolute idealism and the absorption of negative dialectics into a totalizing synthesis. Although he welcomes Husserl's theory of categorical intuition and the concomitant rejection of scientific positivisms and reductionisms of every kind, he objects to its still rather Cartesian epistemological focus. Finally, although he affirms Heidegger's purported attempt to make philosophy more responsive to the phenomenal structures of existence and history, he protests the construction of a mystifying poetic ontology that would seem to fail miserably in this regard.[19]

---

[17] Ibid., 5.

[18] For a comparable Catholic theological confrontation with the same tradition of modern identity philosophy, see Hans Urs von Balthasar, *The Glory of the Lord: A Theological Aesthetics*, vol. 5: *The Realm of Metaphysics in the Modern Age*, trans. Oliver Davies, Andrew Louth, Brian McNeil, John Saward, and Rowan Williams (San Francisco: Ignatius Press, 1991), 429–596.

[19] Theodor Adorno, *Negative Dialectics*, trans. E. B. Ashton (New York: Continuum, 1987), 39, 67–69, 104, 120, 265, and 334.

Adorno suggests that each of these modern philosophies finds a way to deny the concrete matter on which their thinking nevertheless depends. For Adorno, this concrete matter is inseparably subjective, objective, individual, and social; hence, his "materialism" is not a crassly reductivist materialism. He argues that these philosophies deny this concrete matter by failing to deal rigorously enough with its constitutive moments of nonidentity. They interpret each given phenomenon as an expression of some prior, stipulated sameness in consciousness, being, the singular, or the collective, and thereby do not sufficiently negate what demands to be negated in it and in their own theorizing. The consequence, on Adorno's account, is not merely a lack of honesty with what appears. It is complicity with the powerful cultural, existential, and political negativities permeating concrete material reality that these philosophies both conceal and abet. As examples of such negativity, he cites the deadening homogenization of bourgeois life and, more horrifically, the incineration of Jewish lives in Auschwitz. According to Adorno, any philosophy of identity—which is to say any philosophy not characterized thoroughly by negative dialectics—falters at these points of overwhelming negativity; even if it remains silent, it colludes.[20]

A critical Catholic theology can join Adorno in each of these arguments while working from its own prophetic, apocalyptic, ascetical, and mystical sources. By extension, it can advance similar negative dialectical arguments in other theoretical and practical situations throughout a diverse, globalized world (thereby surpassing his Eurocentrism, androcentrism, and other delimiting types of narrowness). To recognize this possibility, one needs to be able to distinguish such a critical Catholic theology from the sorts of idealistic and mythological metaphysics that Adorno rightly resists. I claim that this can be done and that a negatively purified doxological hope is the key to doing so. Unlike any given species of identity philosophy, this precise sort of hope humbles one and makes one confront with uncompromising seriousness the moments of nonidentity that pervade concrete historical and material reality. This is the sort of hope that we see (with various accents) in Schillebeeckx, Ellacuría, Metz, Boff, Marion, and Bingemer—and, to be sure, they are not its only witnesses.

---

[20] Ibid., 363 and 367.

One must also be able to distinguish such a critical Catholic theology from Adorno's critical theory. Once again, a negatively purified doxological hope is key here: it opens the possibility for a critique of Adorno and makes clear a distinctive Catholic theological mode of negative dialectics. Adorno is not an explicit or *de jure* nihilist: he rejects such nihilism as another abstract identity philosophy and occasionally lets himself engage in some utopian imagination.[21] He also applies the *negatio negationis* operation to his own critical thinking, thereby shielding himself from any potential charges of hypocrisy or naiveté. Nevertheless, Catholic theologians can legitimately object to Adorno's insistence that "dialectics, the epitome of negative knowledge, will have nothing beside it."[22] This reduction of thought to the work of critical negation guarantees its secularity without demonstrating any necessity of doing so and without questioning any costs of this decision.[23] Along similar lines, Adorno restricts the meaning of hope to persistence: "It lies in the definition of negative dialectics that it will not come to rest in itself, as if it were total. This is its form of hope."[24] Hope, for Adorno, is constituted by a relentless will to critique, even one's own critiques. It coincides with permanent dissatisfaction. By contrast, for Catholic theologians, hope has a doxological character. It is theocentric. It takes us beyond ourselves and our own critical and self-critical capacities. I contend that this crucial difference need not diminish but may in fact strengthen the Catholic theological claim for a liberative *negatio negationis*.

Insofar as it is able to agree with Adorno's negative dialectical repudiation of multiple forms of modern identity philosophy, a critical Catholic theology can distinguish itself (at least as successfully as Adorno's critical theory can) from any *de facto* nihilism of permanently tolerated negativity—that is, from an ideological sanctification of the contradiction-rife *status quo*. At the same time, insofar as it disagrees

---

[21] Ibid., 150 and 381.

[22] Ibid., 405.

[23] Traces of some sort of "negative theology" or "minimal theology" in Adorno's work (as detailed, for example, in Christopher Craig Brittain, *Adorno and Theology* [New York: T&T Clark, 2010], 83–98) do not alter the overarching secularity of his project, which is to say its refusal of any explicit doxological hope in a saving God revealed historically in glory and word.

[24] Adorno, *Negative Dialectics*, 406.

with Adorno's methodological absolutism that asserts that negative dialectics should have "nothing beside it"—and must disagree because of its doxological hope—the very same critical Catholic theology can defend itself more successfully than Adorno's critical theory can against the charge of a *de facto* nihilism of interminable negativity. Both agreement and disagreement are therefore necessary.

Paul Ricoeur and the Place of Hermeneutics within a Critical Catholic Theology

Having defined, illustrated, and argued for the possibility of a critical Catholic theology that would be in certain (but not all) respects concordant with Adorno's critical theory, it remains necessary to consider what relationship such a theology would have with hermeneutics. More specifically, we need to discern where critical Catholic theology stands in the debate between critical theory and hermeneutics (as symbolized by the conceptually productive tension between Gadamer and Habermas). While working from the hermeneutical (i.e., Gadamerian) side of this debate, Ricoeur nonetheless seeks a mediating position that can incorporate some of the concerns of critical theory (i.e., Habermas and, before him, Adorno).[25] My question is whether Ricoeur's particular mediating position is the one best suited to a critical Catholic theology. This question is especially pertinent given the major influence that Ricoeur's hermeneutical theory has had on contemporary theology in general and Catholic theology in particular.[26]

According to Ricoeur, to understand any text (whether biblical, philosophical, literary, or otherwise) is to discover oneself through it and to be transformed through self-implicating reflections on the

---

[25] In the following discussion I leave aside Habermas because the present argument has already focused on Adorno and because Adorno's version of critical theory is less amalgamated with a distinct theory of communicative rationality that would need to be addressed on its own terms.

[26] In addition to the countless students and scholars who have been influenced by Tracy's *Analogical Imagination* and Schneiders's *Revelatory Text*, one might also consider more recent studies such as Dan Stiver, *Theology after Ricoeur* (Louisville, KY: Westminster John Knox, 2001); Stiver, *Ricoeur and Theology* (London: Bloomsbury, 2012); and Boyd Blundell, *Paul Ricoeur between Theology and Philosophy: Detour and Return* (Bloomington: Indiana University Press, 2010).

world that it opens up. In this respect, he proposes something similar to a Gadamerian fusion of horizons. Nevertheless, he distinguishes his hermeneutical theory from Gadamer's by placing a greater emphasis on the sharpening functions of explanation, distanciation, and ideology critique.[27] He believes that these dialectical negations are productive of more precise world- and self-understanding and that they contribute to more ethically engaged subjects. In this way, without relinquishing his affiliation with Gadamer, he concedes some ground to Habermas and critical theory. In short, he calls for a "critical hermeneutics."[28]

Nevertheless, one is still left with the impression that negative dialectics intervenes in Ricoeur's hermeneutical theory, as it does very differently in Hegel's metaphysics, mainly to serve the possibility of a greater synthesis. Ricoeur seeks an actualization of the self through its other, a mediation of identity by nonidentity, a designated place for the hermeneutics of suspicion within a larger self- and horizon-affirming hermeneutics of charity. This moderated use of the *negatio negationis* within a hermeneutical identity philosophy would not satisfy Adorno just because it is hermeneutical (admittedly a critical advance over metaphysics). To formulate his objection, Adorno would not need to argue (unconvincingly) that Ricoeur's hermeneutics is thoroughly uncritical. Rather, he could simply point out that its efforts at critique are generally counterbalanced and subordinated by a prior commitment to what Ricoeur calls "the creative renewal of cultural heritage."[29] I want to suggest provocatively here that Adorno would be right both to understand Ricoeur's meditating position in this way and to advocate a negative dialectical response to it—and right not only on his own terms but also on those of a critical Catholic theology.

The argument would be that Ricoeur shelters the hermeneutical subject (i.e., the interpreter who seeks meaning by blending his or her horizon of consciousness with the horizon of a text or tradition) in two problematic ways that diminish the import of negative dialectics and doxological hope, respectively. Only the first of these types of

---

[27] Ricoeur, "The Hermeneutical Function of Distanciation," in *From Text to Action*, 75–88, at 88.
[28] Ricoeur, "Hermeneutics and the Critique of Ideology," 294–99.
[29] Ibid., 306.

sheltering would concern Adorno, who would worry that Ricoeur coddles the hermeneutical subject too much by suggesting that whatever concrete contradictions or experiences of nonidentity may surface in his or her lifelong practice of interpretation will, as a rule, serve mainly as productive detours on the way toward a satisfying actualization of the self. By encouraging negation to be interpreted as distanciation, Ricoeur makes negation appear less threatening to whatever cultural heritage forms the basis of one's narratival development of identity. This heritage will, for *methodological* reasons (i.e., reasons supplied by hermeneutical theory), win out in the end, no matter what critical interruptions may divert it or enhance it in the meantime. The subject traveling this path seems to be guaranteed victory in advance by having a capacity (analogous to Hegelian *Geist*) to appropriate without serious loss anything that initially appears alien to it.

Ricoeur likewise seems to insulate the same hermeneutical subject against the most radical implications of doxological hope. This is the second problematic sort of shielding, which, though perhaps a matter of indifference to Adorno, would concern Catholic theologians: in a word, it is the problem of anthropocentrism. The God whose coming greatness cannot be conceived (*Deus semper maior*) may find in the hermeneutical subject a creature still too attached to the stories, meanings, and structures it has produced and inherited to be genuinely receptive to the fullness of life, freedom, and charity which are in store. In other words, Ricoeur's proposed agent of interpretation, a self-in-the-making who strives to contain negativity by categorizing it as an intermediate step along the path to the fusion of horizons (Gadamer's *Horizontsverschmelzung*), may thereby achieve a "self" (i.e., acquire a sense of identity) without any apparent need for a prophetic, apocalyptic, ascetical, or mystical intervention of the divine other that would surpass all previously given horizons and modes of subject-formation.

All in all, the *somewhat* sheltered status of Ricoeur's hermeneutical subject orients it toward conceptions of selfhood that are not sufficiently challenged or determined by the unity of negative dialectics and doxological hope, which we have seen is essential to critical Catholic theology. From the perspective of critical Catholic theology, therefore, Ricoeur's hermeneutical subject requires a twofold critique. As a counter-proposal, I would suggest that we reverse Ricoeur's priorities and treat the hermeneutical subject's fusion of horizons as a mediating moment *within* a simultaneously dialectical and doxological practice of self-critical thought. Interpretation would on this account be validated in a limited way as a productive, conceptually clarifying instrument of negative dialectics and doxological hope, rather than being accepted as an all-embracing method which would (intentionally or not) blunt the critical edge of both.

One might object that the doxological hope essential to Catholic theology makes it vulnerable to the very critiques of identity philosophy that Adorno would level against Ricoeur's hermeneutics. Similarly, one might object that doxology and hermeneutics are natural bedfellows: the glory of God and the word of God are transmitted to us through texts, symbols, and traditions that call for interpretation. In response to these two objections, I contend that a clear understanding of the theocentric character of doxological hope significantly changes the terms of the debate. The living God of doxological hope is not an identity we can grasp, even if the word "God" is sometimes used by certain identity philosophies. Moreover, this living God must therefore be sought at least as much by the negation of our textually and traditionally mediated interpretations as by their affirmation. The same points could not be made if the reasons for our hope were merely the preservation of some particular "cultural heritage." If that were the full meaning of Catholic theology, then Adorno would be correct to oppose it as an identity philosophy, and Ricoeur's hermeneutical theory would perhaps give us sufficient tools to think it rigorously (without perhaps saving it from Adorno's criticism). But the fact that God is in question here makes all the difference.

To mistake our interpretation of any worldly object for an adequate comprehension of the divine addressee of doxological hope is precisely idolatry. For any similarity or analogy that we might perceive (for example, in narratives, doctrines, experiences, and so on) which may truly communicate this mystery, there is an ever-greater dissimilarity kept intact by God's almighty transcendence.[30] Even if the worldly

---

[30] By making this point in the "theological language" of analogy (as Tracy calls it in *The Analogical Imagination*, 405), I intend to show that the sort of critical Catholic theology I propose in this chapter is not bound to be an exclusively dialectical (which is to say analogy-refusing) theology, à la the early Karl Barth. Rather, there is room for analogies (of being and grace), and the interpretive possibilities that they open up, within the critical unity of negative dialectics and doxological hope that constitutes critical Catholic theology. But this critical unity must be recognized to have a certain

presence of Christ in his historical and eucharistic bodies must for Catholics be exempt from the purifying work of negative dialectics, insofar as Catholics believe that in both of these modes Christ is really present as the word and glory of God made flesh, our interpretations of this mystery of Christ must nonetheless be subject to the highest scrutiny, since deadly worship of a false Christ is certainly conceivable. It is for these reasons (i.e., inevitable dissimilarity and corruptible Christology) that Catholic theologians can genuinely welcome the radicality and comprehensiveness of Adorno's negative dialectics without jeopardizing doxological hope. If our hope is truly *for God*, and not some idol of our own fashioning, it will be untouchable by any convincing dialectical critique of some concrete negativity operative in historical realities.

By the same token, this doxological hope will resist any attempt to define Catholic theology exhaustively as an act of hermeneutics performed by a human agent seeking self-understanding through the worlds opened up by texts, even biblical texts, to which Ricoeur admittedly gives some special attention.[31] However, we must consider precisely how far his theory extends. In his study of biblical hermeneutics, he acknowledges that faith involves a "movement of hope . . . following the paradoxical laws of a logic of overabundance" and insists that, for this reason, "faith eludes hermeneutics and attests to the fact that the latter has neither the first nor the last word."[32] Here Ricoeur

---

priority over any given analogy. Tracy himself acknowledges that "all the classic systematic theologies from Paul and John to our own day are *de jure* inadequate" (407). Tracy's analogical hermeneutics has value only in the search for *de facto* relative adequacies. Such a search is justified by "the always-already, not-yet event of the yes disclosed in the grace of Jesus Christ," and this search is necessary to avoid the "chaos of pure equivocity" (421). This is sound reasoning. Although Tracy's argument in this text supports a largely Ricoeurian approach to hermeneutics, it does not diminish the urgent need for negative dialectics (which he may nonetheless underemphasize; cf. 394–98), nor does it grant hermeneutics any power to attain a fully adequate understanding of the addressee of doxological hope. These are the main points that need to be emphasized here in order to defend a critical Catholic theology (*inclusive* of analogy and hermeneutics) against Adorno's legitimate critiques of identity philosophy.

[31] See, for example, Paul Ricoeur, *Figuring the Sacred: Religion, Narrative, and Imagination*, trans. David Pellauer, ed. Mark Wallace (Minneapolis: Augsburg Fortress Press, 1995), 129–201.

[32] Ricoeur, "Philosophical and Biblical Hermeneutics," in *From Text to Action*, 99.

seems to concur that his hermeneutical theory cannot be absolutely decisive for a faithful theology, which must operate by a different "logic of overabundance." To be sure, some highly sophisticated sort of hermeneutics must remain part of any critical Catholic theology (otherwise it will have no understanding of what it seeks to discuss), but in the final analysis this hermeneutics will have to be tested (and ultimately be found wanting) in the blinding, fiery, purifying presence of God's glory and word. A prophetic, apocalyptic, ascetical, and mystical theology puts lasting hope in nothing else.

Conclusion

In this chapter, I have attempted to clarify the idea of a critical Catholic theology composed of the equally necessary elements of negative dialectics and doxological hope. This sort of critical Catholic theology can be accented in various ways. I have pointed toward certain prophetic, apocalyptic, ascetical, and mystical accents, but there may be others. It can also be developed concretely to meet the needs of a wide variety of historical communities struggling with diverse (and sometimes intersecting) crises. I have not offered much specific analysis in this area, leaving it for other scholars and for other occasions. My decision to focus here on the very idea of a critical Catholic theology stems from a desire to contest the un-argued assumption, which both Catholics and non-Catholics may be tempted to hold, that critical theory and Catholic theology are strictly opposed and perhaps even irreconcilable discourses. This assumption cedes the practice of critique to the realm of modern secularity and reinforces an unsatisfactory view of Catholic theology as an uncritical and hence morally compromised endeavor. Secular theorists may be happy to promote such a picture, but I do not see any reason why Catholic theologians would give credence to it. My hope is that the idea of a critical Catholic theology will grant some *prima facie* legitimacy to various concrete uses of negative dialectics within the field of Catholic theology, shifting the argumentative terrain away from any abstract doubts about critical theory and toward more specific debates about what sorts of experiences of negativity require what sorts of critical yet doxologically conditioned responses.

The sort of critical Catholic theology I propose is not inimical to hermeneutics or, for that matter, to analogy; on the contrary, it depends on both hermeneutics and analogy. Nonetheless, it does ask the hermeneutical subject to surrender her- or himself both to the full force of ideology critique and to the radical theocentrism (including disquieting adventures of divine unknowing) implied by doxological hope. Even though it is inclusive of hermeneutics, the sort of critical Catholic theology that I have sought to articulate in this text should be able to be recognized as a genuine mode of critical theory by both secular thinkers and theologians (even though the former will likely question its theocentrism). It deserves this recognition as a type of critical theory because its methodological commitment to negative dialectics (in other words, its broad agreement with Adorno's thoroughgoing critique of identity philosophy) is real and serious. In view of this agreement, it cannot be easily accused of a *de facto* nihilism of permanently tolerated negativity. Nevertheless, such a critical Catholic theology also identifies and seeks to avoid the particular nihilistic threat that comes with severing negative dialectics from doxological hope, namely, the threat of an interminable practice of negativity. In this respect, it moves beyond Adorno and can articulate good reasons for doing so.

More discussion would be needed in order to weigh the differences between a distinctively Catholic expression of negative dialectics and doxological hope and similar ideas coming from other traditions (including perhaps certain secular forms of utopian thinking, which I have not sufficiently considered here). By focusing on critical Catholic theology in this paper, I certainly do not wish to exclude the more inclusive possibility of a critical Christian theology or, for that matter, a critical comparative theology drawing on multiple traditions. The narrowness of focus in this case is meant merely to emphasize that Catholic theology can recognize and develop its own intrinsic critical capacities.

In the twenty-first century, we seem to be approaching a broad consensus regarding the question of whether Catholic theology can in some sense be considered a hermeneutical practice. Across various sorts of dividing lines, many Catholic theologians seem willing to say "yes" to this proposition. To be sure, some may want to hold the hermeneutical task in tension with other more deductive methods of theological reasoning characteristic of some sort of scholasticism. I do not want to deny here the relative value that may still be found in these sorts of reasoning, but I do want to emphasize what seems to be the clear predominance of a hermeneutical approach, in which Catholic theology is construed as a self-implicating interpretation of scripture, tradition, and experience. Can any near consensus of this sort be reached on the question of whether Catholic theology may be understood, perhaps even more crucially, as a critical-theoretical exercise? It is difficult to discern how close we may be to such a possibility. But at least the idea of a critical Catholic theology should no longer appear inconceivable.

CHAPTER 8

A Synodal Church
On Being a Hermeneutical Community

Ormond Rush

A third phase in the reception of Vatican II is beginning. After initial enthusiasm fifty years ago, and then—*de facto,* despite the rhetoric—official caution for thirty-five years, now it would seem greater freedom to implement the full vision of the council is enthusiastically promoted in the pontificate of Pope Francis. Like his predecessors, he also often quotes Vatican II; but there is something different. The shift could well be described as a move toward a more listening church. And, if there is one above all who is being officially invited into the conversation, then it is the third person of the Blessed Trinity—the Holy Spirit.

"Listen to what the Spirit is saying to the churches." The cry rings out seven times in the last book of the New Testament, the book of Revelation.[1] The essential medium through which the Spirit speaks to the churches is the Spirit's gift of *sensus fidei*. The ecclesial reality of the *sensus fidei*, given by the Holy Spirit to baptized Christians and to the church as a whole, is affirmed in *Lumen Gentium* 12.[2] This "sense

---

[1] Rev 2:7, 11, 17, 29; 3:6, 13, 22 (all biblical references use the New Revised Standard Version translation).

[2] *Lumen Gentium* 12 states: "The holy people of God has a share, too, in the prophetic office of Christ, when it renders him a living witness, especially through a life of faith and charity, and when it offers to God a sacrifice of praise, the tribute of lips that honour his name. The universal body of the faithful who have received the anointing of the holy one, cannot be mistaken in belief. It displays this particular quality through *a supernatural sense of the faith in the whole people* [*supernaturali sensu fidei totius populi*]

of/for the faith," the council teaches, enables the church to continue responding faithfully to God's loving self-revelation, i.e., to be infallible in believing. In the reception of the Council over the past fifty years, the implications of this teaching have hardly begun to affect the official learning and teaching processes of the Catholic Church. However, it certainly appears that the Catholic Church is entering into a new phase in the reception of LG 12. The faithful have an increasing awareness of the importance of their own sense of the faith for revitalizing the church in an age of unbelief; theologians are giving more attention both to the *sensus fidei* as a topic for systematic reflection and, accordingly, to the *sensus fidei* of their own local communities; and, among the hierarchy, Vatican II's doctrine of the *sensus fidei* seems to be receiving greater acknowledgment. Of significance here is the prominent role the *sensus fidei* of the whole people of God plays in the ecclesial vision of Pope Francis. His favorite passage would surely be LG 12 on the *sensus fidei*; and his favorite image of the church is that of "the people of God," the title of the chapter in which LG 12 is situated.

Early in his pontificate, in an August 2013 interview with the editor of the Jesuit periodical *La Civiltà Cattolica*, Pope Francis revealed something of his personal ecclesiology being grounded in Vatican II:

> The image of the Church I like is that of the holy, faithful people of God. This is the definition I often use, which is the image of *Lumen Gentium*, no. 12. Belonging to a people has a strong theological value. . . . The people themselves are the subject. And the Church

---

when 'from the bishops to the last of the faithful laity,' it expresses the consent of all in matters of faith and morals. *Through this sense of the faith* which is aroused and sustained by the Spirit of truth, the people of God, under the guidance of the sacred magisterium to which it is faithfully obedient, receives no longer the words of human beings but truly the word of God; it adheres indefectibly to 'the faith which was once for all delivered to the saints;' it penetrates more deeply into that same faith through right judgment and applies it more fully to life." Second Vatican Council, Dogmatic Constitution on the Church (*Lumen Gentium*) 12, in *Decrees of the Ecumenical Councils*, vol. 2: *Trent to Vatican II*, ed. Norman P. Tanner (London: Sheed & Ward; Washington, DC: Georgetown University Press, 1990), 858. Hereafter Vatican II documents are cited by abbreviation and paragraph in the text; e.g., (LG 12), and all subsequent translations are from the Tanner edition: LG = *Lumen Gentium*; DV = Dogmatic Constitution on Divine Revelation (*Dei Verbum*); GS = Pastoral Constitution on the Church in the Modern World (*Gaudium et Spes*).

is the people of God on the journey through history, with joys and sorrows. *Sentire cum Ecclesia* [to think and to feel with the Church], therefore, is my way of being a part of this people. And all the faithful, considered as a whole, are infallible in matters of beliefs, and the people display this *infallibilitas in credendo*, this infallibility in believing, through a supernatural sense of the faith of all the people walking together. This is what I understand today as the "thinking with the Church" of which St Ignatius speaks. When the dialogue among the people and the bishops and the Pope goes down this road and is genuine, then it is assisted by the Holy Spirit. So this thinking with the Church does not concern theologians only. . . . And, of course, we must be very careful not to think that this *infallibilitas* of all the faithful I am talking about in the light of Vatican II is a form of populism. No, it is the experience of the "holy mother the hierarchical Church," as St Ignatius called it, the Church as the people of God, pastors and people together. The Church is the totality of the people of God.[3]

A few months later, Pope Francis echoed these same thoughts in his Apostolic Exhortation *Evangelii Gaudium*.[4]

In this chapter, I propose that the ecclesial reality and authority of the *sensus fidelium* can be fruitfully explored by employing the "background theory" of hermeneutics.[5] Of course, as Jürgen Habermas

---

[3] Pope Francis, *My Door Is Always Open: A Conversation on Faith, Hope and the Church in a Time of Change; Pope Francis with Antonio Spadaro* (London: Bloomsbury, 2014), 49–50. This interview took place over three meetings in August 2013.

[4] "In all the baptized, from first to last, the sanctifying power of the Spirit is at work, impelling us to evangelization. The people of God is holy thanks to this anointing, which makes it infallible *in credendo*. This means that it does not err in faith, even though it may not find words to explain that faith. The Spirit guides it in truth and leads it to salvation (*Lumen Gentium*, 12). As part of his mysterious love for humanity, God furnishes the totality of the faithful with an instinct of faith—*sensus fidei*—which helps them to discern what is truly of God. The presence of the Spirit gives Christians a certain connaturality with divine realities, and a wisdom which enables them to grasp those realities intuitively, even when they lack the wherewithal to give them precise expression." Pope Francis, Apostolic Exhortation *Evangelii Gaudium*, §119, http://w2.vatican.va/content/francesco/en/apost_exhortations/documents/papa-francesco_esortazione-ap_20131124_evangelii-gaudium.html.

[5] On the function of "background theories" in theological method, see Francis Schüssler Fiorenza, "Systematic Theology: Task and Methods," in *Systematic Theology: Roman Catholic Perspectives*, ed. Francis Schüssler Fiorenza and John P. Galvin, 2nd ed. (Minneapolis: Fortress Press, 2011), 1–78, at 56–58.

noted in his critique of Hans-Georg Gadamer's hermeneutical notion of tradition: "Hermeneutic consciousness remains incomplete as long as it does not include a reflection upon the limits of hermeneutic understanding."[6] Other background theories, such as critical theories, can well aid the church in developing its theology of the *sensus fidei*, by opening up further perspectives on the complexity of the world in which the faithful live the Gospel.

The background theory of hermeneutics I believe is especially relevant for interpreting four major teachings of the Second Vatican Council. First, divine revelation is not only, nor primarily, a series of doctrines and morals formulated throughout church history, although it includes these in a secondary and qualified sense. Rather, revelation is primarily a personal encounter with the Living God in all ages throughout history, and it is the Holy Spirit who enables the human reception of this personal revelation by bestowing the gift of faith (DV 2, 5). Second, along with the gift of faith (*fides*), the Holy Spirit gifts baptized individuals and the whole community of faith with a hermeneutical skill, a *sensus fidei*, i.e., "a sense for" understanding, interpreting, and applying the faith through time (LG 12). With the gift comes the ability both to receive the gift and to contextualize the gift. Third, this divine revelation and its accompanying gift of *sensus fidei* are communicated not only to the pope and bishops (as if we were some gnostic sect of select *Illuminati*) but to "the whole body of the faithful," the *universitas fidelium* (LG 12). Fourth, in this way "the God who spoke of old still maintains an uninterrupted conversation with the bride of his beloved Son [i.e., the church]. The holy Spirit, too, is active, making the living voice of the gospel ring out in the church, and through it in the world, leading those who believe into the whole truth, and making the message of Christ dwell in them in all its richness" (DV 8). In other words, divine revelation is happening here and now, and the Spirit's gift of *sensus fidei* enables its faithful interpretation.

---

[6] Jürgen Habermas, "The Hermeneutic Claim to Universality," in *The Hermeneutic Tradition: From Ast to Ricoeur*, ed. Gayle L. Ormiston and Alan D. Schrift (Albany: State University of New York Press, 1990), 245–72, at 253. For Gadamer's approach, see Hans-Georg Gadamer, *Wahrheit und Methode: Grundzüge einer philosophischen Hermeneutik* (Tübingen: Mohr, 1960); ET: *Truth and Method*, 2nd rev. ed., trans. Joel Weinsheimer and Donald G. Marshall (New York: Crossroad, 1989 [based on the 5th German ed., 1986]).

And in the here and now, God may just be teaching the church new perspectives on God's plan for humanity as history unfolds.

Reading these four teachings in a hermeneutical key opens up avenues for exploring the ecclesial implications of the dialogue that God continues to have with the church in our own time. And, it thus opens up ways of understanding the eschatological character of Christian truth; the story is never finished, until the eschaton. God continues to surprise us and to provoke us. And the *sensus fidei* is the antenna for sensing those surprises and provocations.

Around the time of his appointment as archbishop of Chicago in September 2014, Blase Cupich spoke of the uncomfortable challenge Pope Francis is currently presenting for the Catholic Church. He said: "One of the lines that [Pope Francis] uses [is] '*realities* are greater than ideas.' . . . I think the pope is giving us *a new epistemology, a new way of learning, of knowing—another way in which we're informed*. We can really get caught up in living in our own little bubble of an idea or an illusion of things the way they have been in the past. It's important not to have just a 30,000 feet perspective on life but to really be there in the reality of the situation and pay attention to the observables right now around you."[7]

Hermeneuts reading this may have sensed that in Cardinal Cupich's words there is an evocation of something of the so-called "hermeneutical circle" or "spiral": i.e., we get a sense of the whole (in theological terms, the doctrinal perspective) by getting down into the detail (the pastoral perspective); and from the perspective of the detail, we have to form a revised and more "real" sense of the whole; and so it continues in an ongoing hermeneutical circle. Observing a valley below from a plane 30,000 feet up gives *one* sense of context. Landing the plane, getting out, and walking through a village in the valley gives a very different sense of things. But, then again, this gives only one sense of context on the ground—there are other villages in the valley.

Let's put this another way. According to the notion of the hermeneutic circle, understanding is a circular movement from "the whole"

---

[7] Joshua J. McElwee, "Exclusive: Chicago's New Archbishop Talks About 'Stepping Into the Unknown,'" *National Catholic Reporter*, Sep. 21, 2014, http://ncronline.org/news/people/ exclusive-chicagos-new-archbishop-talks-about-stepping-unknown (emphasis added).

to "the part" and back to the whole again. For example, I may come to a topic with only a vague knowledge of the subject matter. The "whole" of my knowledge is limited; my current position is one of "not-knowing." I may go to a dictionary or an encyclopedia to get an overview, thus broadening my knowledge of "the whole." Perhaps one particular aspect of the topic grabs my attention, and a question may formulate in my mind about the matter. So I telescope in on the narrower question, seeking an answer. My knowledge of the whole already gained gives some kind of context to what I now learn about the partial detail. I understand the detail in terms of the general view I already have; I understand the part in terms of the whole. The consequence of this narrower enquiry is an expansion of my knowledge of the whole. This back and forth process of questioning, from whole to part and back again, from general to particular and back again to general knowledge, is the rhythm of the hermeneutical circle. Some authors prefer to speak of "the hermeneutical spiral," an expression that perhaps better captures the ongoing dynamic of understanding. We don't just return to the same point in a circle—we now see differently than before. This circle or spiral is similar to the way we come to know the past and the present. We only know the present out of the past, and we only know the past out of the present. This interrelationship of past and present is also a hermeneutical circle.

The church well knows this dynamic, with its ongoing challenge, however much it might sometimes try to avoid the challenge. But, *from its very origins*, the church has always been a "hermeneutical" community—it is embedded in the church's DNA. As it moves through history, it is always necessary that the church interpret the Gospel for new times and contexts. Indeed, this hermeneutical task "must ever be the law of all evangelization" (GS 44). In the very process that gave rise to the New Testament, those early disciples, even pre-Easter, were interpreting Jesus, trying to "make sense" of his words and deeds, and of his identity in relationship with the God whose kingdom he was so focused on. But a decade or so later, someone like a Paul or an evangelist was asking, what does all that mean for my community? The New Testament canon (the finally-agreed-upon collection of twenty-seven writings), chosen by the early churches to stand thereafter as the ultimate benchmark regarding the faith for all time, is a testament to diverse "senses of the faith" in the church's earliest proclamations of the one faith in Jesus Christ. These writings are the classic examples of the *sensus fidei* at work in the life of the early churches. During the so-called Apostolic Period of the first and second centuries CE, we see local hermeneutical communities, *from within* and *for* their own contexts, interpreting and interrelating both their experience of divine revelation and the formulations of the faith and Christian practices that they have had passed on to them.

There is at work here what I have called elsewhere an "apostolic hermeneutic," an interpretive dynamic within the first few generations of the church regarding Jesus Christ and the implications of his teaching and way of acting within the changing circumstances of economic, social, cultural, and political life.[8] The results of this "apostolic hermeneutic" become normative for all times, including our own. We too must operate out of an apostolic hermeneutic and be equally creative for the sake of fidelity to the same God, who is still revealing and saving in Christ through the Spirit in our own time.

The two synods of bishops on marriage and the family in 2014 and 2015 were not only about moral and sacramental theology, nor simply about the church's past doctrinal teaching. They were, at a more fundamental level, about *hermeneutics*—and the ramifications of one's particular hermeneutic for key issues in fundamental theology (revelation and faith) and ecclesiology (the salvific mission of the church in a complex and constantly changing world). The 2014 synod had already exposed deep conflicts in interpretation, deep rifts regarding what the church should be all about, and in particular the interrelationship between doctrine and pastoral "realities" (as Pope Francis likes to call them). All this has ignited *a hermeneutical battle* that rages on even now, as we try to assess the implications of these two synods.

The German philosopher Odo Marquard, in his essay "The Question, To What Question Is Hermeneutics the Answer?" situates a significant point in the origins of the modern hermeneutical tradition in the religious wars of the seventeenth century following the Reformation.[9] He depicts the devastating Thirty Years' War (1618–48) as

---

[8] See Ormond Rush, *The Eyes of Faith: The Sense of the Faithful and the Church's Reception of Revelation* (Washington, DC: The Catholic University of America Press, 2009), 116–29.

[9] Odo Marquard, "The Question, To What Question Is Hermeneutics the Answer?," *Farewell to Matters of Principle: Philosophical Studies*, trans. Robert M. Wallace (New York:

"a civil war of the absolute text" between Catholics and Protestants.[10] The Latin word for "hermeneutics" (*hermeneutica*), he notes, is first found in 1654, six years after the end of the Thirty Years' War and the so-called Peace of Westphalia. Marquard's thesis is that "hermeneutics gives an answer to this experience of the deadliness (*Tödlichkeitserfahrung*) of the hermeneutic civil war over the absolute text by inventing—thus turning itself into pluralizing, which is to say literary, hermeneutics—the nonabsolute text and the nonabsolute reader."[11] He makes a distinction between "singularizing hermeneutics" and "pluralizing hermeneutics." For singularizing hermeneutics, on the one hand, there is only "the one correct reading . . . the one absolute reading (for salvation) of the Bible."[12] Pluralizing hermeneutics, on the other hand, "traces out many possible meanings and the most various kinds of spirit in one and the same literal form."[13] In the religious wars, both sides were working out of their own singularizing hermeneutics, with tragic consequences, as Marquard observes:

> The dogmatic quality of the claim to truth that is made by the unambiguous interpretation of the absolute text can be deadly: that is the experience of the religious civil wars. When, in relation to the sacred text, two interpreters assert, in controversy, "I am right; my understanding of the text is the truth, and in fact—and this is necessary for salvation—in this way and not otherwise": then there can be hacking and stabbing. Hermeneutics, when it turns into pluralizing hermeneutics, gives an answer to precisely this situation when it asks: Could this text not be understood, after all, in still another way, and—if that is not sufficient—still another way, and again and again in other ways?[14]

Oxford University Press, 1989), 111–37; *Abscheid vom Prinzipiellen* (Stuttgart: Reclam Verlag, 1981).

[10] Ibid., 122. On the religious wars and their aftermath, see particularly Peter H. Wilson, *The Thirty Years War: Europe's Tragedy* (Cambridge, MA: Belknap Press of Harvard University Press, 2009); Benjamin J. Kaplan, *Divided by Faith: Religious Conflict and the Practice of Toleration in Early Modern Europe* (Cambridge, MA: Belknap Press of Harvard University Press, 2007).

[11] Marquard, "The Question," 122. Translation corrected.

[12] Ibid., 121.

[13] Ibid., 122.

[14] Ibid., 123. Marquard's approach has affinities with that of Paul Ricoeur's notion of a text's "surplus of meaning," by which the reader makes of the text. See, for example,

A text thus invites a dialogue with future generations down through history. This ongoing process of pluralizing hermeneutics is evident within the Bible itself.[15] Applying such a pluralizing hermeneutics, as a background theory, to the human interpretation of divine revelation is not a denial of the status for Christians of the Bible as the written Word of God and its function as the canon of the Christian faith.[16] Nor is it some capitulation to a dictatorship of relativism in interpretation. Rather, it is a recognition that "realities are greater than ideas" in the transmission of revelation in new contexts.

Certainly the distinction between singularizing and pluralizing hermeneutics captures something of the tension within the Catholic Church in our own time. There have been some who have publicly voiced their concern over the present pope, his privileging of "mercy" in the interpretation of Scripture and tradition, and what they perceive as his promotion of "a weaker, pastoral permissiveness and a Christianity-lite, a way of being Christian at a reduced cost. So they see in mercy a kind of 'fabric softener' that undermines the dogmas and commandments and abrogates the central and fundamental meaning of truth."[17] Cardinal Walter Kasper speaks of the pope's lens for interpreting and applying the Gospel in a new context as a "hermeneutical principle" in a way that appears to want to avoid any singularizing hermeneutics:

> One can . . . characterize this highlighting of mercy—as a foundational hermeneutical principle—as a paradigm shift: from a deductive method to a method in the sense of see-judge-act, which begins inductively at first and, only in a second step, introduces theological criteria. Such a paradigm shift can elicit irritations and

---

Paul Ricoeur, *Interpretation Theory: Discourse and the Surplus of Meaning* (Fort Worth: Texas Christian University Press, 1976).

[15] See, e.g., Mogens Müller and Henrik Tronier, eds., *The New Testament as Reception* (New York: Sheffield Academic Press, 2002).

[16] On the Bible as not being "revelation" as such for Christians, but rather a "revelatory text," requiring interpretation from different worlds "in front of the text," see Sandra M. Schneiders, *The Revelatory Text: Interpreting the New Testament as Sacred Scripture*, 2nd ed. (Collegeville, MN: Liturgical Press, 1999).

[17] Walter Kasper, *Pope Francis' Revolution of Tenderness and Love: Theological and Pastoral Perspectives*, trans. Willam Madges (New York: Paulist Press, 2015), 34. On the opposition to Pope Francis from certain cardinals and bishops, see, e.g., Massimo Faggioli, "The Italian Job: Can Pope Francis Manage His Local Opposition?," *Commonweal* (August 15, 2014): 17–20.

misunderstandings . . . , as if what had been previously said was no longer valid. However, rightly understood, the paradigm shift does not change the previously valid content of what has been taught, but certainly changes the perspective and the horizon in which it is seen and understood.[18]

The appeal of Pope Francis's opponents to the absolute character of Scripture, as well as the absolute character of the church's doctrinal tradition on those texts, does sound a bit like a "singularizing hermeneutics," and indeed, a declaration of war—without perhaps the actual "hacking and stabbing" of 1614–48.[19] And it does seem to be an ecclesial conflict as significant as that hermeneutical battle in the early church between Paul and Peter over circumcision and the implications of the Gospel in a new non-Jewish context.[20] In tension here were appeals to "the Law of Moses" (Acts 15:5) and appeals to "the truth of the gospel" (Gal 2:14). In the midst of such hermeneutical battles, the New Testament does provide us with a model for coming to a *consensus fidelium*. At the so-called Council of Jerusalem, "after there had been much debate" (Acts 15:7) and sharing of the diverse *sensus fidei* of the community gathered in "council," together they were able at the end of it all to say: "For *it has seemed good to the Holy Spirit and to us* to impose on you no further burden than these essentials" (Acts 15:28). Openness to a pluralizing hermeneutics can lead to dialogue and, through dialogue, to a *consensus fidelium*. Dialogue is the means through which the Spirit communicates.

Cardinal Luis Tagle has recently made a distinction between "problems" and "dilemmas." "Problems," he said, can be solved, but "dilemmas" don't have clear and universal solution. Learning how the faithful have faced dilemmas, he went on, can only be accessed by listening

---

[18] Kasper, *Pope Francis' Revolution*, 35.

[19] Marquard, "The Question," 123.

[20] Gal 2:11-14: "But when Cephas came to Antioch, I opposed him to his face, because he stood self-condemned; for until certain people came from James, he used to eat with the Gentiles. But after they came, he drew back and kept himself separate for fear of the circumcision faction. And the other Jews joined him in this hypocrisy, so that even Barnabas was led astray by their hypocrisy. But when I saw that they were not acting consistently with the truth of the gospel, I said to Cephas before them all, 'If you, though a Jew, live like a Gentile and not like a Jew, how can you compel the Gentiles to live like Jews?'" On these issues, see Ian J. Elmer, *Paul, Jerusalem and the Judaisers: The Galatian Crisis in Its Broadest Historical Context* (Tübingen: Mohr Siebeck, 2009), 81–116.

to their stories. "Tell stories of people who have navigated through those murky waters of dilemmas. . . . You don't need a solution. You need meaning. You need hope."[21] Listening to the stories of the people of God and the dilemmas they have faced in their journey through the murky waters of their lives is simply listening to their *sensus fidei*, their "senses of the faith."[22] Those *sensus fidei* may very well have been formed in prayerful conversation with the Holy Spirit who graced them with that gift in their baptism. Their *sensus fidei* reveal how they have sensed the Gospel and have decided to act in their circumstances. Hearing those stories is hearing stories of *the Holy Spirit at work*, the one who is the Enlightener, the Interpreter, the Hermeneut. Through the exercise of their sense of the faith, in the reality of their constrained lives in the changing contexts of human history, God is in dialogue with humanity throughout that history (DV 8). This is not to be cheaply dismissed as some "situation ethics" or just one more example of the "dictatorship of relativism" but rather *a deeply theological affirmation*, grounded in the New Testament and the tradition of the church, concerning the activity of the Holy Spirit whose enlightenment brings about understanding, interpretation, and application of the Christian Gospel in the realities of life in sinful, yet grace-filled and often selflessly loving, human lives—down in the valley, in their particular situations.

And here we get to the rub—*history*. The hermeneutical tradition is above all concerned with having an historical consciousness at all turns, and even—in more recent times, with the "urging" of critical theories—turning historical consciousness critically upon ourselves as interpreters of the past in the present. On this score, I think the present pope is once again prophetically messing with the minds of Catholics, bringing us back to basics. Like the historian pope he seems to be modeling himself on, St. John XXIII, Pope Francis wants to bring into play the Holy Spirit, who urges us to descend the plane from 30,000 feet and land down in the valley, and then, from the valley—where Jesus walked—to go back up to a renewed perspective on reality from 30,000 feet. From Pope Francis's perspective, there are lots of smelly sheep wandering across this valley; and the hermeneutical church must

---

[21] Joshua J. McElwee, "Cardinal Tagle: Church Should Not Look to 'Idealized Past' with Nostalgia," *National Catholic Reporter*, May 22, 2015, http://ncronline.org/news/global/cardinal-tagle-church-should-not-look-idealized-past-nostalgia.

[22] The nominative plural form of the singular *sensus* is also *sensus*.

take on "the smell of the sheep."²³ That hermeneut Martin Heidegger continues to challenge us as an ecclesial hermeneutical community: "What is decisive is not to get out of the [hermeneutical] circle but to come into it in the right way."²⁴ And the privileged way for us as a church to get into the hermeneutical circle of interpreting God's revelation is the *sensus fidelium*. And becoming a synodal church is the privileged way of listening to the *sensus fidelium*.

Toward the end of the 2015 synod, at a ceremony to commemorate the fiftieth anniversary of the creation by Paul VI of the Synod of Bishops, Pope Francis outlined his vision of "a synodal church."²⁵ Yet again he cited LG 12 on the *sensus fidei* of the whole people and quoted his own commentary of the passage from *Evangelii Gaudium* 119. The pope linked the importance of the Council's teaching with his desire to access the worldwide *sensus fidei* before the synod, albeit in some basic way:

> Such was the conviction [regarding the *sensus fidei*] underlying my desire that the people of God should be consulted in the preparation of the two phases of the Synod on the family, as is ordinarily done with each *Lineamenta*. Certainly, a consultation of this sort would never be sufficient to perceive the *sensus fidei*. But how could we speak about the family without engaging families themselves, listening to their joys and their hopes, their sorrows and their anguish? Through the answers given to the two questionnaires sent to the particular Churches, we had the opportunity at least to hear some of those families speak to issues which closely affect them and about which they have much to say.

The pope went on to present the implications of his vision of a synodal church: "A synodal Church is a Church which listens, which realizes that listening 'is more than simply hearing.' It is a mutual listening in which everyone has something to learn. The faithful people, the college of bishops, the Bishop of Rome: all listening to each other, and all listening to the Holy Spirit, the 'Spirit of truth' (Jn 14:17), in

---

²³ *Evangelii Gaudium* 24.
²⁴ Martin Heidegger, *Being and Time*, trans. John Macquarrie and Edward Robinson (New York: Harper and Row, 1962), 195.
²⁵ Pope Francis, Address to the Ceremony Commemorating the Fiftieth Anniversary of the Institution of the Synod Of Bishops, October 15, 2015, http://w2.vatican.va/content/francesco/en/speeches/2015/october/documents/papa-francesco_20151017_50-anniversario-sinodo.html.

order to know what he 'says to the Churches' (Rev 2:7)."²⁶ "Synodality," he stated, is "a constitutive element of the Church." Indeed, "in this Church, as in an inverted pyramid, the top is located beneath the base." From the local level to the universal, whether it be parish councils, diocesan councils, episcopal conferences, synods of bishops, each of these are "an opportunity for listening and sharing," and so contribute to a more synodal church.

Determination of the *sensus fidelium* at all of these levels is not easy, because it a diffuse sense.²⁷ Beginning at the local level, it involves different "agents" and "instruments," including "the listening bishop" and "the listening theologian."²⁸ But we must not forget that already, within faith and the functioning of the *sensus fidei*, there is "theologizing" being done, before the scholarly theologians get to work.²⁹ The *sensus fidei* is already itself a capacity for intuitive judgment of what rings true to the Gospel, and what doesn't. Theologians must tap into the trajectory of this intuitive theologizing. At the local level they have a particular role to play in bringing to systematic expression the oftentimes-diffuse expressions of insight into the Gospel by the faithful. In this way, theologians help to coalesce these insights into "local theologies," which are genuine expressions of the lived faith inspired by the Holy Spirit through the exercise of the *sensus fidei*. Theologians,

---

²⁶ The quotation is taken from *Evangelii Gaudium* 171.

²⁷ On the determination of the *sensus fidelium* through ongoing dialogue between the *sensus fidelium*, theology, and the magisterium, see Rush, *The Eyes of Faith*, 241–91.

²⁸ On "the listening bishop" and "the listening theologian," see ibid., 274–75.

²⁹ Karl Rahner writes: "Since the analysis by the hearer of what he is told is an inevitable moment in the process of hearing itself, and since utter non-understanding destroys even the hearing itself, *a certain degree of theology belongs as an inner moment to hearing itself,* and the mere hearing in faith is already a human activity in which man's own subjectivity, together with its logic, its experience, native concepts and perspectives, already enters into play. What we call theology and hence dogmatic statement in the strict sense is therefore merely a further development, an unfolding, of that basic subjective reflection which already takes place in the obedient listening to the Word of God, i.e. in faith as such. From this it follows, however, that dogmatic reflection and its statement can and must never separate themselves completely from the source from which they spring, i.e. from faith itself. This refers always, as has been said, not merely to the object of faith but also to its exercise. The latter remains the basis and support of the dogmatic statement as such itself." Karl Rahner, "What Is a Dogmatic Statement?," in *Theological Investigations*, vol. 5: *Later Writings*, trans. Karl-H. Kruger (New York: Seabury, 1975), 42–66, at 49 (emphasis added).

then, are mediators of the Holy Spirit in helping to bring international awareness across the universal church of the particularities of the one faith in different contexts. And bishops, assisted by the same Holy Spirit, are called to listen to the lived faith of the church local and universal and are aided by theologians to be open to the possible challenges coming from the Spirit-inspired *sensus fidelium*.

Thus, the church's interpretation of divine revelation can be imagined as a circle—a hermeneutical circle—of understanding. And around the circle are the five constitutive points of reference: Scripture, tradition, the *sensus fidelium*, theology, and the magisterium. Getting into the hermeneutical circle marked by these five points can only be via those who live in the valley; it must be through the lived faith of the church in history enabled by the Holy Spirit, i.e., via the *sensus fidelium*. This, of course, does not make the *sensus fidelium* the final arbiter in the formulation of matters of faith and morals. But even though the magisterium is that final arbiter, its role is to safeguard the church's *faith*. And faith has its sensing organ that the Spirit has guaranteed. The guarantee to the magisterium of a "charism of truth" (DV 8) and of an "infallibility in teaching" (LG 25) is not a guarantee over and above the guarantee of "infallibility in believing" assured of the church as a whole, through the *sensus fidei* given to all the baptised (LG 12). There is a condition to the charism of truth that must be realized: "in maintaining, practicing and professing the faith that has been handed on there is a unique interplay [*conspiratio*] between bishops and the faithful" (DV 10). Truth, as the "council" of Jerusalem found, is arrived at through dialogue. And theologians too, in their "faith seeking understanding," are beholden not only to their own perceptions but more so to the faith of the communities of faith they serve. Through their attention to the *sensus fidelium*, their local theologies can contribute to a so-called "development" of doctrine.

Development of doctrine can come through new encounters with God's otherness within human history, and new perceptions of the meaning of Scripture and tradition.[30] It is incumbent on all the baptized

---

[30] For a hermeneutical approach to the organic notion of "development," see Ormond Rush, "Reception Hermeneutics and the 'Development' of Doctrine," *Pacifica* 6 (1993): 125–40.

to be attentive to these "signs of the times,"[31] especially the signs of God's presence which the Spirit reveals.[32] As the council highlights, the activity of the Holy Spirit is vital. Yves Congar writes of the promise of *new knowledge* that the Holy Spirit reveals to the church:

> In his discourse on the coming of the Spirit, Jesus combines the affirmation of a non-autonomy of the Spirit with the promise of new knowledge: "He will guide you into all the truth; for he will not speak on his own authority, but whatever he hears he will speak, and he will declare to you the things that are to come. . . . He will take what is mine and declare it to you." Such a pendulum-swing between *the already acquired* and *the new*, between what has preceded and what has yet to come, should not perplex anyone with a sense of Tradition, *for it is the very law of Tradition*. To be the genuine transmission of something, Tradition must be at once criticism, creativity and reference. It is the active presence of a principle at every moment of its history, the permanence of identity in what renews itself and changes.[33]

This element of criticism is fundamental for the vitality of the living tradition. The *sensus fidelium*, actively at work receiving the Gospel and passing it on to others in a meaningful and truthful way, constitutes the living tradition of the church. This *sensus fidelium* therefore should function in a critical way in the processes of the church learning and teaching, in its hermeneutical circle of understanding. In his commen-

---

[31] "In every age, the church carries the responsibility of reading the signs of the times and of interpreting them in the light of the Gospel, if it is to carry out its task. In language intelligible to every generation, it should be able to answer the ever recurring questions which people ask about the meaning of this present life and of the life to come, and how one is related to the other. We must be aware of and understand the aspirations, the yearnings, and the often dramatic features of the world in which we live" (GS 4).

[32] "The People of God believes that it is led by the Spirit of the Lord who fills the whole world. Impelled by that belief, they try to discern the true signs of God's presence and purpose in the events, the needs and the desires which it shares with the rest of humanity today. For faith casts a new light on everything and makes known the full ideal which God has set for humanity, thus guiding the mind towards solutions which are fully human" (GS 11; translation corrected).

[33] Yves Congar, "Renewed Actuality of the Holy Spirit," *Lumen Vitae: International Review of Religious Education* 28, no. 1 (1973): 13–30, at 24 (emphasis added). Congar quotes from John 16:13-14 and cites John 14:26.

tary on *Dei Verbum*, Joseph Ratzinger noted that unfortunately it did not allow for a critique of tradition by Scripture.[34] A similar statement can be made regarding the role of the *sensus fidelium* as a necessary critique of tradition. DV 12 intimates the role of the Holy Spirit for a proper ecclesial reading of Scripture: that Scripture must be interpreted with the same Spirit with which it was written. The same Holy Spirit, who inspired the Scriptures—which, as Ratzinger highlights, must act as a critical norm of the tradition—evokes in believers, through the gift of *sensus fidei*, interpretations and applications of Scripture which must be allowed to function as a critique of the tradition.

The cry still challenges the Catholic Church: "Listen to what the Spirit is saying to the churches." Becoming a synodal church and finding better ways to listen to, discern, and determine the sense of the faithful throughout the world church is fundamental for responding to that scriptural injunction—and for implementing the vision of the Second Vatican Council fifty years on.

---

[34] "Not every tradition [in the narrow sense of a particular formulation, discipline, or practice] that arises in the Church is a true celebration and keeping present of the mystery of Christ. There is a distorting, as well as a legitimate, tradition. . . . Consequently, tradition must not be considered only affirmatively, but also critically; we have Scripture as a criterion for this indispensable criticism of tradition, and tradition must therefore always be related back to it and measured by it. . . . On this point Vatican II has unfortunately not made any progress, but has more or less ignored the whole question of the criticism of tradition." Joseph Ratzinger, "Chapter II: The Transmission of Divine Revelation," in *Commentary on the Documents of Vatican II*, vol. 3, ed. Herbert Vorgrimler (New York: Herder, 1969), 181–98, at 185–86.

PART 3

Rewriting the Questions

CHAPTER 9

Revealing Subversions
Theology as Critical Theory

Judith Gruber

Theology has very good reasons to be skeptical of critical theory. The tradition of critique, after all, was inaugurated by Immanuel Kant with the explicit goal to curb the influence of religious authority. More recent strands of critical thought, such as feminist and postcolonial theories, have pushed this agenda only further; they have traced the impact of male and ethnic privilege on the formation of the Christian tradition and have thus massively complicated the claim of the church to be the universal representation of God's salvific presence in the world. The tenets of critical theory, it seems, are a direct attack on the epistemo-political foundations of the Christian faith.[1]

It is against the odds, then, that in this chapter I will argue that theology lives up to its own normative foundation *only if* it is done as radical critique. I will develop this argument in three steps: First, an outline of a genealogy of critical theory will show that the driving force in the development of critique is the problematic relation between knowledge and power. A second step will outline how profoundly critical theory unsettles theology: a critique of Christian tradition exposes its deep-running complicity with hegemonic power but also

---

[1] The hyphenated term "epistemo-political" anticipates the crucial presupposition of radical critique. It is used to resist the idea(l) of pure reason and instead highlights the inextricable entanglement and mutual reinforcement between knowledge production and the (asymmetrical) power regimes which make up any social group (i.e., politics).

uncovers resources for counter-hegemonic strategies at its very heart. A third step will argue that it is in its counter-hegemonic, rather than in its hegemonic form, that theology lives up to the normative foundations of the Christian faith.

An Outline of a Genealogy of Critical Theories

What is reason? What is emancipation? These are the two crucial questions that drive the project of critique. Critical theory does not consider them separately. On the contrary, it derives its distinct intellectual scope from the postulate that there is an intimate connection between reason and emancipation, between knowledge and liberation. Critical theory is an *epistemo-political* project and it has been so from its Enlightenment inception. Kant argued that it is the use of reason that allows for emancipation from heteronomy inflicted by the exercise of authority, and especially religious authority. For the sake of emancipation, therefore, the scope of reason has to be gauged: it is with this political agenda in mind that Kant developed his epistemology.

Mediating between rationalism and empiricism, Kant's critique of reason credits reason with the decisive role in the generation of knowledge.[2] While he holds that understanding does not arise independently from empirical facts, he privileges reason in the process of knowledge generation. It is reason that systematizes sensory perceptions and thus, ultimately, leads to understanding: "Though all our knowledge begins with experience," Kant says, "it by no means follows that all arises out of it."[3] Through processes of abstraction, pure theoretical reason has the potential to arrive at knowledge, which does not come by way of sensory perceptions. Theoretical reason meets its limits, however, at the question of ethics. It cannot provide norms for our acting, because these are of a metaphysical scope, to which pure theoretical reason has, by Kant's very definition, no access. It takes, instead, practical reason to ascertain the foundations of ethical practice. And while Kant explicitly strives to hold on to the claim that there can be "only one and the same reason, differentiated solely in its

---

[2] "Thoughts without content are empty, intuitions (perceptions) without concepts are blind." Immanuel Kant, *Critique of Pure Reason* [1781], trans. Norman Kemp Smith (New York: St. Martin's, 1965), A 51/B 75.

[3] Ibid., Introduction I.

application,"[4] his approach ultimately does not succeed in reconciling the two kinds of reason it presupposes.[5] The unity of theoretical and practical reason remains a desideratum.

Kant's approach to critique thus introduces a twofold separation between the knowing subject and the objects of knowledge: First, it holds that sensory perceptions do affect the generation of knowledge, but only insofar as they trigger the process of reasoning and systematization through reason. Ultimately, their relation is unidirectional: reason shapes perception, but perceptions do not shape reason. On the contrary, the ideal for pure reason is to transcend sensory perceptions and to arrive at understanding independent and purged from the senses. The knowledge generated through theoretical reason, in turn, does not directly translate into practice. The bifurcation between theory and practice isolates reasoning from (inter)acting with the objects of knowledge. In Kant's critique, reason thus rules over the process of knowledge generation in an absolute (literally: detached) fashion: it is unafflicted by the sensory perceptions which it systematizes, and it is dissociated from the subject's interaction with the objects of knowledge.

In the wake of the Enlightenment, Kant's twofold absolutization of reason has come under stark critique. His presupposition of pure theoretical reason, twentieth-century critical theories argue, allows him to conceal, first of all, that (his and any) critique is a (specific, and therefore contingent) practice and, second, that knowledge is always and inextricably conditioned by social, historical, and economical forces.[6] Through the absolutization of knowledge,

---

[4] Immanuel Kant, *Groundwork of the Metaphysic of Morals* [1785], trans. H. J. Paton (1964; reprint, New York: Harper, 2009), 59 (4:391).

[5] Cf. Gerold Prauss, "Kants Problem der Einheit theoretischer und praktischer Vernunft," *Kant-Studien* 72, nos. 1–4 (1982): 286–303. Rex Gilliland, however, argues that Kant does succeed in establishing a "soft" form of unity in his philosophical system. See Rex Gilliland, "Kant's Doctrine of the Primacy of Pure Practical Reason and the Problem of a Unitary System of Philosophy," in *Kant und die Berliner Aufklärung: Akten des IX. Internationalen Kant-Kongresses*, ed. Volker Gerhardt, Rolf-Peter Horstmann, and Ralph Schumacher (Berlin: de Gruyter, 2001), 29–38.

[6] "The facts which our senses present to us are socially performed in two ways: through the historical character of the object perceived and through the historical character of the perceiving organ. Both are not simply natural; they are shaped by human activity, and yet the individual perceives himself as receptive and passive in

Kant's theoretical system fails to acknowledge (and succeeds in hiding) its own "impure" contingency. Moreover, and crucially, post-Enlightenment critical theories expose that this "blind spot" in Kant's critique is not politically innocent.[7] In fact, quite the contrary: Max Horkheimer and Theodor Adorno, who are crucial in exposing some of the issues at stake, argue that the original emancipatory notion of enlightenment (emancipation through the use of reason) endorsed repressive and oppressive behaviors. They interpret these behaviors not as an unfortunate perversion of pure and innocent reason but argue that they arise from the very heart of Enlightenment critique: by conceiving reason as a tool of domination over nature, Enlightenment has instrumentalized reason—and reason then, in turn, instrumentalizes and reifies the objects of its knowledge production.[8] By advancing understanding and control of nature, enlightenment thus becomes, as Jürgen Habermas puts it, "domination over an objectified external nature and a repressed internal nature."[9] Ultimately, enlightenment produces a positivist rationality which, rather than criticizing the factual conditions of society, affirms them as necessary. The use of instrumental(ized) reason does not bring about emancipation; on the contrary, it is a hegemonic instrument for the perpetuation of oppressive and repressive conditions.

With this critique of Enlightenment's own critique, the hegemony of modern rationality is exposed.[10] Contemporary critical theories

---

the act of perception." Max Horkheimer, "Traditional and Critical Theory" [1937], in *Critical Sociology: Selected Readings*, ed. Paul Connerton (Harmondsworth: Penguin, 1976), 206–24, at 213.

[7] François Laruelle argues that *all* forms of philosophy are structured around a prior decision and remain constitutively blind to this decision. See Laruelle, "A Summary of Non-Philosophy," *Pli: The Warwick Journal of Philosophy* 8 (1999): 138–48, at 138: "Philosophy is practise, affect, existence, but lacking in a rigorous knowledge of itself, a field of objective phenomena not yet subject to theoretical overview."

[8] Max Horkheimer, *Eclipse of Reason* (New York: Oxford University Press, 1947), 32.

[9] Jürgen Habermas, *The Philosophical Discourse of Modernity: Twelve Lectures*, trans. Frederick G. Lawrence (Cambridge, MA: MIT Press, 1987), 110.

[10] See Jürgen Habermas, "The Entwinement of Myth and Enlightenment: Re-Reading Dialectic of Enlightenment," *New German Critique* 26 (1982):13–30, at 22: Contemporary critical theory "breaks down the barrier between truth and power and thereby annihilates that fundamental differentiation which the modern decentered understanding of the world thought it had gained definitively by overcoming myth. Reason,

reveal its "blind spot" to be an intimate connection between power and knowledge generation, which Kant has hidden by absolutizing reason. While he strove for emancipation through the use of reason, contemporary critical theories have exposed an intimate connection between reason and oppression. The crucial question that critique faces after this exposure, then, is: How can it hold on to the normative goal of critical theory (critique facilitates liberation) without concealing the intimate connection between knowledge and power? On which grounds can we establish a politics of liberation after the epistemological breakdown of the power of reason?

The Frankfurt School declared its adherence to the belief in the emancipatory power of critique: Adorno and Horkheimer do not understand their critique of Enlightenment as geared toward its destruction but consider it as a preparation for reframing rationality in liberative terms.[11] Hence, they supplement their astute empirical social analysis of instrumental reason with a normative search for an *opposite* understanding of reason that does not fall victim to the trap of instrumentalization.[12] In a way, then, an absolutization of reason is again at work: reason is to be purged, this time not of the contingent conditions of its operations, but of the hegemony which has inscribed itself deeply into reason through its instrumentalization by Enlightenment.

The generation of critical theorists that have come after the Frankfurt School has further pushed the critique of knowledge and power as a resource of liberation. Two opposing lines of thought have developed. On the one hand, Jürgen Habermas, proponent of critical social theory, has further pursued the bifurcation of instrumentalized and emancipatory reason. For him, a radicalized critique of the hegemony of reason cannot provide resources for emancipation from oppression and does not elicit agency and resistance. Instead, he argues that, in order to allow for liberation, critique has to establish normative and universalizable claims which transcend the power-ridden factual conditions of society.

---

once instrumentalized, has become assimilated to power and has thereby given up its critical power—this is the final unmasking of a critique of ideology applied to itself."

[11] Theodor Adorno and Max Horkheimer, "Dialektik der Aufklärung," in Max Horkheimer, *Gesammelte Schriften*, vol. 5: *"Dialektik der Aufklärung" und Schriften 1940–1950*, ed. Gunzelin Schmidt Noerr (Frankfurt: Fischer Taschenbuch-Verlag, 1987–96).

[12] Ibid., 21. They want to "einen positiven Begriff von ihr vorbereiten, der sie aus ihrer Verstrickung in blinder Herrschaft löst."

Habermas, therefore, develops a contrast between a critical description of instrumentalized reason and a normative concept of communicative, non-hegemonic reason. This bifurcation, he is convinced, is necessary to generate the emancipatory thrust of critique and to overcome the hegemonic conditions produced and legitimized by instrumentalized reason.[13]

Ironically, then, Habermas becomes one of the most ardent defenders of Enlightenment ideals and its epistemo-political procedures. In adopting Kant's affirmation that the correct (i.e., communicative) use of reason will lead to liberation from oppression, Habermas builds the same blind spot into his approach to critical theory as did Kant: the critique of reason is no longer applied to itself. As Kant absolutized pure reason from sensory perceptions, theory from practice, and ultimately, epistemology from politics, so does Habermas absolutize (communicative) reason from hegemony.[14] His critical theory, therefore, is truncated. It can conceive of the normative goal of critique only by splitting it from the findings of his profound socio-empirical analysis of the epistemo-political conditions of society. This raises crucial questions: Can the normative goal of critical theory really be achieved if it is detached from the critical analysis of the epistemo-political conditions of society? Does the bifurcation between descriptive rigor and normative claims really allow for a *consistent* critique of reason?

The optimism with which Habermas could put forth, in the 1980s and 1990s, his project of mapping a normative foundation for critique has waned since: "The predominantly confident defense of the universalistic content of reason typical of *The Theory of Communicative Action*

---

[13] "The concept of a communicative reason that transcends subject-centered reason . . . is intended to lead away from the paradoxes . . . of a self-referential critique of reason." Habermas, *The Philosophical Discourse of Modernity*, 341. See note 9.

[14] Habermas's position is more complex than can be outlined here. As Michael Kelly shows, Habermas cannot simply be called an "absolutist." "Habermas . . . refers to universals as 'stand-ins' (and even describes modern philosophy itself as a 'stand-in'), emphasizing that universals are subject to revision. That is, philosophy raises universals as hypotheses to be confirmed or not by (the logic of) historical developments. In short, Habermas's universals are 'strong (i.e. universal) propositions with weak (i.e. fallibilist) status claims.'" Michael Kelly, "Foucault, Habermas, and the Self-Referentiality of Critique," in *Critique and Power: Recasting the Foucault/Habermas Debate*, ed. Michael Kelly (Cambridge, MA: MIT Press, 1994), 389. Kelly cites Habermas, *The Philosophical Discourse of Modernity*, 409n28.

is strikingly out of tune with post-1989 and post-9/11 modernity."[15] The search by critical theorists today for a framework of the emancipatory import of critique is more contextualized, situated, and pragmatic.[16] In pursuing this focus, they can draw inspiration from Michel Foucault's approach to critique, who—challenged through his dispute with Habermas—tried to pave a way for theorizing the emancipatory potential of critique without concealing its irresolvable entanglement into hegemonic epistemo-politics. While Habermas maintained that critique can unfold its transformative power only once it is extracted from the power ploys of instrumentalized reason, Foucault insisted that critique, too, is a discursive practice and, as such, irresolvably entangled into the relations of knowledge and power. Critique, Foucault says, does not transcend the hegemonic relation of society but can only be at work within it; it is and remains *local* critique.[17] It is pursued in detailed genealogies of the formation and mutual consolidation of knowledge and power in particular historical-cultural situations. And, as Michael Kelly argues in his reading of Foucault,[18] from these descriptions, resources for the transformation of the hegemonic relations at work in these situations can arise, because "the history of various forms of rationality is sometimes more effective in unsettling our certitudes and dogmaticism than is abstract criticism."[19] As Kelly shows convincingly, Foucault thus holds on to the normative claim of critical theory by locating the liberative potential of critique *within*, not detached from, the critical exposure of genealogy:[20] The historical

---

[15] Nikolas Kompridis, "Rethinking Critical Theory," *International Journal of Philosophical Studies* 13, no. 3 (2005): 299–301, at 299.

[16] See the contributions in *International Journal of Philosophical Studies* 13, no. 3 (2005).

[17] Foucault introduces the idea of *local critique* in Michel Foucault, "Two Lectures," *Power/Knowledge: Selected Interviews and Other Writings 1972–77*, ed. Colin Gordon (New York: Pantheon Books, 1980), 78–108.

[18] See Kelly, "Foucault, Habermas, and the Self-Referentiality of Critique."

[19] Michel Foucault, "Politics and Reason," in *Politics, Philosophy, Culture: Interviews and Other Writings, 1977–1984*, ed. Lawrence D. Kritzman (New York: Routledge, 1988), 57–85.

[20] "If the Kantian question was that of knowing what limits knowledge has to renounce transgressing, it seems to me that the critical question today has to be turned back into a positive one: in what is given to us as universal, necessary, obligatory, what place is occupied by whatever is singular, contingent, and the product of arbitrary restraints? The point, in brief, is to transform the critique conducted in the form of

recovery of local forms of discourse undermines the reigning discourse and its master narratives and makes hitherto subjugated knowledges, discourses, and practices visible—*and therefore possible*. Radical critique "discloses" alternatives to the hegemonic rationality *within* concrete historical-cultural situations.[21] The questioning of hegemonic epistemo-political conditions thus opens up space a "space of concrete freedom, i.e., of possible transformation."[22]

When liberative critique is at work, the hegemonic proclivity of reason is not suspended but subverted: The radicalization of critique as subversion ties its liberative practice right into the midst of the powerful forging of knowledge. It is conceived no longer as detachment from but as an intimate familiarity with the hegemony of reason.[23] It no longer looks for a non-hegemonic form of rationality but discloses counter-hegemonic practices of knowledge generation. Because of its irreducible contingency, (radical) critique cannot be defined absolutely, independent of the contingent conditions of its operations.

---

necessary limitation into a practical critique that takes the form of a possible transgression. . . . Criticism is no longer going to be practiced in the search for formal structures with universal value, but rather as an historical investigation into the events that have led us to constitute ourselves and to recognize ourselves as subjects of what we are doing, thinking, saying. . . . It will not deduce from the form of what we are what it is impossible for us to do and to know; but it will separate out, from the contingency that has made us what we are, the possibility of no longer being, doing, or thinking what we are, do, or think. It is not seeking to make possible a metaphysics that has finally become a science, it is seeking to give new impetus, as far and as wide as possible, to the undefined work of freedom." Michel Foucault, "What Is Enlightenment?," in *The Foucault Reader*, ed. Paul Rabinow (New York: Pantheon Books, 1984), 45–46.

[21] See Nikolas Kompridis, "Disclosing Possibility: The Past and Future of Critical Theory," *International Journal of Philosophical Studies* 13, no. 3 (2005): 325–51. However, as Kelly points out, "even if historical knowledge acquired through genealogy can open our eyes to a critique of present forms of rationality and the possibility of their transformation, critique and change do not automatically follow genealogy. Foucault is aware of this, and he explicitly argues that . . . genealogy is not yet critique and critique is not yet transformation. Ethical-political action fills the gap in both cases, making possibilities opened up by genealogy into actualities confirmed by critique and then put into transformative practice" ("Foucault, Habermas, and the Self-Referentiality of Critique," 373.)

[22] Michel Foucault, "Critical Theory/Intellectual History," in Kritzman, *Politics, Philosophy, Culture*, 36.

[23] See Kompridis, "Disclosing Possibility," 337.

As the subversion of specific contexts, it does not have a clearly and absolutely discernible foundation or telos—its liberative power is relative to the situation it critiques. It cannot promise emancipation once and for all but remains provisional, limited to the subversion of a specific epistemo-political constellation. It operates on a humbler scale than Habermas's grand project of critique as non-hegemonic communicative action—and is, precisely for that reason, all the more unsettling. It does not counter hegemonic reason with an opposite understanding of reason as purified of power relations. This anti-hegemonic understanding of reason is, in effect, still defined by the logic of hegemony; here, the polarities remain. Habermas's modernist critique brings reversal instead of transformation, and ultimately is prone to becoming the new hegemony.[24] A radical critique, on the other hand, questions and undermines the very epistemology on which hegemonic politics is founded: the idea that there is one (one right) form of reasoning that is absolutely true and universally valid and that can operate independently from historical, social, economic, and hegemonic conditions.

Yet radical critique still holds on to the normative perspective of critical theory: critique of knowledge is geared toward the liberation from oppressive powers. Because radical critique presupposes that there is no escape from power in the forging *and evaluation* of knowledge, it locates the potential for liberation in the exposure of contingency. Because hegemonic narratives consolidate their epistemo-political position through concealing the historical, cultural, and economic conditions of their emergence, exposing their contingency undermines their sovereignty. The de-absolutizing strategy of radical critique (descriptively) resurfaces excluded narratives and, through this very act, simultaneously grants them (normatively) a right to exist, because de-absolutization questions and subverts the epistemo-political preconditions of hegemonic power. Through the exposure of contingency, radical critique argues, epistemo-political justice can be brought about.[25] Yet radical critique does not consider these subversive narratives as liberative per se. This would cut short the critical

---

[24] See Walter Mignolo, *The Darker Side of Western Modernity: Global Futures, Decolonial Options* (Durham, NC: Duke University Press, 2011). Mignolo argues that coloniality is integral to modernity.

[25] See Shiv Visvanathan, *A Carnival for Science: Essays on Science, Technology, and Development* (Delhi and New York: Oxford University Press, 1997). Visvanathan calls for

thrust of the exposure of the hegemoniality of *all* narratives. It is the *act of subversion*, not the *content* of subversive narratives, which makes emancipation possible. Radical critique is a specific *form*, not a specific narrative. In Foucault's words, "The point, in brief, is to transform the critique conducted in the form of necessary limitation into a practical critique that takes the *form of a possible transgression*."[26]

Since its inception in European Enlightenment, then, critical theory has gone through profound conceptual shifts, and, as Nikolas Kompridis puts it, "quite unexpectedly, critique has been much more successful in undermining the hopes of the Enlightenment than in justifying them."[27] From the initial belief that the use of reason will lead to emancipation, it shifted to the exposure of an unholy (but purifiable) alliance of reason and oppression and ultimately acknowledged that reason is irresolvably tied to power—and, through its entanglement with power, it can be both liberative and oppressive. Through these shifts, critical theory has thus exhumed a profound ambivalence at the heart of reason, which deprives knowledge of an absolute foundation: critical theory's self-critique has triggered a paradigm shift toward a non-foundational, post-metaphysical epistemology. Critical theory no longer looks for the one universal form of reason, knowledge, or truth which is believed to facilitate emancipation but in reality reinscribes the epistemo-political logic of hegemony; instead, it traces the forging of knowledge in an—uneven—tug of war between hegemonic and subversive narratives. Critique is "not the exposure of error; it is constantly and persistently looking into how truths are produced."[28]

A Critique of Theology

This critical search for the *construction* of truth has not stopped short of the Christian tradition. Historically, it was the rise of contextual

---

"cognitive justice" in view of the destructive impact of hegemonic Western science on developing countries and non-Western cultures.

[26] Foucault, "What Is Enlightenment?," 45 (emphasis added).

[27] Kompridis, "Disclosing Possibility," 332. See also Reinhart Koselleck, *Critique and Crisis: Enlightenment and the Pathogenesis of Modern Society* (Cambridge, MA: MIT Press, 1998).

[28] Gayatri Chakravorty Spivak, "Bonding in Difference," in *An Other Tongue: Nation and Ethnicity in the Linguistic Borderlands*, ed. Alfred Arteaga (Durham, NC: Duke University Press, 1994), 273–85, at 285.

theologies since the mid-twentieth century that has questioned and undermined the master narrative of Christian tradition and exposed its hegemoniality. The emergence of alternative, hitherto silenced voices from the margins of the theological "establishment" has thereby followed the epistemo-political pattern of radical critique: The rather sudden visibility of these *other* (feminist, postcolonial, queer, etc.) theologies has not so much exposed the "error" of hegemonic church tradition but shows how it has been forged in an entanglement of power and knowledge. These alternative theologies expose how the master narrative of the Christian tradition has been shaped through the exclusion of other voices. Their existence, now made visible, reveals that the logic of orthodoxy relies on strategies of epistemo-political hegemony: the epistemo-theological ideal of one universally true narrative builds on and reinforces a politics of exclusion of all other stories.[29] By surfacing excluded traditions, therefore, a critical genealogy of church history reveals that *orthodox tradition is, in a very literal sense, heresy*: it is forged through powerful choices (*hairesis*); it takes its shape in epistemo-political strategies of in- and exclusion. A radical critique of church history thus discloses that structures of oppression have inscribed themselves deeply *into* the texture of its master narrative—and, once in place, have served to perpetuate the hegemonic forces which gave it its shape. Christian tradition, too, is exposed as a discourse, governed by a fundamental epistemo-political law: Those in power have the power to shape knowledge in a way that reinforces their power.[30]

Yet, not only does a critical genealogy of Christian history compromise its master narrative by exposing an interplay of power and truth at work in its formulation. The reemergence of silenced theologies troubles the established tradition in an even more profound way: their critique reveals just how deeply and inextricably Christian tradition is entangled in the particular social, historical, and economic situations

---

[29] For case studies, see Catherine Keller and Laurel C. Schneider, eds., *Polydoxy: Theology of Multiplicity and Relation* (New York: Routledge, 2011).

[30] The discursive history of the concept of original sin is one of many examples for this epistemo-political dynamics at work in the Christian tradition. Feminist theologians have exposed the interplay of patriarchal power and theological knowledge in the formation of the dogma of original sin. Cf. for an overview Tatha Wiley, *Original Sin: Origins, Developments, Contemporary Meanings* (New York: Paulist Press, 2002), 153–78.

out of which it has been forged. Feminist theologians, for instance, have shown how the normative texts of the church are imbricated with the patriarchal structures of their contexts. Similarly, postcolonial critics have uncovered structures of racism, which undergird the formation of Christian tradition.[31] In short, not only does a critical genealogy reveal conflicting narratives of uneven power *within* the theological tradition; it also exposes the fact that this tradition has not developed in an epistemo-political vacuum. Instead, it highlights political, social, historical, and economic conditions as *decisive* factors in the forging of the church. This "impurifies" the master narrative of tradition and compromises its claim for universality (understood as absolutization and detachment from contingency), which has buttressed its hegemonic position as the one, orthodox truth. Against the hegemonic concealment of the contingency of ecclesial texts and practices, the radical critique of marginalized traditions makes visible that the Christian tradition has never existed independently from the all-encompassing interplay of power and knowledge.

Even more disturbingly, the entanglement of Christian tradition in politics can by no means be understood as secondary—as the political "impurification" of an originally unpolitical "theology." More recent critical historical Bible studies have traced the entanglement of theology and politics right into the heart of the origins of the Jesus movements as portrayed in the gospels. They have highlighted the eminent relevance of the wider Roman imperial context for an interpretation of the New Testament and argue that the ecclesial witness of birth and life, ministry and message, death and resurrection of Jesus the Christ from Nazareth cannot be understood independently from the hegemonic power of the Roman Empire which pervaded the historical, social, political, and economic dimensions of life in the Mediterranean world.[32] Until recently, the hegemonic narrative of the *Imperium Romanum* as a "period of unprecedented political stability

---

[31] J. Kameron Carter, *Race: A Theological Account* (Oxford: Oxford University Press, 2008). Willie James Jennings, *The Christian Imagination: Theology and the Origins of Race* (New Haven: Yale University Press, 2010).

[32] See, among others, Warren Carter, *The Roman Empire and the New Testament: An Essential Guide* (Nashville: Abingdon, 2006). Stephen D. Moore, *Empire and Apocalypse: Postcolonialism and the New Testament,* Bible in the Modern World 12 (Sheffield: Sheffield Phoenix Press, 2006).

and prosperity" after an era of severe political destabilization through civil war and political conflict has been influential in historical studies. However, the political tensions in first-century CE Judaea and Galilee reveal that the *Pax Romana* was established through brutal and unrestrained oppression.[33] Through their subjection to Roman *hegemone*, the addressees of the gospels were intimately and painfully familiar with the lethal workings of hegemonic power and its inseparability from theology: divine justification, which the Roman emperors claimed for their power, made Israel's monotheism an uneasy theopolitical tool of resistance against colonial oppression. Once these political realities are resurfaced through a critical genealogy of the texts, and once the gospel is no longer purified of the contingent conditions of its formation, the profound theopolitical import of the Jesuanic proclamation of the coming of *God's basileia* comes to the fore: both its political context and its political terminology clearly imbue the theology of the New Testament Jesus with political implications. In the New Testament texts, God's *basileia* is sketched as contesting Roman imperial power; it imagines an *alternative* vision of power and carries hope and promise for a *different* reign—a reign which does *not* rule through oppression, which does *not* establish peace through violence.[34] Yet the texts and practices of the *basileia tou theou* in the gospels do not simply pitch God's reign versus Roman reign in a binary fashion. They do not envision God's kingdom as a reversal and replacement of the Roman Empire but develop a more complex and profound critique of its hegemonic rule.

This initially becomes apparent through a linguistic analysis of the textual evidence. As Keith Dyer shows:

> [T]here are very few instances in the Greek texts or inscriptions of the first century (including the Biblical texts and Josephus) where *Basileia* has been used explicitly to refer to Rome and its empire. Occasionally, *basileius* is used of a Roman ruler or of kings in general including Romans (Lk 17:7; 1 Tim 6:15; Rev 17:14; 19:16), but it is used in the Gospels primarily to refer to Herod and his successors, and elsewhere to other client kings who ruled with Rome's permission. *Kaisar* and

---

[33] Philip L. Tite, *Conceiving Peace and Violence: A New Testament Legacy* (Dallas, TX: University Press of America, 2004), 39–41.

[34] See the contributions to Michael L. Budde and Robert W. Brimlow, eds., *The Church as Counterculture* (Albany: SUNY Press, 2000).

hegemone are used consistently in first-century texts to describe the overarching dominance of Rome and its Caesars. . . . From the second century the influence of classicism and the ideals of Hellenistic kingship lead to the *basileia* word group being used more frequently of Rome, and even by Romans, until it becomes commonplace in the writings of Eusebius. . . . This later development should not be permitted to blur the meaning and careful use of *basileia* in first-century texts in order to heighten the opposition between kingdom of God and the empire of Rome, or between the kingship of Christ and the emperor of Rome, as a primary hermeneutical paradigm for interpreting the early New Testament documents.[35]

Instead, Dyer argues for reading the *basileia* texts as a more localized critique of hegemonic rule: "The most significant oppositions in the earliest Jesus 'kingdom of God' traditions focus on the Pharisees/Herodians/Sadducees—with occasional swipes at their Roman overlords—and are then recast in subtle and subversive ways as later Gospel accounts take shape in imperial contexts more distant from Judea and Galilee."[36] The linguistic evidence thus supports an interpretation of the New Testament *basileia* message as *local critique*, directed against hegemonic power *as it occurs in specific situations*.

This is further substantiated through a distinct theological motif developed across the *basileia* texts of the gospels. As John Dominic Crossan has proposed in a number of publications, the Jesuanic *basileia* message remodels widespread contemporary apocalyptic eschatological visions into an ethical eschatology. Defining "eschatology" as a fundamental negation of the hegemonic master narrative about "the world,"[37] Crossan argues that "apocalyptic eschatology . . . negates this world by announcing that in the . . . imminent future, God will

---

[35] Keith Dyer, "The Empire of God, the Postcolonial Jesus, and Postapocalyptic Mark," in *Colonial Contexts and Postcolonial Theologies: Storyweaving in the Asia-Pacific*, ed. Mark G. Brett and Jione Havea (New York: Palgrave MacMillan, 2014), 81–97, at 83–85.

[36] Ibid., 81.

[37] "It is a profoundly explicit no to the profoundly implicit yes by which we usually accept life's normalcies, culture's presuppositions, and civilization's discontents. . . . It indicates a vision and/or program that is radical, counter-cultural, utopian, or this-world-negating. It presumes that there is something fundamentally wrong with the way of the world." John Dominic Crossan, *The Birth of Christianity*: *Discovering What Happened in the Years Immediately after the Execution of Jesus* (Edinburgh: T&T Clark, 1999), 260.

act to restore justice in an unjust world. . . . [An] intervening act of overwhelming divine power is imagined and invoked. . . . Apocalyptic eschatology almost inevitably presumes a violent God who establishes the justice of nonviolence through the injustice of violence."[38] The ethical-eschatological thrust of the gospels, on the other hand, "negates the world by actively protesting and nonviolently resisting a system judged to be evil, unjust, and violent. It . . . is directed at the world's *normal* situation of discrimination and violence, exploitation and oppression, injustice and unrighteousness. It looks at the systemic or structural evil that surrounds and envelops us all and, in the name of God, refuses to cooperate or participate any longer in that process. Instead, it sets out to oppose systemic evil *without succumbing to its own violence*. . . . Ethicism is present wherever nonviolent resistance to structural evil appears in this world."[39]

By advocating an ethical rather than an apocalyptic eschatology, the *basileia* texts and practices of the New Testament become a theopolitical tool which transforms rather than replaces the violent logic of hegemonic power: the Roman Empire is not simply to be substituted by God's kingdom; instead, the texts envision a more profound critique of hegemony. They employ strategies that undermine the structures of oppression necessary to establish and keep imperial power in place:

> We glimpse some [of these strategies] . . . in the growing body of literature that hears the stories with the ears of the oppressed/minority/subaltern, alert to hidden transcripts, parody, and satire. The legion of drowning pigs, the anti-climactic entry into the Temple, and the farcical representation of Jesus' trial have revealed undercurrents of subversive hope and humor when seen in this light. The results are diverse and not uniformly "anti-imperial"—though Rome is the butt of the jokes. . . . Nor is it possible to argue from these accounts . . . that Mark envisages a bipolar reversal whereby the Kingdom of God through the parousia of Jesus defeats the Empire of Rome so that Christ takes his place at the head of the new patriarchal hierarchy. The hope that the "last becomes first and the first last" is a parody of what it means to be first and last (as the extraordinary sequence Mk 9:35; 10:31, 43-4 demonstrates) and empties social rank of its

---

[38] Ibid., 283.
[39] Ibid., 284 (emphasis added).

meaning, just as the kingdom of God as a mustard seed and shrub (Mk 4:31-2) parodies and redefines the great nesting trees of the Daniel (4:9-12) and Ezekiel (17:23-4) visions of universal empire.[40]

God's kingdom, these texts suggest, will not simply mirror and reflect the power of Rome but (already) works differently. Its counter-imperial (rather than anti-imperial) strategies critique hegemonic power *locally*, as it takes its shape in specific situations. They do not envision its replacement in one cataclysmic event[41] but work at its transformation in concrete contexts. As a local and radical critique of hegemonic power, *God's kingdom takes place where Empire is subverted*.

This, in turn, implies that, because they take their shape as its subversion, the manifestations of *God's* basileia *remain dependent on hegemonic politics*. This is the truly unsettling outcome of a radical critique that exposes the entanglement of power and knowledge in the Christian tradition. It shows that from its very inception in the Jesuanic proclamation of the coming of God's kingdom, the Christian tradition has derived its existence and shaped its normative texts from an epistemo-political positioning in relation to hegemonic discourses. As a subversion of the established epistemo-politics in a specific situation, it cannot be traced back to one independent foundation which then gave rise to conflicting interpretations but has *always already* owed its formation to *other* narratives, *other* discourses, *other* epistemo-political formations. This deprives the church of an absolute and pure origin, and a definite telos (which could also serve as a norm for evaluating the disparate narratives within its tradition). A radical critique of Christian theology exposes an "impurity" at its very foundation—its origin cannot be had absolutely but is contingent upon epistemo-political power.

This state of affairs, of course, massively complicates the orthodox master narrative of the church. Through its genealogical analysis, a radical critique of Christian tradition shows that if this narrative of the church is claimed to be absolutely true and universally valid (as opposed to contingently conditioned), it relies, in fact, on hegemonic strategies of oppression and exclusion. This entails a profound destabilization of tradition as we know it; however, it also offers resources

---

[40] Dyer, "The Empire of God," 89.
[41] Cf. Crossan, *The Birth of Christianity*, 258.

for reconceiving Christian theology in a new way: Once *other* stories are no longer silenced by the hegemonic master narrative of the church, it becomes visible that Christian tradition has taken its shape *in resistance to the exclusivist epistemo-politics of hegemony*. A critique of the hegemonic narrative of Christian tradition discloses a counter-hegemonic thrust at the heart of this tradition—a critical description of Christian theology reframes Christian theology *as radical critique*.

Theology as Radical Critique

We can draw on a theology of incarnation to argue that this reconfiguration of theology as critical theory suggests itself not only as the result of a critique of Christian tradition but can be tied back to the normative core of theology. Its foundational belief that God revealed God's self in the historical event of life, death, and resurrection of Jesus the Christ prescribes a pattern for theology which is congenial to radical critique. The historical event of incarnation puts theology into a non-foundational, counter-hegemonic framework. Let me outline this in more detail.

Historical events, Michel Foucault argues, are instances of radical critique. They emerge *as* a clash of interpretations within particular discourses.[42] The emergence of events depends on a particular discourse, and at the same time they subvert the established narratives within this discourse: "How can the inseparability of knowledge and power in the game of multiple interactions and strategies induce at once singularities that fix themselves on the basis of their conditions of acceptability and a field of possibilities, of openings, of indecisions,

---

[42] Foucault's approach to the event contrasts with that of Ricoeur, for whom the event is a "manifestation of the absolute" that triggers historiography as a "conflict of interpretations" (Paul Ricoeur, "Hermeneutics of Testimony," *Anglican Theological Review Evanston* 61, no. 4 [1979]: 435–61, at 454). Ricoeur thus does take the interpretative character of history into account, but in trying to locate the absolute within the event, he interrupts the chain of interpretations and thereby undermines the very contingency which constitutes history. Hence, Ricoeur makes the absolute immune to historical particularity; he does not expose it to real, actual contingency. Translated into incarnation theology: it is the attempt to understand God's incarnation in Jesus the Christ not as a human being but like a human being—it implies an understanding that God did not really become human but appeared to be human. This interpretation of the incarnation was excluded from Catholic tradition as the heresy of Docetism.

of reversals, and of eventual dislocations that make them fragile, that make them impermanent, that make of these effects events—nothing more, nothing less than events?"[43]

The event of incarnation is a prime example of this logic of the event: the belief that God revealed God's self in Jesus from Nazareth could emerge only against the discursive background of revelation as understood in the Hebrew Scriptures. It depends on the Hebrew belief that God's salvific presence becomes manifest in the history of God's people. Yet, at the same time, the event of incarnation shifts and unsettles this discourse: proclaiming the crucified as the Messiah (and the Messiah as the crucified) is "impossible" for Hebrew theology,[44] which tends to conceive of the messiah as a powerful, kingly figure.[45] The Christ event thus addresses and subverts temptations of hegemonization inscribed into the Hebrew discourse of revelation history.[46] Just like the event of the coming *basileia* of God, which emerges when Roman *hegemone* is subverted, incarnation is thus contingent upon an *other* theopolitical discourse. As a historical event, it both rests on and "scandalizes" (1 Cor 1:23) the theopolitical discourse of Hebrew theology. There is, in short, an irresolvable and mutual dependence between event and discourse: an event subverts the established narratives, which allow for its emergence in the first place.

If we want to hold on to the historicity of incarnation as the foundation of the church, we can therefore not assume a linear relation between the historical event of revelation and the theological discourse of the church. Instead, there is a *hermeneutical circle between revelation and theology*, in which God's revelation and ecclesial theology are in a relation of mutual dependence. As an event in history, incarnation pro-

---

[43] Michel Foucault, "What Is Critique?," in *Philosophical Traditions: Eighteenth-Century Answers and Twentieth-Century Questions*, ed. James Schmidt (Berkeley: University of California Press, 1996), 382–98.

[44] On the (im)possibility of conceiving events, see Jacques Derrida, "A Certain Impossible Possibility of Saying the Event," *Critical Inquiry* 33, no. 2 (2007): 441–61.

[45] "The expectation of the Messiah was most often of a royal (kingly) role, occupied by a human being who would be a new (and better) David: a great warrior, a righteous man of God, a wise and just ruler who would bring back the days of glory and power to oppressed Israel." Mark C. Black, *Luke* (Joplin, MO: College Press, 1996), 88.

[46] Israel Selvanayagam, "Interpreting a Riddle: Jesus' Subversion of the Davidic Legacy," *Black Theology* 6, no. 2 (2008): 262–68.

vides a foundation for the church which manifests itself only through its proclamation by the church.[47] Theologically speaking: the body of Jesus the Christ is available only as the ecclesial body of Christ; *incarnatio* necessitates the *incarnatio continua* of the church.

Its foundation in a historical event thus puts the church at first sight into a very strong theological position: *extra ecclesiam nulla revelatio*. Yet, at the very same time, the logic of its founding event proves to be profoundly unsettling for the church: Because the event takes its manifestation only through its interpretations, it is marked and marred by a *tension of presence and absence* or, as Michel de Certeau puts it, "a relation of kenosis to glory, of disappearance to manifestation." He explains it this way:

> The "truth" of the beginning of an event is revealed only through new possibilities which it opens. That truth is both *shown* by the differences in relation to the initial event and *hidden* by new elaborations (differing from the first evangelical testimony). . . . It is the *condition* and not the *object* of the operations which flow from it. Thus the event is lost precisely in what it authorizes. It somehow dies to its own historical specificity, but this happens in the very discoveries which it provokes. The process of death (the absence) and the survival (the presence) of Jesus continues in each Christian experience: What the event makes possible is different each time, as a new remoteness from the event and a new way of erasing it.[48]

While God's revelation finds its manifestation only through the theology of the church, they never coincide. There is always already an interpretative break at work in the ecclesial proclamation of God's revelation: the logic of the revelatory event inscribes an (only eschatologically redeemable) absence into the heart of the representation of the church. God's self-revelation in radical contingency does not provide the church with one readily available narrative for its proclamation but takes its shape only *through* its erasure by the church.

---

[47] This epistemo-theological principle has been constitutive for the self-understanding of the church throughout its tradition: "Good" Christian theology starts with the presupposition that knowledge of God is accessible only on the basis of faith (cf. Anselm's axiom: *credo ut intelligam* [*Proslogion*, 1]).

[48] Michel de Certeau, "How Is Christianity Thinkable Today?," in *The Postmodern God: A Theological Reader*, ed. Graham Ward (Oxford: Blackwell, 1997), 142–55, at 145.

Built on this lack of one absolute narrative, the Christian proclamation is not accessible as a specific content but can manifest itself (only) as a specific form. Because the church has no absolute narrative at its disposal, it has developed a strategy of drawing on *other* discourses and establishing a difference *within* them—ecclesial theology reiterates its founding event by "fragilizing" (in Foucault's terms) the narratives of *other* discourses. As de Certeau puts it, the distinct Christian *modus loquendi*[49] can be characterized as "displacement" or "conversion" of existing discourses.[50] This form of speaking is biblical in origin, or, better, it is the origin of the Christian Bible,[51] and it bears a strong resemblance to radical critique: it does not establish one autonomous discourse but interrupts the established narratives of these discourses and is, therefore, a subversive act. Its original *modus loquendi* prefigures theology as subversion.

It is at this point that we can begin to make crucial connections between the theological form of speaking and radical critique. For Foucault, subversion offers a potential for the liberation from oppressive forces. Theologically speaking, the liberation from oppressive forces is salvation.[52] The subversive activity of the church in other

---

[49] "Mystic discourse is a *modus loquendi*. It is the outcome of an entire set of operations on and in the shared social text. It is an *artifact* (a production) created by the labor of putting language *to death*." Michel de Certeau, *Heterologies: Discourse on the Other*, Theory and History of Literature 17 (Minneapolis: University of Minnesota Press, 1986), 159. *Mutatis mutandis*, the same can be said of Christian discourse in general.

[50] De Certeau, "How Is Christianity Thinkable Today?," 153–55.

[51] Ibid., 153–54: "By [this] movement alone it conforms to the way in which the entire Christian faith is articulate in the conversion of the Old Testament into the New Testament. . . . Jesus does not cease to hold on to the uniqueness of the Jewish institution, while he creates the beginning of another meaning for it. His act brings about a displacement which gives birth to a new law. . . . This type of conversion inaugurated by the act of Jesus is to be continued indefinitely. [. . .] The essential here is not a new content, . . . but the conversion of relationships."

[52] One of the oldest soteriological concepts of the Christian tradition is *apolutrōsis*, which is now commonly translated as "redemption" and has taken on distinctly religious (as opposed to *political*) connotations. However, in its original meaning (i.e., before its adoption by theological discourse), it denotes the release from slavery and thus brings very concrete situations of oppression and exclusion into play. The Christian concept of salvation thus shares a surprising affinity with the normative framework of critical theory: to express the political import of critique, Kant used the concept of "emancipation," which also refers to the release from slavery. Also, many other of the

discourses has a potentially liberative, a *salvific* quality. We can thus qualify the *extra ecclesiam nulla revelatio* statement: *If* the God-talk of the Church subverts established powers, it manifests God's salvific presence. *If* theology is done as radical critique, it (re)presents God's salutary revelation.

The parallels between theology and radical critique go further. As long as it does not succumb to the temptation to absolutize one of the narratives which emerge from its subversive activity within other discourses, theology is, like radical critique, *local* critique, and therefore necessarily pluriform and open-ended. The logic of its founding event has always already forced the church to rely on other narratives, in which it establishes a difference in order to find a representation of God's revelation. The normative Christian form of speaking continues to challenge the church to look elsewhere for its theology, because only if it continues to subvert established narratives (including its own narratives) can and does the church (re)present revelation.[53] Incarnation, therefore, compromises the definitions of the visible church: it makes for a church which manifests God's presence only insofar as it subverts and transgresses itself. The Christian *modus loquendi* produces revelatory events which unsettle and fragilize the established discourse of the church.

Here, the mutual dependence between theology and revelation comes full circle. The hermeneutical circle of theology is carried out through subversions, propelled by the constitutive lack at the heart of ecclesial theology which it has to maintain lest it becomes idolatrous and replaces God's (absent) revelation with its own contingent God-talk. This hermeneutical circle is, therefore, not a closed circle but an open-ended spiral, in which the church is not in sovereign control of the revelations which it facilitates, because God's presence takes its manifestation through the subversion of hegemonic narratives.[54]

---

soteriological metaphors of the Christian tradition sketch salvation as a subversion of established power structures, e.g., the heavenly banquet, to which *all* will be invited.

[53] De Certeau goes as far as saying that theology *is* conversion. De Certeau, "How Is Christianity Thinkable Today," 152–54.

[54] This also implies that the church might find manifestations of God's revelation outside its established borders. If subversion is, indeed, the decisive criterion for authentic God-talk, discernment becomes a crucial task of the church in its representation of God's revelation: Are there "other" stories, outside the boundaries of the visible

God-talk in *genetivus subjectivus* (revelation) thus does not smoothly translate into God-talk in *genetivus objectivus* (theology), and vice versa. As subversive critique of *hegemone*, the eschatologically open spiral of theology produces always new God-talk. God's *basileia* has already, but not quite yet, arrived.

Conclusion

If we are to follow the challenging outcome of a critical genealogy of theology and indeed reframe theology as critique, we will have to expose it to both massive political *and* epistemological reconfigurations. These shifts mutually depend on each other as two sides of one coin. Theology will first have to switch, politically, from an epistemological framework which advocates one orthodox tradition to a "polydox" discourse which acknowledges the multifaceted narratives within the Christian tradition and, moreover, is sensitive to asymmetries of power between them. Reframed as critical theory, theology makes explicit that it has taken its shape in an uneven tug of war between hegemonic and subversive voices within the Christian tradition.[55] This political reconfiguration goes hand in hand with a profound epistemological shift: as outlined above, the exposure of the polydoxy of Christian tradition ultimately reveals an irreducible contingency at the heart of Christian God-talk; a radical critique of theology shows that Christian God-talk has always already been contingent upon established epistemo-political power. Theology has to reposition itself within a non-foundational epistemological paradigm.

Because it acknowledges contingency as a formative factor of Christian tradition, theology as radical critique can easily be seen to be *in conflict with the established theological narrative* which claims normative

---

church, which subvert hegemonic narratives and must therefore be appropriated by the church as theology? This further unsettles the established discourse of the church. When the subversion of hegemonic narratives facilitates the liberation of oppressive powers, the church finds resources for its theology by interpreting them as manifestations of God's salvific presence. Not only is theology to be done as radical critique; radical critique, in turn, is theology. John Caputo's project of a "weak theology" can, among other approaches, be read as explorations of the "theologicality" of radical critique. See John D. Caputo, *The Weakness of God: A Theology of the Event* (Bloomington: Indiana University Press, 2006).

[55] See the contributions to Keller and Schneider, eds., *Polydoxy.*

status for itself as the faithful and truthful representation of Christian God-talk. This master narrative tends to absolutize God-talk from the contingent conditions of its emergence and to pitch absolute transcendence against contingent immanence; it is highly suspicious of theological frameworks which run counter to this bifurcation. This should not come as a surprise. As we have seen above, hegemonic narratives rely on strategies of absolutization to legitimize their exclusive and exclusivist epistemo-political status. Like all hegemonic narratives, the master narrative of the Christian tradition, too, is prone to succumb to the temptation to purify God-talk from its constitutive contingency in order to establish itself as its one legitimate, "orthodox" representation.[56] Having established itself as the hegemonic narrative by concealing the contingency of its formation, the master narrative of Christian tradition is in a position to push this absolutization from contingency as normative for Christian God-talk. Those in power have the power to shape knowledge in a way which reinforces their power. In contrast to this *hegemonialization* of theology based on its *absolutization*, I have argued in the last part of this chapter that an exposure of its own contingency is *the* crucial criterion for ecclesial God-talk. Only if it acknowledges its own contingency can the church remain a faithful representation of God's (absent) presence.

Yet is this an argument we can make at all within the theoretical framework of radical critique? Critical theory, after all, highlights the irretrievable hegemonic character of knowledge. Its crucial argument is that there is no "power-free" base from which to evaluate a discourse, and it therefore maintains that criteria too are forged from the irresolvable entanglement of power and knowledge. Hence, from the perspective of radical critique, it is safe to expect that norms and criteria privilege the epistemological position of power within a discourse. How can we assume, then, that the norm of the theological discourse favors the *counter*-hegemonic strategy of radical critique, rather than offering a legitimization for the established master narrative of tradition? Can we really argue that theology proper calls for an exposure of contingency rather than the absolutization of power/knowledge?

---

[56] See the argument Mark Lewis Taylor makes in his *The Theological and the Political: On the Weight of the World* (Minneapolis: Fortress Press, 2011).

From the perspective of radical critique, it would involve less argumentative effort to answer this question in the negative.[57] However, we would then give up the normative claim of the Christian tradition that theology has a soteriological underpinning. When we want to hold on to the belief (i.e., the normative claim) that Christian God-talk is done in the interest of salvation and that salvation is, in a very broad sense, redemption from oppressive powers, we have to assume that the Christian tradition has resources for counter-hegemonic strategies built into its normative core. After a radical critique has exposed the deep entanglement of theology with hegemony, our task, therefore, is to develop an understanding of theology which neither conceals the complicity of theology with hegemonic power, nor completely surrenders Christian God-talk to it. In this chapter I have argued that radical critique provides an epistemo-political tool for both the exposure of hegemonic elements within the Christian tradition and the mobilization of its counter-hegemonic resources. It is through the subversion of hegemonic narratives that the church can be a faithful representation of God's salutary self-revelation in the historical event of the life, death, and resurrection of Jesus the Christ. Critical theory thus gains a normative status for theology. Not only does a reformulation of theology as critical theory suggest itself based on the outcome of a critical genealogy of Christian tradition, this reformulation is also crucial for theology in order to comply with the normative parameters of Christian God-talk. *Only when it is understood and practiced as radical critique does theology live up to its constitutive norms.*

---

[57] There are critics and theologians who answer this question in the negative. Mark Lewis Taylor, for example, argues in *The Theological and the Political* that there is an inextricable and unsalvageable link between the theological discourse of transcendence and the maintenance of sovereignty, which fosters a "necropolitics" of oppression and exclusion. For Taylor, the normative framework of Christian God-talk has no resources to offer to counter hegemonic power. Instead, he calls on us to abandon theology and to search elsewhere (particularly in literature and the arts) for liberative strategies. On the other hand, Marianne Sawicki does painstaking work to recover counter-hegemonic currents underneath the potentially oppressive discourse of the established tradition. See Sawicki, *Seeing the Lord: Resurrection and Early Christian Practices* (Minneapolis: Fortress Press, 1994).

CHAPTER 10

Postcolonial Hermeneutics and a Catholic (Post)Modernity

Susan Abraham

Critical theories that investigate the connection between knowledge and power arise from within Western modernity. Postcolonial hermeneutics is an offshoot of Western critical theories, arising in the late twentieth century from contexts that share a historical connection to modern Western and European colonialism. It is avowedly "secular" while critically assessing notions such as "religion," "theology," and "mission" as deeply implicated in European colonialism. Postcolonial theory and hermeneutics challenge Christian and, in a particular way, modern Catholic theology to provide an account of itself against the charge of colluding with modern European colonialism. Yet, as I shall argue, critical theory is not an undifferentiated and homogenous discourse that mounts a univocal challenge to Western modernity. Precisely because critical theory advocates for acute attention to be paid to context, we can discern important variations in their particular emphasis. The goal of such critical theory is decolonizing Western frames of knowing. Catholic decolonial theology that is attentive to contextual concerns including economic, political, cultural, and multi-religious ones will resonate with the goals of postcolonial critical theory.

While contemporary Catholic theology must take such decolonizing attempts seriously, its limits must also be tracked in view of global Catholic theology. In particular, one of the more salutary features of contemporary postcolonial hermeneutics is its range of regional variation expressed globally. Such variations complicate the notion that postcolonial theory and hermeneutics have unified or singular goals. Precisely because the colonial experience was different in different contexts, strategies to decolonize Western modernity are different. All postcolonial critical thinkers complicate the narrative of Western modernity through critiques of identity, difference, colonial history, and neocolonial economic relations. For example, Walter Mignolo presents one particular account of decolonizing "Western modernity."[1] Decolonizing modernity entails a critique of Western metaphysical assumptions while also reconstructing metaphysics for a global ethic that is attentive to context. Mignolo's impact on contemporary critical studies of religion is growing. For example, the inclusion of an essay by Mignolo in the acclaimed *Postcolonial Philosophy of Religion* indicates his relevance and importance to the study of religion.

Richard King, moreover, in the same volume, addresses Mignolo's emphasis on "border *gnosis*" that interrogates the geopolitics of knowledge, exposing how "local histories" present themselves as "global designs" as the way that philosophy of religion decolonizes. "Border *gnosis*," moreover, calls into question what we would call "religion" and "secularism" and the relationship between the two. As King writes, "It is a critical reflection upon knowledge production from both the interior borders of the modern/colonial world system and from its exterior borders (that is, knowledge production related to the impact of the colonial encounter between cultures)."[2] Nevertheless, contemporary postcolonial theory also mandates a self-reflexive and critical examination of how postcolonial theory itself is implicated in contemporary colonial relations. Therefore, on closer examination, I shall show that Mignolo's postcolonial hermeneutical strategies assert a problematic "difference" in comparison with those from South Asia. He privileges the category "(Latin American) decolonial" over "(South Asian/Black) postcolonial," which seems to claim that decolonization was not part

---

[1] Walter D. Mignolo, *The Darker Side of Western Modernity: Global Futures, Decolonial Options* (Durham, NC: Duke University Press, 2011), 161 (emphasis in the original): "At the end of the sixteenth century Mathew Ricci suggested that Chinese science was *falling behind* that of the West, since the Chinese had no conceptions of the rule of logic, and because their science of ethics was merely a series of confused maxims and deductions. Ricci's observations were not isolated, but complemented Christian discourses about the Moors and about Incas and Aztecs."

[2] Richard King, "Philosophy of Religion as Border Control: Globalization and the Decolonization of the 'Love of Wisdom' (*Philosophia*)" in *Postcolonial Philosophy of Religion*, ed. Purushottama Bilimoria and Andrew Irvine (Breinigsville, PA: Springer, 2010), 51.

of South Asian postcolonial theory from its inception. In my reading, therefore, Mignolo's postcolonial hermeneutics results in a form of critique based in identity politics that elides the reality of contemporary colonial relations—a strategic failure.

Decolonizing strategies cannot be in competition for a "better than yours" truth. For a Catholic, sacramental, and incarnational theology, the starting point for decolonizing hermeneutics has always to be the particularity and contingency of the context from which it speaks. South Asian and Latin American Catholic theologians do not speak from the same context. However, their theological articulations necessarily use a common grammar of sacramental and incarnational theology. The differences that they exhibit, however, reveal a range of contemporary political concerns. These political concerns, I shall argue, impact what Anthony Godzieba calls "a broadly liberal theological reflection that developed in response to Vatican II's call for theological renewal."[3] History, culture, and hermeneutical strategies that contextualize the Catholic understanding of the mystery of salvation demand attention to the concrete and particular body. Decolonizing contemporary and global Catholic theology cannot uncritically utilize a singular postcolonial theoretical framework, prizing one way of envisioning liberation and salvation over others. Rather, employing what Godzieba identifies as the Catholic sacramental imagination, I bring a postcolonial critique to Mignolo's otherwise important work. Such a continuing critique of important voices in postcolonial theory sharpens the possibility of constructing the good news of a "critical and hopeful" Catholic theology.[4]

Identity, Deconstruction, and *Différance*: Debating the "Postcolonial"

> Necessarily, we must dismiss those tendencies that encourage the consoling play of recognitions.
>
> — Michel Foucault, "Nietzsche, Genealogy, History"[5]

---

[3] Anthony Godzieba, "Incarnation, Theory, and Catholic Bodies: What Should Post-Postmodern Catholic Theology Look Like?," *Louvain Studies* 28 (2003): 217–31, at 218.
[4] Ibid., 222.
[5] Epigraph to Stuart Hall's essay "When Was the Postcolonial? Thinking at the Limit," in *The Post-Colonial Question: Common Skies, Divided Horizons*, ed. Iain Chambers

In literary and cultural theory, the term "postcolonial" refers to both an identity category and a methodological one. Suspicion was cast on the term from very early on. For example, in an essay now almost twenty years old, the recently deceased British and Black cultural theorist Stuart Hall argues that the status of the "postcolonial" is best understood as an "episteme in formation."[6] His argument reveals, first, the extent to which suspicion is cast on the "post" in postcolonial; second, that the term "postcolonial" seems to be preoccupied with Eurocentric time; and, finally, that the term proffers a double inscription of the colonial encounter leading not to the easy polemics of "difference" of identity but to a *différance*. I draw on the work of Stuart Hall not because he was the first person to use the term,[7] nor because he is the most well-known of postcolonial theorists, nor even because he

---

and Lidia Curti (New York: Routledge, 1996), 242–60; quoted from Michel Foucault, "Nietzsche, Genealogy, History," in *Language, Counter-Memory, Practice: Selected Essays and Interviews*, ed. Donald F. Bouchard, trans. Donald F. Bouchard and Sherry Simon (Ithaca, NY: Cornell University Press, 1977), 139–64, at 153.

[6] Hall, "When Was the Postcolonial?," 255.

[7] Various archeological endeavors attempting to trace the genealogy of postcolonial theory exist. In one of the more proximate analyses, Sankaran Krishna in his *Globalization and Postcolonialism: Hegemony and Resistance in the Twenty-first Century* (Lanham, MD: Rowman and Littlefield, 2009), 63–104, argues that it depends on one's lens. If one begins with a form of Third-World Marxism, the term was used (and this was its first appearance) by Marxist scholar Hamza Alavi, to describe societies such as India, Pakistan, and Bangladesh. Here, the term was primarily geographical. If "postcolonial" refers to an internal dissent of European colonialism, then the anti-colonial tract written by the Iberian Catholic bishop Bartolomé de Las Casas in 1542 inaugurates another intellectual moment of emergence. As a literary movement, postcolonial theory is the phenomenon of "The Empire Writes Back" in the writing and discursive freedom in the literatures of the former colonies. The critique of Orientalism in the work of Edward Said, which argued that knowledge or representation is always intertwined with issues of power, social class, and materiality is another thread to follow. A distinct and foundational work for contemporary postcolonial theory is advanced by yet another perspective, that of the Subaltern Studies group which emphasized critical method over political critique. They emphasized the notion that Western modernity as a global process depended on colonialism and conquest. Homi Bhabha's notions of ambivalence, mimicry, and hybridity present the next strand of contemporary postcolonial theory, arguing that colonialism brought modern notions of identity and subjectivity into deep crisis. The postcolonial self for Bhabha is not a "sovereign" being, a subject of coherence.

shows up in "genealogies" of postcolonial theory. I introduce his work because he was one of the original "border" thinkers, one who most certainly has influenced the work of Walter Mignolo, and also as one who understands postcolonialism to be a process of decolonization.[8]

In the first place, the prefix "post" represents ambivalence because it marks a "shift in global relations, and the necessarily uneven transition from the age of Empires to the post-independence or post-decolonization moment."[9] "Postcolonial," then, refers to a process of agents who delink from any colonial power through self-governance exercised by a newly emerged nation-state. What is important, however, is that delinking from colonial power simultaneously marked both decolonizing societies and colonizing societies, thus subverting the old colonizer/colonized binary. An allied issue raised by the use of "post" is whether the post refers solely to the moment of the *European* history of colonialism. Such a provenance for other modernities from within a European context obscures the proliferation of modernities, traditionalisms, and histories competing for discursive supremacy. As Hall suggests, the "deconstruction of core concepts" in the "post" discourses reveals not a temporal and linear history but a proliferation and decentering of any singular temporal narrative.[10] For this reason, the "difference" presented by the "postcolonial" is better understood as *différance*. It is such *différance*, a concept Hall derives from Derrida and employing the method of deconstruction, that has relevance for postcolonial hermeneutics.[11] Deconstruction, then, is one form of postcolonial hermeneutics. The method actively inhibits the category being mobilized solely as an identity marker.

A useful explicatory essay by Stanley E. Porter and Jason C. Robinson in their *Hermeneutics: An Introduction to Interpretive Theory* makes the

---

And finally, Gayatri Chakravorty Spivak's "double negative" understands postcolonialism in the context of globalization. Consequently, she understands hegemonic structures be they economic or cultural to be simultaneously empowering and impoverishing.

[8] Hall, "When Was the Postcolonial?," 246. Important here is to note that the idea of decolonization has always been part of postcolonial theory.

[9] Ibid., 246.

[10] Ibid., 248.

[11] See, e.g., Jacques Derrida's classic essay "Différance," in *Margins of Philosophy*, trans. Alan Bass (Chicago: Chicago University Press, 1982), 1–27.

notion of *différance* central to any analysis of postcolonial hermeneutics.[12] *Différance* is a "quasi-transcendental" word that does not "constitute understanding or knowing in the typical sense."[13] As a quasi-transcendental word, it is the condition for the possibility of knowing as in the Kantian sense. It is also a term under which meaning, identity, and presence occurs while simultaneously disrupting, destabilizing, decentering binary oppositions to undermine the myth of full presence. It is anti-foundational from the outset. Derrida was, of course, very pessimistic about the very possibility of hermeneutics.[14] The authors assert, however, that Derrida's insistence that there cannot be a transcendentally signified grounding of the kind assumed by Western metaphysics is not radically new. Hans-Georg Gadamer, in the move from an epistemological to an existential hermeneutics based in dialogue, does not assume that interpretation can be based in a firm grounding of meaning. What is important in Porter and Robinson's analysis is that they point out that deconstruction's impetus to destabilize and decenter Western rationality has already been intimated in Gadamer's philosophical hermeneutics.

Both Derrida and Gadamer, for example, have common concerns for language and texts. Both share a common concern to challenge the metaphysical bias of presence. Both challenge the metaphysical tradition by destabilizing its confidence in presence by placing an emphasis on the experience of otherness and difference. Neither is agreed that there is a transcendental vantage point from which to understand, nor that there is a language or discourse that privileges understanding. While both agree that meaning is ambiguous, Derrida believes that Gadamer does not go far enough because of his reliance on a dialogical model of understanding. Nevertheless, Porter and Robinson assert that the novelty ascribed to deconstruction is overestimated. They point out that, for Gadamer, dialogue with a text or a person is not a simple uncovering of the truth. Dialogue will also not guarantee perfect understanding. The point, then, is that the notion that deconstruction is some kind of new mode of challenging herme-

---

[12] Stanley E. Porter and Jason C. Robinson, *Hermeneutics: An Introduction to Interpretive Theory* (Grand Rapids, MI: Eerdmans, 2011).

[13] Ibid., 201.

[14] Ibid., 15.

neutical theory is overdrawing the distinction between Derrida and Gadamer. In deconstruction, Derrida asserts that all understanding is predicated on non-understanding and incompleteness. Gadamer, say Porter and Robinson, already stands in such a place. "Otherness" and the undecidablity of it is no stranger to interpretation and hermeneutics. Why, then, the disdain of deconstruction?

Stuart Hall points to the debate surrounding the term "postcolonial" and its origins in post-structuralist discourse as one reason for the disdain of deconstruction. When deconstruction dissolves binary oppositions, it is a reminder that binary oppositions were what were put in place to represent cultural difference.[15] Thus, the term "postcolonial" now is a "bearer of unconscious investments, a sign of desire for some and equally for others, a signifier of danger."[16] Among those presenting the dangers of the term are Ella Shohat and Arif Dirlik who, respectively, point to the temporal linearity of the term and the implication that "post" means "past" and to the dissolution of a political Marxist stance in favor of a culturalism that is now commodified by a neo-liberal American academy.[17] Hall, in accepting the stance of deconstructive post-structuralism, is more sanguine about the term because the nostalgia of binary politics comes at a price: "Isn't the ubiquitous, the soul-searing lesson of our times the fact that political binaries do not (do not any longer? Did they ever?) either stabilize the field of political antagonism in any permanent way or render it transparently intelligible?"[18]

A very interesting *elision* in Hall's essay and simultaneously reflected in postcolonial theoretical analyses that came after him is that of a specifically feminist analysis informing postcolonial literary theory from the outset. Deconstruction in postcolonial theory is not limited solely to a critique of metaphysics of knowledge. Deconstruction's social and cultural utility reveals the presence of multiple oppressions of women, reflecting the presence of a metaphysics of "Self" and "Other." In his essay, Hall makes reference to Ruth Frankenberg and Lata Mani's essay "Crosscurrents, Crosstalk: Race, 'Postcoloniality' and the

---

[15] Hall, "When Was the Postcolonial?," 249.
[16] Ibid., 242.
[17] Ibid., 243.
[18] Ibid., 244.

Politics of Location,"[19] which complicates the "post" of "postcolonial" by pointing to the globalized context in which it circulates and its particular effects on women. While Hall refers to feminist deconstruction approvingly, he does not incorporate its salient proposals.

Among Frankenberg and Mani's suggestions is that "postcolonial" is a term that ought to be contextualized: when too hastily globalized, it blurs the locatedness of the "postcolonial" in India, Britain, and the United States. Contextualizing the term reveals that there are multiple implications of the "post-ness" in relation to colonialism in each of these three venues. Hence they propose a "feminist conjuncturalist" approach to the issue of postcolonial context.[20] Feminist conjuncturalism is feminist postcolonial analysis which "neither conceives domination in single axis terms, nor falsely equalizes the effects of these relations on subjects. . . . There is (consequently) an effective but not determining relationship between subjects and their histories, a relationship that is complex, shifting and yet not free."[21] In other words, feminist postcolonial theory points to a distinct lack of independence or freedom in decolonized spaces for women and other minoritized groups in domestic social, political, and cultural contexts. Of course, domestic national contexts are in turn affected by global capitalism and global militarism. Key here is their insistence that the "post" in postcolonial signifies not an "after" but marks "spaces of ongoing contestation enabled by decolonization struggles both globally and locally."[22] A feminist conjuncturalist politics reveals the necessity of the prefix "post" in conjunction with the suffix "ity," thus, postcolonialism is best understood as a conjuncture of various forms of oppression, domination, resistance, *and* revisioning. Postcoloniality, therefore, presents an occasion for constructive politics, a move that a narrow view of deconstruction fails to acknowledge. What is important again is that "postcolonial" from the outset was not a term that was theorized as a totality. Neither is "deconstruction" solely in reference to the deconstruction of Western metaphysics of meaning. As postcolonial feminists argue, it can also be used to deconstruct analyses of gender oppression and resistance.

---

[19] Ruth Frankenberg and Lata Mani, "Crosscurrents, Crosstalk: Race, 'Postcoloniality' and the Politics of Location," *Cultural Studies* 7, no. 2 (1993): 292–310.
[20] Ibid, 292.
[21] Ibid., 306.
[22] Ibid., 294.

That deconstruction and post-structuralism in South Asian postcolonial theory results in a "paradoxical parochialism" is an argument presented by Richard King, who provides four cogent reasons for such a development.[23] First, he argues, poststructuralist thought has been useful in the South Asian context to destabilize and challenge universalist pretensions of Western intellectual traditions. Second, it is the use of post-structuralism and a perception of its use as avant-garde politics that has raised postcolonial theory's profile in a largely Euro-American academy. Third, post-structuralism has been a way for South Asian Marxists to move beyond a merely economics-centered reading of Marx in favor of a Gramscian reading of culture. Finally, King points out that the South Asian strand represented by Homi Bhabha, Gayatri Spivak, and the Subaltern Historians resonates with post-structuralism because the rhetoric of "civilizing the rest of the world" in the eighteenth and nineteenth centuries is precisely what created the context for colonialism in South Asia.

The paradoxical parochialism of South Asian postcolonial theory leads to competing emphases in postcolonial analyses. King points out that Latin American liberation philosophers such as Mignolo and Enrique Dussel evaluate the colonial context in Latin America as properly belonging to the first stage of modernity, whereas in South Asia it was more the second stage of modernity. Thus, postcolonial South Asia aptly draws on internal-to-Europe dissenting epistemological traditions such as post-structuralism. As first stage colonialism, Latin American postcolonialism necessarily deals with Christian missions and colonization for religious conversion. Postcolonial criticism in Latin America, unlike that derived from post-structuralist postcolonial criticism of South Asia and its secular allegiances, consequently is far more invested in Christian liberation theology. Conversely, the uncritical retrieval of religious and theological traditions in South Asia and West Asia has resulted in "atavistic indigenism" in the form of Hindutva or Islamism.[24] The religious retrieval of cultural traditions, however, creates much anxiety among postcolonial theorists.

Once again, a Western notion of "religion" invigorates such (oxymoronic) modern atavisms. As King points out, "religion" bears the

---

[23] King, "Philosophy of Religion as Border Control," 35–53.
[24] Ibid., 43.

brunt of the weight of the category "tradition." In many postcolonial contexts, the nation-state becomes the bearer of such tradition, closely yoking modernity, secularism, and tradition together. King points out that Mignolo would characterize such modern atavisms as "local histories with global designs" and suggests instead that "tradition" should mean more than "religion" and refer to "cosmographic wisdom traditions" instead.[25] These more-than-religion analyses would indeed be able to shoulder the urgent need to consider the impact of neoliberal capitalism, consumerism, and global capitalism on identity, ethics, and the differences embodied in its articulation. "Wisdom" thus is the hermeneutical lens—a "planetary approach to philosophical debate"[26]—to overturn the effects of colonialism. A "loving pursuit of wisdom, nourished by a clearer self-critical grasp of its historic situation and limitations" deconstructs the binary oppositionality of "religion," "secularism," "tradition," and "modernity."[27]

Deconstruction is unavoidable in dismantling the paralyzing logics of oppositional binaries at play in social contexts. *Différance* illumines the dissolution of these binaries and becomes useful for a complex politics that provides the basis for both critique as well as resistance. In what follows, I argue that Mignolo's notions of border *gnosis*, decolonial philosophy, and elision of gender issues (save for those essays or books written together with Madina Tlostanova) do not decolonize in the way that he hopes. "Decolonization" in the context of postcolonial analyses is not new. Among South Asian postcolonial theorists, Gayatri Spivak articulated decolonization as the goal of postcolonial theory as early as 1983. Nowhere does an analysis of Spivak's work appear in Mignolo, though there are bibliographic references to her work. Finally, Mignolo also disavows deconstruction even as he asserts that "deconstructing colonial discourse" is a central task.[28] My argument is that the litmus test of decolonial proposals is, to use Spivak's felicitous phrase, the case of the "gendered subaltern." Mignolo stops short at any feminist analysis, arguing instead that colonial difference of culture and epistemology perform the task of decolonizing. The strategic

[25] Ibid., 50.
[26] Ibid., 51.
[27] Ibid., 35.
[28] See Walter D. Mignolo, *Local Histories/Global Designs: Coloniality, Subaltern Knowledges and Border Thinking* (Princeton, NJ: Princeton University Press, 2000), 326.

choice to provide a merely complementary Latin American discourse alongside Western ones does not *decolonize*, which is a specifically political and feminist goal.

Walter Mignolo and Latin American Postcolonial Hermeneutics

> "I am a postcolonial diasporic Indian who seeks to decolonize the mind."
>
> — Gayatri Chakravorty Spivak, *The Postcolonial Critic*[29]

Mignolo argues that a "decolonial philosophy" rather than a postcolonial one is what will dissolve the binary of modernity and tradition.[30] Further, he is leery of deconstruction and its emphasis on what he terms a "world systems analysis."[31] Instead of deconstruction, he proposes that decolonization, initiated by subaltern agency, is border thinking. At the outset, therefore, we note that Mignolo distinguishes himself from the South Asian emphasis on deconstruction. Drawing on Dussel's notion of "transmodernity," Mignolo provides a way to delink the "emancipating promises of modernity" from its more insidious ways of negating and coopting the knowledges and wisdom of colonized others and represents the postcolonial turn to subaltern knowledge. Such a turn in itself is not novel. Spivak, among others, has argued since the early 1990s that crossing borders by delimiting the scope of Western epistemologies and drawing on subaltern languages and knowledge constitute the constructive project of postcolonialism.[32] The project of bringing non-elite knowledges to the foreground of

---

[29] Gayatri Chakravorty Spivak, *The Postcolonial Critic: Interviews, Strategies and Dialogues*, ed. Sarah Harasym (New York: Routledge, 1990), 67.

[30] Madina V. Tlostanova and Walter D. Mignolo, "On Pluritopic Hermeneutics, Trans-Modern Thinking and Decolonial Philosophy," *Encounters* 1 (2009): 11–27.

[31] Mignolo, *Local Histories/Global Designs*, 44.

[32] Cf. a particularly sharp and pointed challenge by Spivak in her "How to Teach a Culturally Different Book" in *The Spivak Reader*, ed. Donna Landry and Gerald Maclean (New York: Routledge, 1996), 252: "If the subaltern is listened to as agent and not simply as a victim, we might not be obliged to rehearse decolonization interminably from above, as agendas for new schools of postcolonial criticism. But the subaltern is not heard. And one of the most interesting philosophical questions about decolonizing remains: *who decolonizes and how?*" (emphasis added).

academic attention is one way to bridge the gap between South Asian and Latin American postcolonial criticisms. What is different about Mignolo's proposal is that he wants to situate Latin American *cultural* knowledges alongside Western ones and to set them in a dialogic relationship. Spivak, conversely, argues that other knowledges, especially those embodied women's knowledges, perform the function of decolonization, *especially* the decolonization of (global) feminism, while deconstructing (national and cultural) identity and gender essentialisms.[33]

Mignolo presents transmodernity as interruptive and transgressive: "it is the epistemic and ontological dwelling of 'the other'" in, with, and through whom decolonization occurs.[34] Transmodernity shows up the provincial nature of European modernity, introduces other voices and languages, and actively rejects the hegemony of European modernity. Delinking from European modernity introduces a decolonial epistemic shift and a different option: "Transmodern futures are built on epistemic and aesthetic disobedience: the disobedience of the other toward imperial designs of the same, disobedience that transforms and converts the imperial same into an equal other. This is, in a nutshell, the process of decolonizing epistemology and aesthetics that we are witnessing at the beginning of the twenty-first century."[35]

In *The Darker Side of Western Modernity*, Mignolo asserts that "modernity" has multiple valences beyond a Western, Euro-American assessment.[36] One of the key distinctions in his body of work is that of *humanitas* and *anthropos*, which has bearing on the project of decolonizing knowledge.[37] *Humanitas* is a concept that is central to the Western modern and epistemological project. It is, for Mignolo, "an

---

[33] See Spivak, "Feminism and Critical Theory," in *The Spivak Reader*, 62: "I am still moved by the reversal-displacement morphology of deconstruction, crediting the asymmetry of the 'interest' of the historical moment. Investigating the hidden ethicopolitical agenda of differentiations constitutive of knowledge and judgment interests me more. It is also the deconstructive moment that keeps me resisting an essentialist freezing of the concepts of gender, race, and class. I look rather at the repeated agenda of the situational production of those concepts and our complicity in such a production. This aspect of deconstruction will not allow the establishment of a hegemonic 'global theory' of feminism."

[34] Tlostanova and Mignolo, "On Pluritopic Hermeneutics," 19.

[35] Ibid, 20.

[36] Mignolo, *The Darker Side of Western Modernity*, 82.

[37] See also Tlostanova and Mignolo, "On Pluritopic Hermeneutics," 11–13.

epistemic style of thinking that hides coloniality and prevents pluriversal, dialogic and epistemically democratic systems of thought from unfolding." *Anthropos*, conversely, is what occupies the space exterior to *humanitas*. Decolonizing epistemology in terms of these two concepts requires that we ask "what are the connections between your body, bio-graphically and geo-historically located in the colonial matrix of power, and the issues you investigate?"[38] Thus, taking the critical theory of Max Horkheimer, who rightly argued that it is not possible to detach the knowing subject from the known object, Mignolo takes it a step further in interrogating the subject of knowledge. He finds this subject to be inadequately theorized because Western critical theory has never truly examined its "deracialized, desexualized, gender-neutral" assumptions.[39] The "decolonial" option for Mignolo, therefore, is an argument from the perspectives of *anthropos*. It is grounded in a geo- and body-politics of knowledge, which is in a direct contest with the theo- and ego-politics of knowledge of *humanitas*. Note that his critique here follows a number of feminist analyses which, as internal-to-Europe's epistemologies, have asked similar questions but do not make an appearance in his work *as* the work of feminists.[40]

Unlike Spivak and other postcolonial feminists, decolonization in Mignolo is not the result of using the method of deconstruction. He argues instead that deconstruction presumes a "monolingual" metaphysics.[41] By this he means that postcolonial deconstruction has narrowly drawn only on Western and Christian metaphysics. Drawing on the work of Abdelhebir Khatibi, a Moroccan philosopher, Mignolo asserts that "an 'other' thinking" is critical to grasping how local histories perform global designs. Khatibi's position that in local contexts other than the "Western Modern" there exist "bilingual" situation for metaphysics—Western and Islamic—in contrast to Derrida, who constructs Western metaphysics, in its variety, as monolingual. It is such a bilingual situation that "allows for a double critique and border thinking." Kahtibi

---

[38] Mignolo, *The Darker Side of Western Modernity*, xxiv.

[39] Ibid. Incidentally, this was exactly the question that Gayatri Spivak asked in 1983: "Can the Subaltern Speak?" (see n. 44). She makes no appearance in Mignolo's *The Darker Side of Western Modernity* other than one bibliographic entry.

[40] For example, his use of Gloria E. Anzaldúa and Cherríe Moraga among Chicana feminists avoids the messier issues of body and sexuality foregrounded in their work.

[41] Mignolo, *Local Histories/Global Designs*, 82.

denotes the conflict that arose in sixteenth century Spain between the Christians and the Moors as the inception of Occidentalism. Border thinking in Khatibi is epistemological and ethical. Since Occidentalism separates Western modernity from Islam and Islamic fundamentalism separates Islam from modernity, Mignolo asserts that Khatibi's ethical and epistemological argument is simultaneously located in all of these contexts as well as in none (no one) of them.[42] Khatibi's decolonizing deconstruction therefore "distinguishes a critique of modernity from the perspective of modernity itself; on the other, he enacts a critique of modernity from the perspective of coloniality . . . marking his alliance with Foucault and Derrida at the same time his detachment."[43]

Another interesting dissonance with Spivak's notion of deconstruction is noteworthy. In Spivak's famous essay "Can the Subaltern Speak?" she tackles head-on whether Derrida's deconstruction has valence for politics and ethics. In other words, querying Derrida has always been part of Spivak's postcolonial feminist methodology. Deconstruction is not for the subaltern. It is a method that *opens* up agential space for the subaltern:

> [In a chapter Derrida composed twenty years ago, "Of Grammatology as a Positive Science,"] he confronts the issue of whether deconstruction can lead to an adequate practice, whether critical or political. The question is how to keep the ethnocentric Subject from establishing itself by selectively defining an Other. This is not a program for the Subject as such; rather, it is a program for the benevolent *Western* intellectual. For those of us who feel that the "subject" has a history and that the task of the first-world subject of knowledge in our historical moment is to resist and critique "recognition" of the Third World through "assimilation," this specificity is crucial.[44]

It is a profound misreading of postcolonial theory and Spivak in particular to charge the method of (South Asian and feminist) deconstruction with failing to provide agency for the subaltern. Spivak's point is that deconstruction is the first phase of decolonization, open-

---

[42] Ibid., 68.
[43] Ibid., 70.
[44] Gayatri Chakravorty Spivak, "Can the Subaltern Speak?," in *Colonial Discourse and Postcolonial Theory, A Reader*, ed. Patrick Williams and Laura Chrisman (New York: Columbia University Press, 1994), 66–111, at 88 (emphasis in the original).

ing up spaces for subaltern agency. How and when the subaltern speaks will be clear when benevolent Western critical thinkers make space for her voice. Spivak's work has always demanded that we do the difficult work of locating the manner in which subjects are formed while attending to the context in which agency is made possible. Mignolo repeatedly asserts that deconstruction is a method followed by South Asian postcolonial theorists and concedes that "the geopolitical distribution of intellectual tasks and disciplinary projects may look suspect, but unavoidable precisely because of the constitution of the imaginary of the modern/colonial world system."[45] Hence he presents deconstruction as a methodological obsession (grounded in Western modernity) of South Asian postcolonial theorists, while arguing that his method of complementing the modern/colonial system with Latin American knowledge is a better way to decolonize.

Mignolo's decolonial project also has the following features. In two similarly titled essays, published two years apart, he situates decoloniality as having its historical grounding in the Bandung Conference of 1955.[46] Decoloniality therefore should be the preferred opposite of Modernity. It is a conscious "delinking" from Western macronarratives and paradigms such as "modern, postmodern, altermodern, Newtonian science, quantum theory, (and) theory of relativity."[47] As mentioned before, the key epistemic dimension of decolonial thought as Mignolo develops it is "border thinking," a notion he has (sometimes) ascribed to Chicana feminist and queer thinkers such as Gloria Anzaldúa and Cherríe Moraga. At other times he ascribes border thinking to Frantz Fanon's query in *Black Skin, White Masks* (1952): "Oh my body, make me one who always questions."[48] He has developed the notion of border thinking extensively in a number of places. In *Local Histories/Global Designs* he explains more fully what it might mean.[49]

---

[45] Mignolo, *Local Histories/Global Designs*, 64.
[46] See Walter D. Mignolo, "Geopolitics of Sensing and Knowing: On (De)coloniality, Border Thinking and Epistemic Disobedience," in *Postcolonial Studies* 14 (2011): 273–83; Mignolo, "Epistemic Disobedience, Independent Thought and Decolonial Freedom," in *Theory, Culture and Society* 26 (2009): 159–81.
[47] Mignolo, "Geopolitics of Sensing and Knowing," 274.
[48] Frantz Fanon, *Black Skin, White Masks*, trans. Richard Philcox (New York: Grove Press, 2008), 206.
[49] Mignolo, *Local Histories/Global Designs*, 49–88.

Border thinking is first a form of *gnosis*. The use of *gnosis* is meant to move beyond the confrontation between epistemology and hermeneutics and to open up knowledge as more than the culture of Western scholarship. Acknowledging that he borrowed the notion of *gnosis* and its potential for intervention from Valentin Mudimbe on the invention of Africa, Mignolo also concedes that *gnosis* has a Christian (and Greek) historical and philosophical provenance. He notes that the Christian and Greek archive maintains that there is a difference between *episteme*, *doxa*, and *gnosis*. For Plato, the distinction between *episteme* and *doxa* is clear: the former refers to a systematic knowledge guided by explicit logical rules, the latter by common sense. *Gnosis*, however, reflected a different sense of knowledge, attained either by mystic contemplation or by mathematical reasoning, a kind of wisdom. Such a form of knowledge, bemoans Mignolo, is unfavorably compared to the ideals of epistemology and metaphysics, which have linked meaning and knowledge in particular ways for Western modernity. Mudimbe's use of the term *gnosis* reflects a negation of the primacy of Western philosophy and epistemology. From these sources Mignolo derives "border *gnosis*":

> [It is] a knowledge from a subaltern perspective conceived from the exterior borders of the modern/colonial world system, and border gnoseology as a discourse about colonial knowledge conceived at the conflictive intersection of the knowledge produced from the perspective of modern colonialisms (rhetoric, philosophy, science) and knowledge produced from the perspective of colonial modernities in Asia, Africa and the Americas/Caribbean. Border gnoseology is a critical reflection on knowledge production from both the interior borders of the modern/colonial world system and its exterior borders.[50]

Such a border epistemology leads to "epistemic disobedience" and is intrinsic to decoloniality.[51] As a decolonizing strategy, it seeks to bring subaltern's voices, knowledges, and politics to elite Euro-American

---

[50] Ibid., 11.

[51] Mignolo, "Geopolitics of Sensing and Knowing," 273–83. Here, Mignolo argues that "decoloniality" is a concept that arises in the "Third world," specifically arising out of the experience of the Bandung Conference. My discomfort with his genealogy is that it leads him to assert a "different" space than South Asian postcolonial theory.

academic conversations. The use of the term *gnosis* signals that Mignolo believes that only those who occupy borders have the potential for epistemic disobedience.

My problem with the presentation of *gnosis* as the preferred decolonial strategy is that it depends on a form of cultural essentialist identity that seeks to trump other cultural identities by asserting a "better than yours" strategy. Postcolonial theorists in the wake of deconstruction of identity are leery of cultural essentialism and culturally supremacist language. Nevertheless, as Spivak has often argued, the strategic mobilization of essentialist categories in view of specific political goals performs its own form of deconstruction, a fragile and strategic essentialism. She would be in agreement with Mignolo that decoloniality (not border *gnosis*) not only changes the content of the transmodern conversations happening with Euro-America but also changes the terms of the conversation.[52] For example, in her essay "Feminism and Deconstruction Again: Negotiations," Spivak argues that deconstruction in postcolonial feminism is best understood as mobilizing a "persistent crisis or unease of the moment of *techné* or crafting."[53] Thus, categories of "self" and "other," most clearly to be seen in the construction of "man" and "woman," are a result of *différance*, not difference. Cultural and gender essentialism, under deconstructive conditions, leads to *différance*. South Asian postcolonial theory would persistently avoid identity claims or knowledge based on cultural identity unless employed in a self-reflexively deconstructive mode.

Mignolo has often presented "decolonial" in contrast and in opposition to "postcolonial." In *The Darker Side of Western Modernity*, he tabulates the differences—the two discourses reflect different *existentia*; decolonial projects are far more disbelieving of the salvation promise of modernity; and decolonializing is always a project that examines the "underside" of modernity.[54] It is clear especially with the last issue that Latin American liberation theology has been a significant influence in his work. While he maintains that the two discourses are not in competition, he does assert that they are "different projects

---

[52] Ibid., 275.
[53] Gayatri Chakravorty Spivak, "Feminism and Deconstruction Again: Negotiations," in *Outside in the Teaching Machine* (New York: Routledge, 1993), 121–40, at 121.
[54] Mignolo, *The Darker Side of Western Modernity*, preface.

that have in common the concern with colonialism, colonial legacies, and above all, for decolonial thinkers, coloniality."[55] In his work, the suffix "ity" to colonial has a specific meaning.[56] Coloniality was a concept introduced by the Peruvian sociologist Anibal Quijano in the late 1980s and 1990s. Mignolo develops it as a concept that grounds Western modernity. That is, there is no modernity that is not aligned with coloniality. He writes:

> Neoliberalism, with its emphasis on the market and consumption, is not just a question of economy but a new form of civilization. The impossibility or lack of credibility of universal or world histories today is not advanced by some influential postmodern theory, but by the economic and social forces generally referred to as globalization and by the emergence of forms of knowledge that have been subalternized during the past five hundred years under global designs. . . . To simplify things, I refer to this double edge as modernity/coloniality. The coexistence and the intersection of both modern colonialisms and colonial modernities . . . , from the perspective of people and local histories that have to confront modern colonialism, is what I understand here as "coloniality," quite simply, the reverse and unavoidable side of "modernity"—its darker side.[57]

Once again, he overdraws the distinction between postcolonialism/postcoloniality and colonialism/coloniality in a manner that ultimately does not serve the goal of decolonization. Spivak, in her *Critique of Postcolonial Reason*, had defined postcoloniality thus: "Postcolonial persons are able to inhabit the global metropolis precisely because imperial culture permits such communication. Such ability is not simplistic privilege or a matter of 'luck.' *Critiquing structures that one inhabits intimately is a deconstructive position which defines postcoloniality*."[58] Mignolo seems to be invested in carving out a separate domain for decolonial strategies while Spivak is far more transparent about the imbrication

---

[55] Ibid., xxvii.

[56] The use of the suffix to complicate the easy mobility of the term "postcolonial" especially in Spivak and even earlier in Frankenberg and Mani's work is never referred to by Mignolo.

[57] Mignolo, *Local Histories/Global Designs*, 22.

[58] Gayatri Chakravorty Spivak, *A Critique of Postcolonial Reason: Toward a History of the Vanishing Present* (Cambridge, MA: Harvard University Press, 1999), 191 (emphasis added).

of postcolonial thought in Western thought. My sense is that Mignolo is representing decolonial thought as a new oppositional binary and its older political style. Who decolonizes? How?

Mignolo's "post-Occidental" thought also invites more pointed feminist philosophical criticism. "Border thinking" is a term originating in Gloria Anzaldúa's *Borderlands/La Frontera* (1987).[59] That border thinking is a notion that arises in the context of Latin American *feminist* and *queer* thought is barely acknowledged by Mignolo (there are a number of references to Anzaldúa and Moraga, but not in terms of their feminism or queer activism). A primary argument made in Anzaldúa's work was that agency is to be grounded in the awareness of multiple oppressions. Gender, race, class, and sexual orientation function in a particular way to create the context of Borderlands. In particular, Anzaldúa is critical of domestic contexts in which queer women resist colonialism, capitalism, and patriarchy even as these transcend geopolitical borders. Anzaldúa's text, which escapes any easy classification, retrieves the bodily identity of the New Mestiza, the feminist on the border, strategically transgressing aesthetic boundaries in her text, gender boundaries with her "choice" to be a lesbian, ethnicity and race in combining native, Spanish, African, and Anglo blood, in order to form the New Mestiza. The bodily transgression which Anzaldúa expresses as a form of agency, however, is subtly repudiated in Mignolo's work because, for him, borders are stable and definite. In Anzaldúa's work, borders behave differently—they are blurry and porous.[60] Anzaldúa, therefore, challenges borders differently; borders are queer.

---

[59] Gloria Anzaldúa, *Borderlands/La Frontera: The New Mestiza* (San Francisco: Spinsters/Aunt Lute, 1987).

[60] Madina V. Tlostanova and Walter D. Mignolo, *Learning to Unlearn: Decolonial Reflections from Eurasia and the Americas* (Columbus: The Ohio State University Press, 2012), 72 (emphasis in the original): "Borders could be 'studied' from the perspective of territorial epistemology (e.g., Western social sciences; Horkheimer's traditional theory) but the 'problem' of the twenty-first century would be not so much to study the life and deeds of the borders but to *think from the borders themselves* and therefore to be the border, in Anzaldúa's words. The main problem of the twenty-first century is not just *crossing* borders but *dwelling in the borders*. We, Madina and Walter, are border dwellers, and hence the argument unfolded here is not an analysis of observers practicing a zero-point epistemology but that of border dwellers engaging in border and decolonial thinking."

Ofelia Schutte in her analysis of Mignolo's contribution to Latin American postcolonial philosophy asserts that there remains a tension between his notion of border knowledges (which retains a Foucauldian flavor) and the structuralist world-systems approach appropriated from Dussel and Quijano.[61] A major problem that she notes in Mignolo's presentation is his dismissal of deconstructive strategies that he dismisses as "blind to colonial difference."[62] As Schutte points out, this is a misreading and misrepresentation of deconstruction methodologies as presented in the work of Spivak and Bhabha, among others (as I have also indicated in my presentation of Spivak). In her estimation, what Mignolo is setting up is a "complementary strategy" to Derridean deconstruction. Thus, his pluritopic hermeneutics is an "interpretive counterstance" in which spatial and temporal concepts are mapped in a side-by-side relation instead of the colonial relation of subordinating the one to the other.[63] Hence Mignolo emphasizes colonial difference which requires decolonial thought to be "post-Occidental" or, to be more precise, contra-Occidental. Schutte's criticism here is gentle, but pointed: "A point that remains ambiguous in Mignolo's presentation of border knowledges is the degree of compatibility he thinks such ways of thinking have vis-à-vis poststructuralist theory in Latin America and its diaspora."[64] Obviously, she points out, since Immanuel Wallerstein, Quijano, and Dussel all employ forms of post-structuralism in their thought, he does not stand in strict opposition to it.

I would take Schutte's criticism even further. Even a cursory familiarity with the complex work of Homi Bhabha and Gayatri Spivak would alert us to the manner in which they approach post-structuralism. South Asian use of post-structuralism is not a simplistic capitulation to Western modernity. Its deconstructive nerve, however, challenges the homogenous certitudes of Western modernity, a condition that all of us (including and especially Mignolo!) occupy. Mignolo's obvious race, ethnicity, class, religious identity (he is white, of Italian Catholic heritage, was raised in Argentina, and is

---

[61] Ofelia Schutte, "Philosophy, Postcoloniality, and Postmodernity," in *A Companion to Latin American Philosophy*, ed. Susana Nuccetelli, Ofelia Schutte, and Otávio Buena (Malden, MA: Wiley-Blackwell, 2010), 312–26.

[62] Ibid., 321, citing Mignolo's *Local Histories/Global Designs*, 38.

[63] Schutte, "Philosophy, Postcoloniality, and Postmodernity," 318.

[64] Ibid., 320.

now teaching at Duke University) seems to play a large role in the unacknowledged privileges marking his work *and* its reception. In my reading, I remain convinced that Mignolo has not only performed misreadings of postcolonial theory to carve a "different" space for decolonial theory, but that he does so by avoiding the messier hermeneutical issues of vulnerable embodiment raised by feminists, queer thinkers, and racially minoritized theorists such as Hall, Spivak, and Anzaldúa.

Who Decolonizes and How for Christian Theology?

At this point I want to ask how decolonization in Mignolo's view will affect Catholic theology. Is Mignolo's emphasis on decolonization in opposition to South Asian deconstruction a productive one for Catholic theology? I do not think so; in my reading, Mignolo's labors to distinguish Latin American decolonial thought from South Asian postcolonial thought represent a capitulation to the Euro-American academy's taste for racialized and minoritized political positions, while simultaneously sidelining gendered ones. For example, when Mignolo refers to "liberation theology," it is often presumed to relate solely to the context of Latin and South America, ignoring the larger theological connotation of "liberation." Liberation theology in Dussel, for example, is not circumscribed by the Latin American context. Dussel's early formulation of the philosophy of liberation took Heidegger's ontological existentialism and Ricoeur's phenomenological hermeneutics as a starting point to think what liberation might mean from the perspective of Latin America without limiting it to that cultural context. It is the ethical emphasis in Dussel that enjoins him to emphasize liberation *as* theology. A deconstructive reading of Mignolo demonstrates that the goal of complementary decolonizing epistemology is a superficial gain for liberation theology. Liberation theology's relationship to its cultural context is an example of contextualization, but reading its scope as limited to the Latin American context contracts its theological vision.

A second worrisome issue is Mignolo's dependence on the diatopical hermeneutics of Raimundo Panikkar.[65] Quoting Panikkar's definition of diatopical hermeneutics as the "thematic consideration of understanding the other without assuming that the other has the same

---

[65] Mignolo, *The Darker Side of Western Modernity*, 61.

self-understanding that I have," Mignolo charges Western modernity of possessing a "monotopic" hermeneutics which animates its epistemological projects on the Right and the Left. Panikkar's diatopical hermeneutics, therefore, advocates an "imparative method" in contradistinction to a "comparative" method and focuses on dialogue, praxis, and existential encounters rather than the dialectics and argumentative reasoning of the latter.[66] Panikkar's work in comparative theology was among the first to challenge the category "religion" and its bounded nature. In a number of his works he has challenged the notion that the secular is separate from the sacred and that the horizontal dimension of human life is distinct from the vertical one. Panikkar's method, in other words, dissolves binaries so dear to Western secular thought. He was a border crosser and not a border dweller. Why, then, is Mignolo hesitant to mobilize Christian theological language which is better able to show the efficacy of diatopic hermeneutics as in Panikkar?

It is not that Mignolo ignores religion entirely. He wants to engage a "spiritual option" provocatively. Hence he advocates "decolonizing religion to liberate spirituality."[67] Interestingly, the move to separate religion from spirituality results in his assertion that cultural forms of religiosity (nodding approvingly toward Andrea Smith's work) do possess the ability to delink from Western modernity. There is little intimation in his work how privileging spirituality will offer key decolonizing options. The example that he offers from Smith, of delinking religious beliefs from the sacredness of land and native relationships to land, is an example of deconstructing "religion" in a postcolonial context. Since Mignolo does not go into any great detail what decolonizing spirituality would look like, I offer here in brief what postcolonial spirituality may entail. Deconstruction aids spirituality, especially the kind of political and decolonial spirituality that Mignolo wants to accomplish.

How may deconstruction decolonize religion? Kevin Hart is of the opinion that deconstruction aids in challenging *idolatry*:

> It may be that *différance* produces "God" in the same way that it originates "identity," "proper," "speech," and "truth" since *différance* generates all conceptual polarities, including those terms associated

[66] Ibid., 208.
[67] Ibid., 62.

with presence. Here Derrida extends Nietzsche's quip, "I fear we are not getting rid of God because we still believe in Grammar"; it is the gnawing suspicion that linguistic structures encourage false dualistic thinking, that the very existence of the word "man" opens the way for people to think of "God," to misconstrue God as a reality.[68]

The point made by Hart (and by others who have examined the role of deconstruction and theology) is that Derrida's critical object is metaphysics, not faith as such. The similarity between deconstruction and negative theology also presents the opportunity to think of theology "post-," that is, after modernity. To be sure, for formal theology, especially in a Thomistic frame, deconstruction and its emphasis on undecidablity simply introduces an inordinate amount of relativism. Further, any theology intending to serve the ecclesial and communal reality of Church grounded in the reality of the incarnation is simply negated by deconstruction and its emphasis on the negation of presence. The relationship between deconstruction and negative theology however is not in a simple commensurability of method and result, or simple opposition. As Hart explains, what religious thought does is to "keep the negative and positive in play," and what Derrida helps to bring into focus is that the positive and negative are not to be resolved dialectically or logically. Postcolonial theological hermeneutics would therefore not advance cultural or geo-political identity but seek to dismantle theological claims that rest on cultural or political imperialism. Thus, deconstruction's effect on epistemology is to diligently interrogate the stated political gain.

But there is another constructive use for deconstruction that is of use to a Catholic postcolonial theology. Here, the incarnational logic that grounds a sacramental imagination of the Church provides the space for what Catholic theologian Anthony Godzieba envisions in a "post-postmodern" Catholic theology. He argues that the incarnation makes it incumbent on us to think theologically by means of the body.[69] I agree. Thinking by means of the body—the bleeding blurry borders of an Anzaldúa, straining to hear the subaltern's speech in Spivak—is a postcolonial feminist hermeneutical lens. Liberation has to be *political*—

---

[68] Kevin Hart, "Jacques Derrida: The God Effect," in *Post-Secular Philosophy: Between Philosophy and Theology*, ed. Philip Blond (New York: Routledge, 1998), 259–80, at 273.

[69] Godzieba, "Incarnation, Theory, and Catholic Bodies," 229.

that is, it has to result in the liberation of gendered bodies and their sacramental potential. Catholic theological anthropology and postcolonial feminist theory have very similar convictions about the body, or, one could say, its *différance* and its necessary presence *as* bodies. Recall, for example, Frankenberg and Mani's use of deconstruction, its social and cultural uses to decolonize the contexts in which gendered bodies attempt to survive: nationhood, citizenship, constitutionality, democracy, and socialism. Deconstruction in such a view challenges both a rationality and theology that denies incarnational grace to some bodies simply because they are female, racially, culturally, sexually, or religiously different. The gendered subaltern, her sacramental potential and her "ontological frailty" *is* the occasion for a Catholic postcolonial theology.[70] In fact, a renewed attention to the gendered subaltern's embodied speech arising from her context, but providing a larger vision of liberation satisfies Mignolo's very account for decolonization: "Border *gnoseology* is a critical reflection on knowledge production from both the interior borders of the modern colonial world system . . . and its exterior borders."[71] The idea that the gendered subaltern is already self-reflexively providing a critical reflection or deconstruction of her own narrative of agency is what decolonizes. Thus, the South Asian gendered subaltern provides a deconstructive sacramental and incarnational standpoint for Catholic theology.

Godzieba's essay is also sharpened by the response provided by Lieven Boeve in his "(Post)Modern Theology on Trial? Towards a Radical Theological Hermeneutics of Christian Particularity" that also has relevance for Mignolo's proposal to decolonize.[72] The postmodern context, for Boeve, demands that Catholic theology become a "radical hermeneutical theology" that does not dismiss the potential of deconstruction for spirituality. However, what can be acknowledged as spirituality depends on the particular languages and grammars of a particular context. Decolonization, in this view, is an articulation from particular contexts that also is deconstructive. In other words, embodied narratives yielding to deconstruction lead to forms of historicized

---

[70] Ibid.

[71] Mignolo, *Local Histories/Global Designs*, 11.

[72] Lieven Boeve, "(Post)Modern Theology on Trial? Towards a Radical Theological Hermeneutics of Christian Particularity," *Louvain Studies* 28 (2003): 240–54.

spirituality: "Recontextualizing theology today means taking seriously the postmodern criticism of master narratives, of the deconstruction of self-securing truth claims."[73] Clearly, Mignolo's decolonial methods do not lend themselves to such a form of recontextualized and historicized spirituality. The claims of South Asian feminists and Latin American queer feminists, however, provide ample ways forward to decolonize religion and theology. They do this by attending to embodied narratives which also deconstruct the relation of their identities to hegemonic power, whether colonial, neo-colonial, global, or national. Of course, they do not envision a theological project precisely because critical secular thought has made room for their insights. A Catholic sacramental imagination is ill-served by the attempt to defeat South Asian feminist deconstruction, because the gendered South Asian body is the locus for a post-postmodern theology, just like its Latin American, Black, and African counterparts. As Godzieba writes: "Finite, particular, fragile embodiment, rather than being considered an epiphenomenon as in continental philosophy of religion, forms the mediating horizon of expectation for the human experience of the infinite and salvific love of God. The incarnation of God confirms the revelatory value of that vulnerable mediation."[74]

---

[73] Ibid., 254.
[74] Godzieba, "Incarnation, Theory, and Catholic Bodies," 229.

CHAPTER 11

". . . And Followed Him on the Way" (Mark 10:52)
Unity, Diversity, Discipleship

Anthony J. Godzieba

Ut unum sint, Ut plures sint

When it comes to unity and diversity in Christianity, how can we have—and think about—both at once?

The catalyst for the question is the emphasis on unity in the Second Vatican Council's Decree on Ecumenism (*Unitatis Redintegratio*), the document which has played such a pivotal role in contemporary ecumenism and whose fiftieth anniversary was recently celebrated.[1] The decree's opening chapter goes right to the heart of the matter by invoking Jesus' prayer to the Father in the Fourth Gospel's last discourse: "that they may all be one, even as you, Father, are in me, and I in you, that they also may be one in us" (John 17:21). The decree calls for "the restoration of unity among all Christians" and judges divisions among the followers of Christ to be a "scandal" that makes

---

[1] Second Vatican Council, Decree on Ecumenism (*Unitatis Redintegratio*), trans. Edward Yarnold, in *Decrees of the Ecumenical Councils*, ed. Norman Tanner, 2 vols. (Washington, DC: Georgetown University Press, 1990), 2:908–20, Latin and English on facing pages (hereafter UR, cited by article). A different translation is available online: http://www.vatican.va/archive/hist_councils/ii_vatican_council/documents/vat-ii_decree_19641121_unitatis-redintegratio_en.html. I cite the translation in the Tanner edition.

it appear "as if Christ himself were divided" (UR 1). To overcome these divisions, the proposed way of unity is that of *communio*, which "finds its highest model and source in the unity of the persons of the Trinity." The signs of this "fellowship in unity" would be the confession of one faith, the celebration of divine worship in common, and the preservation of "the harmony of God's family" (UR 2).

As a fundamental and systematic theologian, I come to *Unitatis Redintegratio* with a view that differs from my colleagues in ecclesiology or ecumenism. My focus here is not on the decree's diagnosis of the ecclesial situation, nor on its prognoses—crucial topics, certainly, but also ground that has already been well-plowed by others. Rather, from my perspective the decree reflects a more general conundrum that inhabits the heart of Christianity and the church, namely, the fraught relationship between unity and diversity and its hermeneutical implications. That relationship appears to some as an exercise of the Holy Spirit's freedom; to others it signals the loss of Catholic identity and a capitulation to relativism. I confess that I am looking for the contradictions that jostle each other for attention, all the little paradoxes that subtly undermine what we are told is the decree's usual meaning and that perhaps reveal another productive approach to the overall meanings of Christian life, the *communio* of those who live it, and the *fides quaerens intellectum* that explores and promotes it.

The decree manifests a crucial dialectic that is emblematic of Christian life, namely, the "unity" proclaimed by the decree as the Christian ideal is closely shadowed by "difference" that cannot be suppressed but is seen as necessary and even an occasion for admiration. Here are three examples. First, along with the opening chapter's emphasis on the Spirit's action of bringing the faithful "into intimate union with Christ, so that he is the principle of the church's unity" (UR 2, citing Eph 4:4-5 and Gal 3:27-28), there is immediate acknowledgment of difference, both in Christ's sending of twelve different apostles on mission (and whose preaching, we are later told, was received "with differences of form and manner . . . explained variously in different places, owing to diversities of character and condition of life" [UR 14]) and in the Spirit's role in "the distribution of graces and offices . . . enriching the church of Jesus Christ with different functions" (UR 2). Thus the Holy Spirit's actions engender both identity and difference. A second example: the "rifts" (*scissurae*) existing in the church are deemed "obstacles" to communion, yet in the midst of these separations we are admonished to recognize that all the baptized "have a right to be called Christians," that "significant elements and endowments" which give life to the church (such as the written word of God and the life of grace) "can exist outside the visible boundaries of the Catholic Church," and that "the separated churches and communities as such . . . have by no means been deprived of significance and importance in the mystery of salvation" (UR 3). The third instance is the most blatant example, and I quote it in full:

> All in the church must preserve unity in essentials. But let all, according to the gifts they have received, maintain a proper freedom in their various forms of spiritual life and discipline, in their different liturgical rites, and even in their theological elaborations of revealed truth. In all things let charity prevail. If they are true to this course of action, they will be giving even better expression to the authentic catholicity and apostolicity of the church. (UR 4)

All three examples underline the fact that the pursuit of authentic Christian unity cannot shake off unity's necessary "other"—diversity, difference, even fragmentation. *Ut unum sint* (that they be one) always includes *ut plures sint* (that they be many), especially since the model for *communio* is the Trinity (UR 2). Cardinal Walter Kasper, who has worked long and hard in the service of Christian unity, puts it this way: "Unity in the sense of full *communio* does not mean uniformity but unity in diversity and diversity in unity. Within the one church there is a legitimate multiplicity of mentalities, customs, rites, canonical orders, theologies and spiritualities."[2] Even amid the single-minded pursuit of Catholic identity, then, difference reveals itself and must be welcomed, not simply accommodated. How are these obviously existing circumstances to be explained?

There have been countless ecclesiological and ecumenical explorations of how unity and diversity can be thought together. But I want to pursue at a deeper level what Kasper has termed the problem of "pluri-

---

[2] Walter Kasper, "The Decree on Ecumenism—Read Anew after Forty Years," in Pope John Paul II et al., *Searching for Christian Unity* (Hyde Park, NY: New City Press, 2007), 18–35, at 30. Also online: http://www.vatican.va/roman_curia/ pontifical_councils /chrstuni/card-kasper-docs/rc_pc_chrstuni_doc_ 20041111_kasper-ecumenism_en.html.

formity" and its limits.³ This analysis is especially necessary in our contemporary context, whether one calls it late modern, postmodern, post-secular, or post-postmodern. Today, aspirations to unity are often considered hegemonic, and "difference" is the default hermeneutic of everyday life. For example, Terry Eagleton notes how the term "culture" has shifted since the 1960s, from its nineteenth-century meaning of high human ideals that grounded a unifying consensus and resolved political strife. It now refers to different and even agonistic national, sexual, ethnic, and regional identities—"culture" now as "difference," and "part of the very lexicon of political conflict itself."⁴ Ever since Martin Heidegger's post-metaphysical arguments for "the ontological difference" (not a concept, but the *process of differentiation itself* that allows us to tell the difference between Being and beings, a "third" that escapes metaphysics' binary thinking) and Jacques Derrida's ode to *différance* (the "play" that makes discourse possible but can never say its own name),⁵ the originary character of "difference" has been considered so self-evident by philosophical, social, and cultural theories that it needs no justification. Arguments for any primordial unity or oneness have been dismissed as Platonic fantasies and considered suspect, even dangerously coercive. Jean-François Lyotard states this in a particularly memorable way when he links what he calls "the transcendental illusion" with terror: "We have paid a high enough price for the nostalgia of the whole and the one. . . . Let us wage a war on totality; let us be witnesses to the unpresentable; let us activate the differences and save the honor of the name."⁶ The current

---

³ See Kasper's address to the Conference of the Society for Ecumenical Studies (May 17, 2003, St. Alban's Abbey, Hertfordshire, England), *"May They All Be One? But how? A Vision of Christian Unity for the Next Generation,"* http://sfes.faithweb.com/ 0305kasper.pdf.

⁴ Terry Eagleton, *The Idea of Culture*, Blackwell Manifestos (Malden, MA: Blackwell, 2000), 38.

⁵ See Martin Heidegger, "The Onto-Theo-Logical Constitution of Metaphysics," *Identity and Difference*, trans. Joan Stambaugh (New York: Harper and Row, 1969), 42–76, at 65; Jacques Derrida, "Differance" [*Différance*], in *Margins of Philosophy*, trans. Alan Bass (Chicago: University of Chicago Press, 1982), 3–27, at 11. See also Anthony J. Godzieba, "Prolegomena to a Catholic Theology of God Between Heidegger and Postmodernity," *The Heythrop Journal* 40 (1999): 319–39, esp. 321–22.

⁶ Jean-François Lyotard, *The Postmodern Condition: A Report on Knowledge*, trans. Geoff Bennington and Brian Massumi (Minneapolis: University of Minnesota Press, 1984), 81–82.

232 *Rewriting the Questions—Part 3*

cultural default in favor of difference renders any argument in favor of Christian unity, and any attempt to see it in a mutual relationship with difference, more difficult to make. It demands a more fundamental analysis than an ecumenical hermeneutics can give. And so the question remains: in Christianity, how can we have both unity and diversity, identity and difference together?

The New Testament Clue: Performance

Scripture provides resources for the first half of the solution that I want to give, and a performance hermeneutic provides the second half.

The New Testament supplies an important warrant by offering what one might consider an exquisite balance between unity and diversity. First, to use James Dunn's formulation, there is "a fairly clear and consistent unifying strand . . . [that] provided the *integrating centre* for the diverse expressions of Christianity,"[7] namely, Jesus himself and *"the affirmation of the identity of the man Jesus with the risen Lord*, the conviction that the heavenly reality known in kerygma and scripture, in community, worship and religious experience generally is one and the same Jesus of whom the Jesus-tradition speaks."[8] That affirmation was not read back into the Jesus-tradition from later insights but rather "was rooted in Jesus' own understanding of his relationship with God, with his disciples and with God's kingdom."[9] In other words, to use Edward Schillebeeckx's pithy formulation, "We must see him like this, because this is the way he is."[10] This christological unity is at the foundation of the unifying roles played by Easter faith and the experience of God's sending of the Spirit throughout all early Christian communities.[11]

But at the same time this unifying conviction was lived out in different situations and expressed in diverse formulations. Most obvi-

---

[7] James D. G. Dunn, *Unity and Diversity in the New Testament: An Inquiry into the Character of Earliest Christianity*, 3rd ed. (London: SCM, 2006), 403 (here and elsewhere, the emphases are Dunn's).

[8] Ibid., 245.

[9] Ibid., 403.

[10] Edward Schillebeeckx, *Interim Report on the Books "Jesus" and "Christ*,*"* trans. John Bowden (New York: Crossroad, 1981), 11.

[11] Dunn, *Unity and Diversity*, 437–42.

ously, there are four canonical gospels and many other gospels besides, each with a particular narrative frame and a distinctive Jesus-portrait. Paul, for his part, identifies God's Son, "descended from David according to the flesh" (Rom 1:3) and "handed over for our transgressions" (Rom 4:25), with the risen Lord who "was raised for our justification" (Rom 4:25). Mark's language is different: his gospel of the Son of God (Mark 1:1) also tells of the suffering Son of Man. Acts contains the very different exhortations to belief in Jesus by Peter in Jerusalem and Paul in the Areopagus (Acts 2:14-40; 17:22-31). The author of John's gospel "presents the earthly Jesus *already* in terms of his exalted glory."[12] And diversity extends far beyond language patterns into practices. As Dunn notes, "*There was no single normative form of Christianity in the first century*," but varied types, "each of which viewed others as too extreme in one respect or other—too conservatively Jewish or too influenced by antinomian or gnostic thought and practice, too enthusiastic or tending towards too much institutionalization."[13] The metaphor that James Robinson and Helmut Koester employed in the 1970s to explain the relationships among early Christian writings—"trajectories"—is helpful here, and can be combined with Walter Kasper's characterization of the Easter event as the "initial ignition" of Christianity, in order to describe its dynamic development in various directions of communities of believers (and not just the literary after-effects).[14] Certain trajectories had the power to shoot out from this origin and become dominant (e.g., Pauline ecclesial organization, Johannine high Christology), while others lost effectiveness for failing to express adequately the essence of Jesus' identity and soteriological significance (e.g., the communities behind Q or the Gospel of Thomas).

Now, none of this ongoing development would happen without *the active reception of Jesus' person, praxis, and message*. In Christianity, this active reception takes the form of embodied, historically situated, temporally extended *performance*; that performance is called "discipleship"—following Jesus, living a Jesus-like life. "Christian identity," William Spohn remarks, "comes from identifying with the person,

---

[12] Ibid., 245.
[13] Ibid., 407.
[14] James M. Robinson and Helmut Koester, *Trajectories through Early Christianity* (Philadelphia: Fortress Press, 1971); Walter Kasper, *Jesus the Christ*, new ed., trans. V. Green (London: T&T Clark, 2011), 112.

cause, and community of Jesus Christ, which are inseparable. Disciples are committed to the person of the master and those whom he is concerned about; his cause is the reconciliation and healing reality of the reign of God."[15] And so alongside Dunn's integrating christological center we must consider this other unifying element, the performative one that includes the possibilities of its own diversity.

The argument about performance that I want to lay out here is a relatively simple one. In making it, I follow two of Hans-Georg Gadamer's cardinal rules about hermeneutical understanding. First, the moment of *understanding* is the moment of *interpretation* is the moment of *application*.[16] Understanding and interpretation are ontological; they pertain to the actualization of the interpreter's temporally situated possibilities-for-being. The truth of any text, work of art, or musical work—and, for our purposes, the values of the kingdom of God preached and lived by Jesus—can only be grasped when applied to the interpreter's own lived experience and possibilities, when there is a fusion of the horizon of the historically situated catalyst with the horizon of the historically situated interpreter. A fusion of horizons does not erase the temporal distance between them, the "pastness" of the past; rather, the temporal distance remains and is productive. It reveals both difference and continuity, allowing the interpreter to see where the past's presence in the present has shaped to some degree the pre-judgments, interests, and questions of the interpreter.[17] The second rule is that any tradition is a "history of effects" (*Wirkungsgeschichte*) and that all understanding is a "consciousness effected by history."[18] To be part of a tradition means that one is, so to speak, standing in a stream with its origins far upstream. What constitutes the stream and flows past one's ankles—that is, what influences the interpreter's pursuit of understanding—is all the material that had originally en-

---

[15] William C. Spohn, *Go and Do Likewise: Jesus and Ethics* (New York: Continuum, 2000), 164.

[16] Hans-Georg Gadamer, *Truth and Method*, 2nd rev. ed., trans. Joel Weinsheimer and Donald G. Marshall (New York: Crossroad, 1989), 307–41, esp. 308.

[17] Ibid., 306: "The horizon of the present cannot be formed without the past. There is no more an isolated horizon of the present in itself than there are historical horizons which have to be acquired. *Rather, understanding is always the fusion of these horizons supposedly existing by themselves*" [emphasis original].

[18] Ibid., 341–79.

tered upstream in time. One can accept, reject, or vary that material, but one is *always already* formed and influenced by it. Thus a double hermeneutic ensues: not only is it necessary to interpret works against the background of their own historical horizon of expectations, but the interpreter has her/his own horizon of expectations against which she/he needs to be interpreted as well.[19]

Discipleship is the Christian applicative moment—embodied, tradition-situated, and temporally saturated. There is no understanding of how God's salvation is revealed to us in Christ without the applicative moment of living a Jesus-like life and imagining one's possibilities in light of the values of the kingdom of God. The New Testament expresses it in many ways: following Jesus, imitating Jesus, living in Christ, remaining in Jesus, being members of the body of Christ, following the example of Jesus, and so forth.[20] Let me focus on one of these, a paradigmatic case from the gospel of Mark, the author who thematizes discipleship to the utmost. Along with Jesus' journey to Jerusalem as the suffering messiah, the entire second half of the gospel foregrounds authentic discipleship, seeing it pointed squarely in the direction of the cross. The episode where the blind Bartimaeus is healed (Mark 10:46-52) leaves us in no doubt about this. Mark's redaction of this miracle story into a discipleship story acts as a corrective to the completely inadequate and perhaps even pernicious understanding of discipleship articulated by James and John in the previous pericope (Mark 10:35-45). Let's call them and the other members of the Twelve the "capital D" disciples, whom we would expect to know precisely what discipleship involves. James and John, however, equate discipleship with eschatological power and control. In the Bartimaeus pericope this definition is swept aside and the true nature of discipleship is again revealed. Mark's narrative quickly

---

[19] On the "double hermeneutic" and its inevitability in theology, see Francis Schüssler Fiorenza, *Foundational Theology: Jesus and the Church* (New York: Crossroad, 1984), 291–92. This can be extended *mutatis mutandis* to all understanding.

[20] For variants of expression, see Fernando F. Segovia, ed., *Discipleship in the New Testament* (Philadelphia: Fortress Press, 1985); Richard N. Longenecker, ed., *Patterns of Discipleship in the New Testament* (Grand Rapids, MI: Eerdmans, 1996), esp. 1–5; Joel B. Green et al., eds., *Dictionary of Jesus and the Gospels*, 2nd ed. (Downers Grove, IL: IVP Academic, 2013), s.v. "Disciples and Discipleship" (M. J. Wilkins), 202–12; Spohn, *Go and Do Likewise*, 164–65.

eliminates the "capital D" disciples as well as the vacillating crowd, leaving only Jesus and Bartimaeus. The question-answer ping-pong effect of their concluding dialogue (Mark 10:51-52) directly equates "faith" with "sight," with spiritual insight. It is with both physical sight and spiritual insight, then, that Bartimaeus, at the close of the episode, "followed him on the way" (*ēkolouthei autō en tē hodō* [Mark 10:52], the most important words in the pericope, placed at the very end for full rhetorical effect)—the way that leads to Jerusalem, to suffering, to the cross, and to resurrection. Authentic discipleship for Mark and his community, then, is embodied in Bartimaeus and in his faith that following in the steps of Jesus, who earlier defined his mission in terms of service rather than power (Mark 10:42-45), is the way to experience God's saving presence. The key in Mark is praxis, living a Jesus-like life, and the responsibility of the gospel's audience as faithful disciples is to spread the good news of salvation.[21] The diversity of forms used by the New Testament books to express particular ways of "following" share this fundamental insight. "Christ also suffered for you," says the First Letter of Peter, "leaving you an example that you should follow in his footsteps" (2:21). Or we can apply Rowan Williams's more contemporary idiom: "Christianity is a contact before it is a message. . . . If the risen Jesus is not an idea or an image but a living person, we meet him in the persons he has touched, the persons who, whatever their individual failings and fears, have been equipped to take responsibility for his tangible presence in the world."[22]

Discipleship shares with Dunn's integrating christological center the same dialectic of unity-and-diversity. In both instances we are confronted with an identity marker as well as the reality of multiple authentic ecclesial variations; the obvious historical variability and even improvisation do not leave identity behind but in fact are the only ways that identity can be experienced. What kind of an explanatory

---

[21] Mark's critique of the misunderstandings of the Twelve has been a staple of Markan scholarship since Theodore J. Weeden's *Mark: Traditions in Conflict* (Philadelphia: Fortress Press, 1971). For a convincing reading of Mark's rhetorical ability to invest his audiences with the responsibility of discipleship, see Paul Danove, "The Narrative Rhetoric of Mark's Ambiguous Characterization of the Disciples," *Journal for the Study of the New Testament* 70 (1998): 21–38.

[22] Rowan Williams, *Tokens of Trust: An Introduction to Christian Belief* (Louisville: Westminster John Knox, 2007), 92–93.

scheme or metaphor can we use to explain how this happens? How do we present this unifying truth of Christian ecclesial life that is not some pure essence or a Kantian *Ding an sich* but that can only be experienced in the midst of shifting historical incarnations? Already in the 1980s Elisabeth Schüssler Fiorenza argued for the advantages of treating the biblical witness as an historical *prototype* allowing variation rather than as an invariant *archetype* to be applied strictly and ahistorically in differing cultural settings. She recognized that one needs to account for the differing historical manifestations of Christian liberative praxis revealed by historical-critical and social-cultural studies of the Bible and its world.[23] But in my view, her insightful suggestion suffers from the same inadequacy that metaphors of "framework," "foundation," and even Dunn's "center" have: they are grounded in either a literary understanding or a visual or mechanical metaphor and thus are too static. They work against what the Tübingen philosopher Manfred Frank has called "the unforseeability of interpretation" that arises from the encounter between a guiding structural form and personal freedom. The result of this encounter is a particular "style" that is determined by neither form nor subjectivity alone and could never be coerced or rigidly codified in a system of rules or discourse.[24] If anything, the diversity of historical responses to the risen Lord demands an explanation that allows more flexibility, more flow, more temporally saturated elements. It must be one that counts difference not as a problem to be solved but as a necessary precondition for any understanding whatsoever of Jesus, his praxis, his preaching, and his death and resurrection.

Ut musica Christianitas: *A Performance Hermeneutic*

Here is my suggested explanation: Christianity is like music. There is a close analogy between the musical work and musical performance and a deeper understanding of the truth of Christian identity as it

---

[23] Elisabeth Schüssler Fiorenza, "Women-Church: The Hermeneutical Center of Feminist Biblical Interpretation," in *Bread Not Stone: The Challenge of Feminist Biblical Interpretation* (Boston: Beacon Press, 1984), 1–22, esp. 9–15.

[24] Manfred Frank, "Toward a Philosophy of Style," trans. Richard E. Palmer, *Common Knowledge* 1 (1992): 54–77, at 54–55, 76.

develops in history.[25] A *performance hermeneutic* is the most adequate way to discern the truth and the underlying logic of the Christian tradition, which is an ensemble of practices, beliefs, and reflections. Christianity is like music because (a) following its own incarnational logic and the New Testament's logic of discipleship, it needs to be performed/interpreted in space and time in order for its intended salvific truth to be fulfilled, and (b) each performance carries with it the history that has preceded it. The comparison works because the "intentional object" that is the musical work is already both a multi-layered *interpretation* of a previously sedimented tradition and an *improvisation* within a historically constituted genre, both of which require duration over time.[26] The intended truth of the musical work occurs in its authentic fulfillment only when realized in particular and therefore varied performances in space and time. Right here is the identity-difference dialectic. Any written score is an historically situated schematic identity (either more or less detailed) that needs to be filled in and concretized by uniquely varied moments of performance.[27] Experiencing the truth of the Christian tradition is a similar process: as a three-dimensional temporal truth it unites a past (that is always already interpretive) with future possibilities, all at the moment of their incipient realization in the always-different present. The key here is *temporality*. In its various guises and various construals of reality, the Christian tradition brings its past—i.e., its origins, the lived experiences of discipleship which effectively and affectively respond to those origins, and the effects of those effects—into a relationship with an ever-changing present by

---

[25] This section borrows some material from my article "*Ut Musica Christianitas*: Christian Tradition as a History of Performances," in *The Shaping of Tradition: Context and Normativity*, ed. Colby Dickinson, Lieven Boeve, and Terrence Merrigan (Leuven: Peeters, 2013), 91–99.

[26] For "improvisation" in this context, see Bruce Ellis Benson, *The Improvisation of Musical Dialogue: A Phenomenology of Music* (Cambridge: Cambridge University Press, 2003); Benson, "The Improvisation of Hermeneutics: Jazz Lessons for Interpreters," in *Hermeneutics at the Crossroads*, ed. Kevin J. Vanhoozer, James A. K. Smith, and Bruce Ellis Benson (Bloomington: Indiana University Press, 2006), 193–210. For the difference between the "intentional" and "real" existence of musical works, see Roman Ingarden, *Ontology of the Work of Art*, trans. Raymond Meyer and John T. Goldthwait (Athens: Ohio University Press, 1989), 27–46, 90–94.

[27] Performances are never identical, even when performers aim for rote repetition ("just like the recording"). They are varied by many factors, such as the acoustic of the space, the mood of the performers and the audience, the physical state of instruments and voices, etc.

means of temporally projected participative acts. With one's performative interpretation of the elements of that tradition—performance in the present—one discloses the past's future possibilities to be discerned, actualized, made effective, and savored.

How might we illustrate this thesis and the principle of variation that, as we have seen, is clearly built into the New Testament witness? Let me offer an example of Western art music where these principles of variation and dialectic are expressed in both text (the musical score) and in performances in real time guided by that text, Johann Sebastian Bach's *Goldberg Variations*, BWV 988 (Bach's title was *Clavier Übung . . . Aria mit verschiedenen Veränderungen* [Keyboard Exercise . . . Aria with Diverse Variations]).[28]

EXAMPLE 1: J. S. Bach, *Goldberg Variations*, BWV 988; title page of original print (Nuremberg: Balthasar Schmid, c. 1741/42).

[28] For the critical edition and facsimile pages, see Johann Sebastian Bach, *Neue Ausgabe sämtlicher Werke* [NBA], Serie V, Band 2: *Zweiter Teil der Klavierübung/Vierter Teil der Klavierübung* [Goldberg Variations]/ *Vierzehn Kanons*, ed. Walter Emery and Christoph Wolff, BA 5048-01 (Kassel: Bärenreiter, 1977). I rely on the following analyses: Ralph Kirkpatrick, preface to Johann Sebastian Bach, *The "Goldberg" Variations*, ed. Ralph Kirkpatrick

Most know that the piece consists of a keyboard "aria" in the guise of a tender sarabande, thirty variations of thirty-two bars each (16+16, with each half repeated), and then a repeat (*da capo*) of the aria at the end. But the movements that follow the aria are not thirty variations on the aria's melody but rather *thirty different melodies* built on the aria's fundamental bass line:

EXAMPLE 2: J. S. Bach, *Goldberg Variations*, BWV 988: Extracted bass line.

A bass line like this, beginning with a descending tetrachord, has a long history stretching back to the seventeenth century and even earlier. The bass line itself is melodious; its first eight notes, in fact, echo the first line of Luther's Christmas hymn tune "Vom Himmel hoch, da komm' ich her" (a melody with which Bach seems to have been preoccupied in his last years). He probes this 32-bar harmonic sequence for every possibility it offers and creates a veritable cornucopia, "thirty distinct essays exploring the language and genres of music as its composer understood them."[29] There is, for example, the boisterous

---

(New York: G. Schirmer, 1938), vii–xxviii; David Schulenberg, *The Keyboard Music of J. S. Bach*, 2nd ed. (New York: Routledge, 2006), 369–88; Peter Williams, *Bach: The Goldberg Variations*, Cambridge Music Handbooks (Cambridge: Cambridge University Press, 2001). For the facsimile title page, see the IMSLP/Petrucci Music Library, http://imslp.org/wiki/Special:ImagefromIndex/74598. Musical examples are taken from Johann Sebastian Bach, *Goldberg Variationen: Aria mit verschiedenen Veraenderungen, Clavicimbal mit 2 Manualen, BWV 988 & Verschiedene Canones über die ersteren acht Fundamental-Noten der Arie, BWV 1087, nach J. S. Bach's Exemplar des Erstdrucks*, ed. Martin Straeten (2010), http://imslp.org/wiki/Special:ImagefromIndex/240148 (reproduced in accordance with Creative Commons Attribution—ShareAlike 3.0 license).

[29] Williams, *Bach: The Goldberg Variations*, 35. The extracted bass line is from Schulenberg, *Keyboard Music of J. S. Bach*, 377.

two-part invention that opens the set (here and in all the examples, the first eight fundamental notes of the bass line are circled).[30]

EXAMPLE 3: J. S. Bach, *Goldberg Variations*, BWV 988: Variation 1, mm. 1–8.

There is a two-part canon built on the bass line, the first of nine canons (every third variation except the last):

---

[30] Reference recording: J. S. Bach, *Goldberg Variations, BWV 988; Toccatas, BWV 912–915*, Bob van Asperen, harpsichord (Virgin Veritas 50999 6 93198 2, 2 CDs). An equally fine recording, also steeped in the style of the period, is Pierre Hantaï's second recording of the work (Mirare 9945). Both players take most of the repeats. (Many listeners associate the *Goldbergs* with Glenn Gould's famous piano recordings of the work. I'm not a fan.)

EXAMPLE 4: J. S. Bach, *Goldberg Variations*, BWV 988: Variation 3 (Canon at the unison), mm. 1–6.

There is a fugue that is both rigorous and playful:

EXAMPLE 5: J. S. Bach, *Goldberg Variations*, BWV 988: Variation 10 (Fughetta), mm. 1–16.

Variation 16 at the midway point is a stunning French overture:

EXAMPLE 6: J. S. Bach, *Goldberg Variations*, BWV 988: Variation 16 (*Ouverture*), mm. 1–8.

There is a heartbreaking *lamento* in the minor key:

EXAMPLE 7: J. S. Bach, *Goldberg Variations*, BWV 988: Variation 25, mm. 1–8.

And the next-to-last variation is a virtuoso *tour de force*:

EXAMPLE 8: J. S. Bach, *Goldberg Variations*, BWV 988: Variation 29, mm. 1–16.

"... And Followed Him on the Way" 245

Thus, thirty *different* melodies built on the same foundational bass line. Bach was so intoxicated with its possibilities that, on a blank page of his personal copy of the print, he composed fourteen more canons on the first eight notes.[31] Even more remarkable is the fact that the bass line never appears in its hypothetical original form, but only as altered with passing notes, chromatic inflections, and embellishments. Any "pure" form of the bass, as shown above, has to be extracted from the thirty-one examples. It is in the nature of the fundamental bass and its implied harmonies to be always in the background, guiding the unfolding logic of the piece while allowing freedom in the creation of the upper melodies. But the bass line is also easily discernible, even

---

[31] Fourteen Canons, BWV 1087. Bach envisioned even more possibilities: in the bottom right corner, he wrote "Et c." He may have stopped because, according to Baroque numerology, "14" was a way of "signing" his name (B [2] + A [1] + C [3] + H [8] = 14). For the critical edition, NBA V/2, see above, n. 28. See also Christoph Wolff, "The Handexemplar of the Goldberg Variations," in *Bach: Essays on His Life and Music* (Cambridge, MA: Harvard University Press, 1991), 162–77.

viscerally felt, since "the harmonic rhythm is consistent throughout the work" and the fundamental notes of the bass are most often on the downbeats.[32]

The point here is not a lesson in music theory. Rather, I want to focus on the unity-diversity dialectic and temporality. If, as I have argued, musical performance in general is the most adequate metaphor for explaining the lived application of Christian truth, the *Goldberg Variations* are an excellent analogue to our specific topic, the unity and diversity of Christianity, its christological claims, and its exhortations to discipleship. This is so because like any musical work, the performance of the score plays out *in time*; it needs actualization in time to reveal its identity and meaning.[33] And this is in addition to the fact that the composition of the score articulates inspiration as it has unfolded over time. In the composition of the *Goldbergs*, the harmonic sequencing that unfolds over time determines the fundamental flow of the composition of the variation but does not predict what the completed form of the variation will turn out to be. Bach's teeming creative imagination—his ability to take the germ of a musical idea and explore it from every angle, exhausting its possibilities while at the same time getting it to transcend its original limitations—is always guided by the underlying harmonic framework but is not scripted by it. Almost anything goes, *as long as it adheres to the rule of the harmonic sequencing of the bass line.* The almost wild diversity of genres attests to this. The canon, the overture, the *lamento*, and the virtuoso showpiece have nothing in common but the harmonic logic of the bass line that structures them and takes time to unfold through a series of dissonances and consonances, tensions and releases, to a satisfying close or cadence. The resulting work is an exemplar of the "unforseeability of interpretation."

The New Testament's christological claim and its call to discipleship have the same function as the *Goldbergs'* bass line: they provide the unifying background shaping impetus to the varied lived experi-

---

[32] Schulenberg, *Keyboard Music of J. S. Bach*, 378.

[33] Even non-tonal pieces follow this prescription. In John Cage's famous 4'33", the pianist, with minimum gestures, sits silently at the instrument for precisely that length of time and thereby "reveals" the ambient sounds around us as music. The subtly shifting (and mesmerizing) percussive and melodic effects of Steve Reich's four-movement *Drumming* need around an hour and a half to unfold.

ences of Christian life throughout the centuries. The truth of Christian life can be expressed with three elements: doxology, soteriology, and liberative praxis. Timothy Radcliffe concisely summarizes the first by identifying what he calls "the point of Christianity": "If Christianity is true, then it does not have a point other than to point to God who is the point of everything."[34] Walter Kasper unites doxology's praise of the triune God with Christianity's salvific intent: "According to the Lord's farewell prayer true life consists precisely in knowing and glorifying God. For its own sake therefore soteriology must pass over into doxology. For amid all the vicissitudes and instability of history man's salvation consists in having communion with the God who through all eternity *is* love."[35] This continual incarnational impetus is never isolatable "as is" but only available in particular embodiments. We experience the love of God through the incarnated grace of Christ offered to us in living a Jesus-like life in light of the paschal mystery. That grace perdures in us and in the world through the power of the Spirit who offers us fellowship, a participation in that divine love (2 Cor 13:13). Discipleship-as-application is thus a necessity, as Jesus tells the lawyer at the close of the Good Samaritan pericope: "go and do likewise" (Luke 10:37). The sole reason for the Christian tradition is to incarnate this participation, and it does so by a series of provocations and receptions: a history of effects. The Christian life is therefore best viewed as the embodied performance of discipleship over time, built on the fundamental logic of the incarnation and its sacramentalizing of particularity, and applied in diverse historical and cultural contexts and as an ensemble of practices, beliefs, and reflections. The tradition never loses sight of its origins in the practices of Jesus of Nazareth and his followers and indeed presents them through the means of effective performative receptions that occur further "downstream." This means that Christianity is always more than "what would Jesus do?" since every present receptive performance responds to all of its pasts, whether overtly or covertly. At the same time, the performers of the tradition also can never ignore the current context in which

---

[34] Timothy Radcliffe, *What Is the Point of Being a Christian?* (London; New York: Burns and Oates, 2005), 1.

[35] Walter Kasper, *The God of Jesus Christ*, trans. Matthew J. O'Connell, new ed., (London; New York: Continuum, 2012), 315.

discipleship is being performed and where the truth of the salvific tradition is being applied.

What is crucial here is the aspect of *temporality*. That is why music and the interpretation of the musical work present the most adequate analogy for understanding the Christian tradition, because only musical performance conveys the combination of unity, variety, and duration that helps explain the authentic diversity of Christian praxis and its ecclesial expressions. The musical work is temporally saturated in two ways: always historically situated, coming out of a particular epoch and interacting with that epoch's genres, but also inherently an *arrangement of time:* it takes time to perform its unique configuration and sequencing of tonal and rhythmic events.[36] We could use words like "concretized," "articulated," "embodied," and "incarnated" to express the historical particularity of Christian lives and to make the necessary connection between those lives and divine revelation's incarnated particularity that is central to Christian belief.[37] But those valid descriptions bypass any acknowledgment that embodied discipleship is constituted and developed individually and communally only over real time. The *ecclēsia* is simultaneously its past, the appropriation of this past through performances in the present, and its eschatological liberative praxis. The ensemble of temporally saturated practices and reflections that constitute the tradition as a history of effects guided by the Spirit unfolds and accumulates receptions in time and over time. The synthesis we make of these practices and reflections—seeing them as an "ensemble"—can be experienced only from particular points in the temporal horizon. Of necessity it is a limited synthesis, much like our experience of any piece of music: we grasp its identity without being able to synthesize all of its performances. So by its very nature the church's incarnational logic and its exhortation to follow Jesus "on the way" are expressed in the dialectic of unity and diversity: *ut unum sint, ut plures sint*. Difference and its counterpart temporality are not problems to be solved and dismissed but rather the necessary

---

[36] This holds true for any musical work, from unmeasured chant to "Happy Birthday" to Beethoven's Ninth Symphony to any pop or rock song played on radio in heavy rotation.

[37] "Incarnated particularity" is fundamental to all Christian faith claims. See Anthony J. Godzieba, Lieven Boeve, and Michele Saracino, "Resurrection—Interruption—Transformation: Incarnation as Hermeneutical Strategy," *Theological Studies* 67 (2006): 777–815.

ways we have access to the plenteous grace of the life of Christ and the Paschal Mystery that confirms our share in it.

The Eclipse of Time and Narrative

Our analysis, though, has omitted one thing: the disturbing eclipse of time and narrative in contemporary culture. The temporal duration necessary for discipleship's implications to unfold and be discerned is becoming literally inconceivable. Christian life is already positioned by a cultural sense and by economic and technological factors that threaten to overwhelm our narrative imaginations.

Recent cultural studies have shown that the accelerated pace of contemporary life leads paradoxically to its "de-temporalization." We complain about "having no time" to get things done, despite the promise of digital technologies to help us control the constant onslaught of fragmentary waves of information. But, as media theorist Douglas Rushkoff notes, it is a false hope: "For not only have our devices outpaced us, they don't even reflect a here and now that may constitute any legitimate sort of present tense. They are reports from the periphery, of things that happened moments ago."[38] Postmodern culture, he says, is characterized by "narrative collapse," due to the loss of optimism about the future and brought on by overwhelming events like 9/11 and the implosion of the economy. That collapse is mirrored in the "presentist" popular culture that shapes much of our everyday experience. For example, goal-directed narrative arcs once used by television dramas and sitcoms have been replaced by shows "characterized by frozenness in time, as well as by the utter lack of traditional narrative goals."[39] Without a *telos*, one's search for meaning looks to drama generated by disconnected spectacles of attention-grabbing behavior, such as reality TV's stock-in-trade of humiliation and personal tragedy.[40] The loss of narrative is also mirrored in contemporary

---

[38] Douglas Rushkoff, *Present Shock: When Everything Happens Now* (New York: Penguin, 2013), 74.

[39] Ibid., 31.

[40] Ibid., 37: "Without the traditional narrative arc at their disposal, producers of reality TV must generate pathos directly, in the moment. . . . What images and ideas can stop the channel surfer in his tracks?"

politics, with its hair-on-fire chaotic decision making and inability to reach or even construct long-term goals.[41]

The social theorist Hartmut Rosa has coined a phrase for the cause of such "now-ism": social acceleration. Such acceleration, he says, has three elements: technical acceleration ("the intentional . . . acceleration of goal-directed processes"), acceleration of social change (where past experiences no longer meet present expectations, causing the present as a time-span of stability to "contract"), and acceleration of the pace of life (where we experience the contraction of the present as "the scarcity of time resources" and the anxious compulsion to "keep up").[42] The way we conceive of both individual and social life thereby changes: "Life is no longer planned along a line that stretches from the past into the future" but rather is governed by short-term decisions in response to an overwhelming number of "unforeseeable contingencies" and the needs and desires of the moment. The result, Rosa argues, is an "incapacity to engage in long-term commitments," which in turn leads to "a paradoxical backlash in which the experience of frantic change and 'temporalized time' give way to the perception of 'frozen time' without (a meaningful) past and future and consequently of depressing inertia."[43] Rosa argues that this "de-temporalization of time" affects not only individual identities; social identities and political decisions are also pervaded by directionless inertia masquerading as frantic change, resulting in the "disappearance of politics."[44] We are left with an apparent unsolvable dilemma: social acceleration reveals a range of human possibilities that is wider than ever, but our abilities

---

[41] Ibid., 47: "Policy, as such, is no longer measured against a larger plan or narrative; it is simply a response to changing circumstances on the ground, or on the tube. . . . What used to be called statecraft devolves into a constant struggle with crisis management. Leaders cannot get on top of issues, much less ahead of them, as they instead seek merely to respond to the emerging chaos in a way that makes them look authoritative."

[42] Hartmut Rosa, *Social Acceleration: A New Theory of Modernity*, trans. Jonathan Trejo-Mathys (New York: Columbia University Press, 2013), 71–80, at 71 (goal-directed), 76 (contraction of the present), 79 (scarcity); Rosa, "Social Acceleration: Ethical and Political Consequences of a Desynchronized High-Speed Society," *Constellations* 10, no. 1 (2003): 3–33, at 6–10.

[43] Rosa, "Social Acceleration," 19–20; see also 25: "The inability to control social change has brought an overwhelming sense of directionless change in an 'iron cage' that itself has become fundamentally inert."

[44] Ibid., 20–22.

to survey these possibilities and decide among them remain as truncated as before. We are overwhelmed and can't keep up. The result is ominous: the pace of everything around us ("increasingly contingent and revisable") accelerates, while our own "loss of direction, priorities, and narratable 'progress'" causes us to decelerate into inertia.[45]

This is the contemporary situation in which Christian discipleship is embedded, at least where consumer capitalism and its technologies prevail. Various forms of contemporary Catholic dogmatism—or, better put, attempts to reduce Catholic identity to a single identity-marker or a "brand"—are capitulations to this inertia, even while claiming to resist the social changes that provoke it. In other words, attempts to "trademark" Catholicism as "settled doctrine" or an ethereal metaphysical realm, or to reduce it to strictly literal readings of Vatican II texts or the *Catechism of the Catholic Church*, or to conflate it with Catholic social thought or inflexible liturgical law are all anxiety-prone reactions to the accelerated speed of social change and overwhelming difference. They are also ways of minimizing the lived performance of discipleship and the basic need for these applicative moments to play out over time in order to clarify their meaning. By understanding unity unilaterally, dogmatist reactions function similarly to Neoscholasticism in its attempt to counteract modernity. As Francis Schüssler Fiorenza has demonstrated, Neoscholasticism relied on modern rationalist means of certainty and thus implicated itself in the very modernity which it tried to condemn.[46] Dogmatist construals of Catholic identity are similarly implicated in postmodern inertia when they conflate a temporally contingent synthesis with the "essence" of Catholicism and go on to claim that synthesis as perennial or absolute. In doing so, the temporally unfolding "harmonic logic" of doxology, soteriology, liberative praxis, and discipleship—the identity-difference dialectic of the New Testament and the ongoing Christian tradition—is betrayed.

The Play of Discipleship

If there is to be any critique of contemporary culture by Catholic theology, the issue is not liberal vs. conservative, pre–Vatican II vs. post–Vatican II, traditionalist vs. progressive. The real point is to critique the

---

[45] Ibid., 27. See also Rosa, *Social Acceleration*, 80–93.
[46] F. Schüssler Fiorenza, *Foundational Theology*, 263.

eclipse of time and narrative that affects our experience of discipleship and the temptation to de-temporalize Christian faith in reaction to what the theologian David Ford has called the "multiple overwhelmings" of the present.[47] If Christianity is indeed like music, then here we need to recall the quasi-temporal structure of the musical work as an intentional object: it contains elements that succeed each other in a determined order and are qualitatively modified by some or all of the preceding and following elements. The Christian tradition as a *Wirkungsgeschichte*, a history of diverse effects and receptions, functions in a similar way. The expression of the fundamental truths of the Christian life as "ecclesial benchmarks" that memorialize the insights the church has gained over a period of time (the creeds, for example) is a valid and necessary exercise deeply embedded in our Christian history. But to express the fundamental truths of Christianity simply as a set of infinitely repeatable identity markers or propositions is an attempt to take an immovable stand within the temporal flow of applications and to articulate a complete synthesis of temporally situated practices and reflections. The gospel injunction to "go and do likewise" always renders such stasis inadequate.

A performance hermeneutic is the most adequate way to explain the variegated play of discipleship that grounds the authentic application of the values of the kingdom of God. For example, John Noonan's *A Church That Can and Cannot Change* can be read as an itinerary of performative moral applications of insights gained from discipleship.[48] The 1999 *Joint Declaration on the Doctrine of Justification* agreed upon by both Catholics and Lutherans is an instance where dissonant theological anthropologies (i.e., diverse performances of the meaning of the paschal mystery) could be brought into harmony after almost six centuries of divergent applications of the notions of faith and grace.[49]

---

[47] David Ford, *Theology: A Very Short Introduction* (Oxford/New York: Oxford University Press, 1999), 7–11.

[48] John T. Noonan, Jr., *A Church That Can and Cannot Change: The Development of Catholic Moral Teaching* (Notre Dame, IN: University of Notre Dame Press, 2005). In speaking of John Henry Newman as the "inventor" of the idea of the development of Christian doctrine, Noonan says, "An Anglican arguing his way into the Catholic Church, Newman saw that the anomalies and novelties of his new spiritual home were the marks of vigor, of maturity, of being alive" (3).

[49] *Joint Declaration on the Doctrine of Justification by the Lutheran World Federation and the Catholic Church* (October 31, 1999), http://www.vatican.va/roman_curia

"... And Followed Him on the Way" 253

And the ongoing reactions to Cardinal Walter Kasper's suggestion at the 2014 Extraordinary Consistory on the Family regarding the readmission of divorced and remarried Catholics to the Eucharist, along with responses to Pope Francis' Apostolic Exhortation *Amoris Laetitia*, have revealed severely different understandings of Jesus' teaching on marriage and the history of exceptions to Jesus' prohibition of divorce, including differences between Western and Eastern Church practices.[50] These divergent applications all claim to be rooted in Jesus' teaching. The continuing discernment of the link between broken married relationships and the reception of the Eucharist, a discernment that needs to delve deeply into Jesus' overall practice and its continued reception among ecclesial communities, will need time to come to fruition.

To explain why and how difference always shadows unity, as both the New Testament and the Decree on Ecumenism acknowledge, a *performance hermeneutic* is needed, a way of articulating the active imitation of Christ and all of its receptions. We thereby can recognize how God's saving grace is revealed in manifold variations over time, and why the central Christian performances of the truths of the tradition which disclose God's rich mercy and the ongoing life of the Spirit—liturgical ritual, sacraments as experiences of the "excess of grace," contemplation leading to action, moral choices leading to actualized participation in divine life—are the fundamental starting points for thinking theologically about the richness, diversity, and temporally saturated character of the Christian tradition and its relation to the world.[51] Discerning the

---

/pontifical_councils/ chrstuni/documents/rc_pc_chrstuni_doc_ 31101999_cath-luth-joint-declaration_en.html.

[50] Cardinal Kasper's address is published as *The Gospel of the Family*, trans. William Madges (New York: Paulist Press, 2014). For a sample of the harsh criticism leveled at Kasper's suggestions, see Sandro Magister, "On Communion for the Remarried, a Letter from Bangladesh," http://chiesa.espresso.repubblica.it/articolo/1350792?eng=y; "For the Record: Full Translation of Cardinal Caffarra's Interview—On the Indissolubility of Marriage, 'Compromise is unworthy of the Lord,'" http://rorate-caeli.blogspot.com/2014/03/for-record-full-translation-of-cardinal.html. For the English translation of Pope Francis's Post-Synodal Apostolic Exhortation *Amoris Laetitia* (March 19, 2016), see https://w2.vatican.va/content/francesco/en/apost_exhortations/documents/papa-francesco_esortazione-ap_20160319_amoris-laetitia.html.

[51] See Walter Kasper, *Mercy: The Essence of the Gospel and the Key to Christian Life*, trans. William Madges (New York: Paulist Press, 2014), 131: "The message of divine mercy is not a theory that is alien to praxis and world realities, nor does it stop at the level

salvific truth of Christian life occurs not merely from the force of rational argument but also from the lived experiences of Christians attempting to follow Jesus, and the unscripted harmonies of grace underpinning those experiences. This is why Christian *performance,* the *play* of discipleship, must be at the heart of any discussion of ecclesial life and the effects of the church in the world. We must be the journeying Bartimaeus, and we cannot leave the active grace of God in Christ to be swept up in any sort of anxious and reactive inertia. In our common attempts to live the values of the kingdom of God, temporality and difference are positive values: they give us access to the unfolding unifying harmonic rhythm of the paschal mystery and the gift of the Spirit that together guide our attempts to live a Jesus-like life. The rest is noise.[52]

---

of sentimental expressions of pity. Jesus teaches us to be merciful like God (Luke 6:36). . . . This motif of *imitatio Dei,* the imitation of God and his actions in Jesus Christ, is foundational for the Bible. Therefore, the message of divine mercy has consequences for the life of every Christian, for the pastoral praxis of the church, and for the contributions that Christians should render to the humane, just, and merciful structuring of civil society."

[52] This chapter was originally presented as a keynote address at the Catholic Theological Society of America 2014 annual convention and published in the *CTSA Proceedings* 69 (2014): 1–22 (http://ejournals.bc.edu/ojs/index.php/ctsa/article/view/5501/4983). It has been revised for this publication.

CHAPTER 12

Lamenting at the Limits of Dialogue in Ecclesiology and Hermeneutics

Bradford E. Hinze

Expressions of lamentations can call into question the promise of dialogue as it has been championed in ecclesiology and philosophical hermeneutics. This paper argues that such grief incites and validates the generation of critical theories that provide both diagnostic resources for dissecting the deficiencies and pathologies of dialogue and also motivates prophetic forms of discourse and action by wrestling with the pain, anger, conflict, and protest associated with laments. In order to advance this thesis I will introduce the shift to a dialogical ecclesiology in the twentieth-century Catholic Church and review selected examples of the attention given to dialogue in hermeneutic theory. The paper will culminate in an exploration of how biblical lamentations provide theological resources for exploring the limitations of the use of dialogue in the church and in hermeneutics and provide incentives for strategic prophetic responses.

To begin let us recall that "dialogue" is a term that is used in a variety of ways.[1] Most often it is identified with the back-and-forth movement between individuals that are acting both as speakers and as listeners. In such cases there is an exchange of messages, sometimes conveying information or directives such as in educational settings, in

---

[1] For further exploration of various meanings of the term dialogue, see Bradford E. Hinze, *Practices of Dialogue in the Roman Catholic Church: Aims and Obstacles, Lessons and Laments* (New York: Continuum, 2006), 8–13, 252–67.

commerce, and in matters of governance. In other instances dialogue provides the conditions for reaching common understandings, judgments, decisions, and actions through deliberative processes. In yet other cases it can provide the medium for bonds of intimacy.

Usually dialogue implies communication, often called a conversation, between two people. But the same dynamics can take place among a group of people, which would need to be small enough for a variety of participants to be speakers as well as listeners in the exchange. Group dialogue is the basic medium of committees, councils, and synods seeking to reach some level of an agreement about matters of policy and goal setting. Dialogue can be used by analogy to describe a public assembly when individuals address a group often who are gathering information in order to make a judgment or decision, such as a legislative body or a research task force, in which case officials can raise questions to the speakers to which the speakers will offer their response.

Dialogue has also come to be used by analogy to describe the relationship between a text and a reader. In such cases the text communicates some sort of message and the reader strives to enter into a dynamic exchange with the text through an implied logic of posing questions that the reader seeks to find answered in the text. When reading narrative forms, a reader can become drawn into a literary dialogue or conversation with a character or between various characters that is conjured in the imagination.

Since at least the tradition of Plato, it has been postulated that people enter into dialogue with the self. This is how the process of thinking and conscience formation has been described. More recently there has been a critique of a unitary view of consciousness and the corresponding stable sense of self-identity associated with many classical and modern theories of the self. As a result psychologists have developed theories positing that people experience themselves composed of (or fragmented by) a plurality of self-identities that are vocal within the self. A person may identify with one of these interior voices (identity postures) at different times or must adjudicate and choose between them. When self-consciousness is considered in this way, the self must negotiate with and adjudicate between this interior set of characters, voices, personas in daily life.

These are some of the major ways dialogue has been understood over the last century that have proven influential for theologians, philosophers, and many others.

Beyond Paternalism and Polemics: Vatican II's Dialogical Ecclesiology

The category of dialogue became very influential in twentieth-century ecclesiology, in significant ways among Roman Catholics. The Second Vatican Council (1962–65) marked a transition for the Catholic Church from a paternalistic approach to communication among members, and from a polemical approach to communication with those outside the church (other Christians, members of other religions, and adherents of other worldviews)—thus, to a dialogical approach both internally and externally. Before the Council, a one-way, monological approach to communication prevailed. Internally, information and directives flowed from centralized and higher levels of authority to those with less or no authority: from Rome to local churches, from bishops to clergy, from clergy to laity. The hierarchy of the church, associated above all with the pope and the bishops, was envisioned as the teaching church, the trusted fathers charged to instruct the children of God, sons and daughters, the lay faithful, understood as the learning church. These fathers were conceived as teachers, leaders, and lawgivers; the children were those who listened and obeyed.

The Council represented a genuine breakthrough to a dialogical ecclesiology, one that promoted collaboration, co-responsibility, and collegiality among all the baptized. This dialogical vision of the church was implemented often slowly and sporadically during the first two decades after the Council, and sometimes not effectively. The fact remains, however, that since the Council great attention has been given to the development of conciliar and synodal models of collective discernment and decision making at every structural level of the church. Vatican II heralded this transformation by the use of the words *dialogus* and *colloquium* in conciliar documents, which led to the development of both structures of participation within the church, and dialogical relationships with other Christians, other religions, and other worldviews.[2]

The development of a dialogical approach to the structure and mission of the church, like the evolution of a classic architectural

---

[2] See Ann Michele Nola, *A Privileged Moment: Dialogue in the Language of the Second Vatican Council 1962–1965* (Bern: Peter Lang, 2006); Bradford E. Hinze "The Reception of Vatican II in Participatory Structures of the Church: Facts and Friction," *Proceedings of the Canon Law Society of America Annual Convention* 70 (2009): 28–52.

form, was advanced on three levels, like three overlapping sheets of an architect's plan. On the first level, the basic communication materials changed: the Council challenged the older approach to discourse in the church that had flourished in response to the Protestant Reformation in the sixteenth and seventeenth centuries, and in response to the developments in the areas of modern science and liberal ideology in the eighteenth and nineteenth centuries. These older styles of ecclesial communication reached their zenith during the second half of the nineteenth century and the first half of the twentieth.[3] To support the sacramental and institutional nature of Catholicism, the hierarchy of the church used a precise propositional and juridical approach to church teachings and policies. Vatican II shifted to a fundamentally dialogical approach to language that was persuasive, technically associated with epideictic rhetoric that used pictorial language, metaphors, and examples to move and convince. Instead of relying on a descending clerical model of authority to provide its credibility, the Council promoted consultation, collaboration, equality, and participation to build bonds of affection, conviction, and legitimacy from within the community. At a second level, the Council reimagined the church's doctrinal foundation. A rhetorically engaging dialogical approach to discourse was utilized in the four main dogmatic constitutions: on liturgy, on revelation, on the church, and on the church in the modern world. These documents provide the four doctrinal pillars for the reformed church structure. At a third level, in its decrees and declarations, the Council set forth specific recommendations for a range of dialogical practices reconceiving the church's processes and purposes: practices of collegiality, synodality, conciliarity, and participatory structures pertaining to the offices of bishops and priests, to religious life, laity, missionary activity, ecumenical and interreligious relations, education, mass media, and civil society.

---

[3] See John W. O'Malley, *What Happened at Vatican II* (Cambridge, MA: Belknap Press of Harvard University Press, 2008), 43–52, 305–13.

A Dialogical Church: A Phenomenological Sketch

An alternate way of exploring a dialogical ecclesiology is to delineate a rudimentary phenomenology of dialogue in the church.[4] The phenomenon of the church's dialogical character can be approached from three different vantage points. These three different perspectives reveal three spheres within the one dialogical reality of the church. Dialogue takes place in all of these spheres, but certain dimensions of dialogue receive special attention depending on one's sphere of engagement or angle of vision.

The first sphere consists of a person's dialogical relationship with God that takes place within, and by means of, a community of believers through participation in Christian traditions and practices. People are invited into this dialogue of faith in numerous ways: through baptism and the Eucharist; through the celebration of feasts and seasons during the liturgical year (Advent, Christmas, Lent, Easter, Ascension, Pentecost); by reading Scripture; through the community's profession of creedal faith; by means of personal and communal practices of prayer and meditation; and through the give-and-take associated with catechesis. The process of handing on the church's living tradition of faith takes place through this variety of dialogical practices.

By these means—ritual behavior, reading, meditation, and catechesis—a person has the opportunity to listen attentively, receive, and respond to the voice of God. This requires cultivating a dialogical imagination by participating in varied religious practices of communication. One is invited, for instance, to participate in the dialogue that takes place between the characters in a biblical story or between liturgical ministers and parishioners in a sacrament. These practices provide a venue that initiates a kind of dialogue between God and believers, where believers address God and they seek to hear God's voice in the Scriptures and sacraments as well as in the voices of others in the church and in the world. Bishops and clergy by their offices, lay leaders by their gifts and appointment, theologians by their calling, charism, and training, and all the faithful by their baptism are charged with fostering and protecting this dialogue of faith, each in

---

[4] For further details, see Bradford E. Hinze, *Prophetic Obedience: Ecclesiology for a Dialogical Church* (Maryknoll, NY: Orbis Books, 2016), 92–98.

one's own way. They are to ensure that the voices of the apostles and other venerated witnesses are remembered so that they may be heard again as a potentially life-giving echo, so that the dynamism and further development of the dialogue of faith may continue unhindered. They are also to pay special heed to the prayers of the faithful, whose aspirations and laments help constitute the living tradition of the pilgrim people of God.

In a second sphere of communication within the church, conversation occurs among members of faith communities. These conversations take place in social settings, whether around informal prayer, meals, or public celebrations, but also in various forms of ministry, especially religious education, works of mercy (with the sick, the poor, the homeless, or the imprisoned), and in the kinds of work for justice and social transformation fostered by community organizing in surrounding neighborhoods and through civic engagement. In this sphere deliberation about the mission and activities of the parish and diocese take place in councils, synods, and other forums. These particular conversations should ideally be places where open and honest dialogue occurs: where people learn to discern and deliberate about pastoral practices and priorities, the needs of the community and the neighborhood, and also honestly evaluate the activities of the parish or diocese and hold accountable people who exercise leadership roles in the community. In these settings people get to know each other and share their faith as it pertains to everyday life, their aspirations and hopes, frustrations and griefs. This is where the community and community leaders get to know each other's concerns. Fostering these connections should contribute to better mutual understanding and more focused decision making about the church's activities and mission outlook. Bishops cultivate such patterns of communication with the members of the local church by means of presbyteral councils, diocesan pastoral councils, diocesan synods, and other forums; among bishops at episcopal conferences, and with the bishop of Rome at synods of bishops. This is the sphere, especially in synodal and conciliar forums, where honest dialogue should take place between various sectors of the people of God, and individuals should be able to raise questions and concerns about pastoral priorities, the signs of the times, and official teachings.

Whereas the first sphere focuses on taking part in the active dialogue of faith in and through traditions of ritualized practices, the second sphere highlights the exchange among participants in the dialogue of faith in everyday existence, wherein participants converse about how traditions and practices move and console, but also where beliefs and practices may elicit pain, doubt, and consternation. This living dialogue of faith among the faithful was a crucial ingredient in the genesis and the early evolution of traditions of belief and practices, beginning with biblical and ancient Christian documents and rituals, and has always been a part of the ongoing exercise of proclaiming the gospel and of evaluating and developing official teaching in the church. Thus, while the first sphere emphasizes the authority of traditions and official mediators and teachers, the second accentuates the contribution and authority of all the faithful in the dialogue of faith.

The third sphere sheds light on marginalized voices, always an ingredient in the two previous spheres, but now as a constitutive domain in the phenomenon of dialogue within the church. In this sphere two questions are posed. First, whose voices have been a part of the dialogue of the church but have been forgotten, excluded, muted, silenced, or repressed either in the first sphere of dialogue or in the second? Second, whose voices at the borders of Christianity have been distorted or prevented from having a creative and constructive role in the dialogue that constitutes Christianity? In every generation, there are dissonant voices, critical voices, voices viewed as strange that are a legitimate part of the ecclesial dialogue but that have been ignored or drowned out both in traditions and practices (first sphere), and in the living practices of discernment (second sphere) in informal settings and official meetings in parishes, in diocesan settings, and larger ecclesial participatory structures. We are more mindful today than in previous generations of how gender, race, sexual identity, and economic and social status have affected and still influence not only the process of listening and receiving traditions and practices but also the ability of some to speak forth and testify from their own local context and experiences of the faith. The voices of members of marginalized and minority traditions can become muted, sometimes inaudible; and sometimes speakers and groups of speakers can be treated poorly, persecuted, and oppressed.

This struggle and failure to enter into dialogue also occurs at the borders of the church, in Christians' interaction with faiths and worldviews of other communities, be they Jews, Hindus, Buddhists, Muslims, animists, atheists, the heterodox, or the hyperorthodox. Dialogue within the church and at the borders of the church with other persons, or with groups that challenge and disorient, can be difficult, tentative, painful, seemingly impossible, and therefore avoided or postponed.

Dialogical Dimensions in Philosophical Hermeneutics

Theories of dialogue and communication became very influential among various Continental philosophers during the twentieth century, and in a special way among theologians and ecclesiologists. Dialogue is a prominent category in the philosophy and religious writings of Martin Buber and other proponents of philosophical personalism. In Buber's analysis of the subject-object relationship identified in terms of an "I" and an "it," in contrast to a subject-subject encounter, an "I" and a "thou," he identified dialogue in-breaking through a person's view of another person as an object, as a catalyst to forming a relationship based on reciprocity and possibly equality, which provides the basis for mutual recognition, individuation, and prayer.[5] Buber influenced many theologians, including key figures involved in the deliberations at Vatican II.

As important as Buber's contribution remains, Emmanuel Levinas throughout his career criticized the prominence given to dialogue in Buber's work as a way to differentiate his own summons to attend to the face of the other and to heed the cry of the other that makes an ethical and religious demand on individuals and communities.[6]

---

[5] Martin Buber, *I and Thou*, trans. Walter Kaufmann (New York: Touchstone Books, 1970), 148, 133; Martin Buber, "Dialogue," and "Afterword: The History of the Dialogical Principle," in *Between Man and Man*, trans. Ronald Gregor Smith (New York: Macmillan Co., 1965), 1–39, 209–24.

[6] In contrast to Buber, for Levinas there is no reciprocity, equality, and intimacy in dialogue; instead we confront the face of the other as in distress, as stranger, in exteriority, that is as one above, who makes an ethical claim on the self. According to Levinas, Buber also threatens God's transcendence through a dialogical view of prayer. See Levinas, *Totality and Infinity*, trans. Alphonso Lingis (Pittsburgh, PA: Duquesne University Press, 1969), 68–70, 154–56; Levinas, "Martin Buber and the Theory of Knowledge" and "Dialogue with Martin Buber," in *Proper Names*, trans. Michael B.

Levinas finds in a classic lamentation a counterpoint and corrective to dialogue: "to give one's cheek to the smiter, and be filled with insults" (Lam 3:30).[7] In prophecy he finds that "the Infinite escapes the objectification of thematization and of dialogue and signifies as *illeity*, in the third person. This 'thirdness' . . . interrupts the face to face of a welcome of the other man, interrupts the proximity or approach of the neighbor, it is the third man with which justice begins."[8] For Levinas, Buber's I-thou cannot avoid the moral and religious duty of facing the irrepressible third that escapes reciprocity. This third gives expression to the marginalized other who is identified in the third sphere of dialogue in the church.

Dialogue has likewise been recognized as a basic feature of philosophical hermeneutics associated with author-centered, text-centered, and reader-centered approaches. Let me introduce these complex fields of inquiry with a few remarks on the contributions of Friedrich Schleiermacher, Hans-Georg Gadamer, and Hans Robert Jauss.

Early in his career, the German Reformed theologian Schleiermacher developed skills as a translator and interpreter of the Platonic dialogues, which instilled in him a dedication to an open-ended dialogical approach to science, in contrast to a more deductive model. His early theological writings, evidenced in *On Religion: Speeches to the Cultured Despisers* (1799) and *Christmas Dialogue* (1806), employed a dialogical rhetorical style.[9] In his lectures on dialectics and on hermeneutics he began to develop a dialogical approach to the science of dialectics and an aesthetic theory of interpretation.[10] Throughout his

---

Smith (Stanford, CA: Stanford University Press, 1996), 32–35, 36–39; Levinas, "Apropos of Buber: Some Notes," in *Outside the Subject*, trans. Michael B. Smith (Stanford, CA: Stanford University Press, 1994), 40–48; Levinas, "Dialogue: Self-Consciousness and Proximity of the Neighbor," in *Of God Who Comes to Mind*, trans. Bettina Bergo (Stanford, CA: Stanford University Press, 1988), 137–51.

[7] All biblical translations come from the New Revised Standard Version.

[8] Emmanuel Levinas, *Otherwise Than Being, or, Beyond Essence*, trans. Alphonso Lingis (Pittsburgh, PA: Duquesne University Press, 2000), 111, 150.

[9] Friedrich Schleiermacher, *On Religion: Speeches to Its Cultured Despisers*, trans. Richard Crouter (Cambridge, MA: Cambridge University Press, 1996); Schleiermacher, *Christmas Dialogue, Second Speech, and Other Selections*, trans. Julia A. Lamm (Mahwah, NJ: Paulist Press, 2014).

[10] Friedrich Schleiermacher, *Dialectic, or, The Art of Doing Philosophy*, trans. Terrence N. Tice (Atlanta: Scholars Press, 1996); Schleiermacher, *Hermeneutics: The Handwritten*

career Schleiermacher devised a hermeneutical method that oscillated between a grammatical approach that aimed at appreciating the distinctiveness of the language of an author in its historical and literary context, working in concert with a technical (also called psychological) method that aimed to understand the distinctiveness of the author's intended meaning. A maxim current in his day captures the dialogical character of Schleiermacher's quest to understand the author in relation to the text: the aim of hermeneutics is "understanding the discourse first as well as and then better than its author,"[11] or as it is often paraphrased, to understand the author better than the author understands her- or himself in their individuality.

In his major work, *Truth and Method*, Hans-Georg Gadamer challenged Schleiermacher's hermeneutical method (unfairly, I would argue, along with others) for being reductionist, too focused on trying to reconstruct the mind of the author through a psychological method, and thereby failing to enter into an authentic dialogue with the subject matter of classic texts. Gadamer's own understanding of dialogue between text and reader was also inspired by the Platonic dialogues and sets up the conditions, through the dynamic of questions and answers, testing and struggling for the subject matter of the text, to communicate a truth claim to the reader. In authentic dialogue, the reader cannot control the text through a method by reconstructing the author's thought process to arrive at the intended meaning but can only discover the strength and power of the subject matter of the text so that the truth of the text calls the reader into question. "What characterizes a dialogue," Gadamer concludes, "is precisely this: that in dialogue spoken language—in the process of question and answer, giving and taking, talking at cross purposes and seeing each other's point—performs the communication of meaning that, with respect to the written tradition, is the task of hermeneutics. Hence it is more than a metaphor; it is a memory

---

Manuscripts, ed. Heinz Kimmerle, trans. James Duke and Jack Forstman (Missoula, MT: Scholars Press, 1977); Schleiermacher, *Hermeneutics and Criticism and Other Writings*, trans. Andrew Bowie (Cambridge, MA: Cambridge University Press, 1998); Schleiermacher, *Vorlesungen zur Hermeneutik und Kritik*, Kritische Gesamtausgabe, Bd. 4, ed. Wolfgang Virmond in collaboration with Hermann Patsch (Berlin: Walter de Gruyter, 2012).

[11] Jean Grondin, *Introduction to Philosophical Hermeneutics*, trans. Joel Weinsheimer (New Haven: Yale University Press, 1994), 137; Schleiermacher, *Hermeneutics: The Handwritten Manuscripts*, 68; cf. Schleiermacher, *Hermeneutics and Criticism*, 107–8.

of what originally was the case, to describe the task of hermeneutics as entering into dialogue with the text."[12] Through this logic of question and answer there emerges the possibility of a fusion of horizons of the effective historical consciousness (*Wirkungsgeschichte*) of the reader with the text, not by avoiding the critical questions of readers, but by having them thought through and transformed through the hermeneutical process. Herein the historical horizon of the reader is projected in the interpretive process and superseded. This fusion of horizons entails understanding, interpreting, and ultimately application.[13] In hermeneutics, "conversation is the process of coming to an understanding about the subject matter."[14]

Hans Robert Jauss was influenced by Gadamer's approach to hermeneutics before he launched his life work on medieval literature, literary history as a basis for an aesthetics of reception, and the development of a literary hermeneutics.[15] Like Gadamer, he emphasizes the importance of dialogue for understanding the hermeneutical endeavor. As he put it, "The history of literature as well as its communicative character presupposes a dialogical and at once processlike relationship between work, audience, and new work that can be conceived in the relations between message and receiver as well as between question and answer, problem and solution."[16] Yet he came to the judgment that Gadamer's dialogical theory of hermeneutics, and particularly his theory of the classic, undergirds and restricts his construal of the dialogical logic of question and answer at work in the history of effects (the influence of the classic and tradition) and the fusion of horizons between the reader and the classic which accentuates the mimetic character of recognition. For Jauss the problem is that Gadamer's

[12] Hans-Georg Gadamer, *Truth and Method*, 2nd rev. ed., trans. Joel Weinsheimer and Donald G. Marshall (New York: Crossroad, 1991), 362–85, at 368.
[13] Ibid., 301–7, 374–75.
[14] Ibid., 385.
[15] On Jauss's contribution, see Ormond Rush, *The Reception of Doctrine: An Appropriation of Hans Robert Jauss' Reception Aesthetics and Literary Hermeneutics* (Rome: Editrice Pontificia Universitá Gregoriana, 1997), 1–64. Jauss collaborated with Wolfgang Iser, who developed his own aesthetic reader response theory. See Wolfgang Iser, *The Act of Reading: A Theory of Aesthetic Reception* (Baltimore, MD: Johns Hopkins University Press, 1978).
[16] Hans Robert Jauss, "Literary History as a Challenge to Literary Theory," in *Toward an Aesthetic of Reception*, trans. Timothy Bahti (Minneapolis: University of Minnesota Press, 1982), 19.

approach fails to acknowledge that "the work of art can also mediate knowledge that does not fit into the Platonic schema if it anticipates paths of future experience, imagines as-yet-untested models of perception and behavior, or contains an answer to newly posed questions."[17] In Jauss's judgment Gadamer privileges a passive form of the fusion of horizons (*Horizontverschmelzung*) at the expense of the clashes and struggles involved between the horizons of text and readers. Thus he comes to emphasize in this encounter of text and readers "the differentiation of horizons" (*Horizontabhebung*), which honors the otherness of those dialogically engaged in this endeavor.[18]

Twentieth-century philosophical hermeneutics thus aimed with various working assumptions and various strategies to interpret texts more adequately by engaging in a dialogue with the authors, with the texts, and with their readers and the history of readers. These assumptions were operative in different ways for historical critical scholars, for literary scholars, and for those academics engaged in social theoretical research, each with their own set of questions about a host of issues: about authors, literary forms, and literary characters and voices operative in historical contexts, in texts, and the claims being advanced through written works; about the kinds of influences these works had on readers and their reception of the texts; and how these generated their own questions, criticism, and creative new efforts.[19]

Philosophical hermeneutics associated with these three trajectories received increasing attention throughout the twentieth century not

---

[17] Ibid., 31.

[18] Hans Robert Jauss, "Horizon Structure and Dialogicity," in *Question and Answer: Forms of Dialogic Understanding*, trans. M. Hays (Minneapolis: University of Minnesota Press, 1989), 205; on Jauss and the influential treatment of dialogue by Mikhail Bakhtin, see Rush, *The Reception of Doctrine*, 111–12.

[19] On hermeneutics and dialogue in poststructuralist theorists, see Hubert L. Dreyfus and Paul Rabinow, *Michel Foucault: Beyond Structuralism and Hermeneutics* (Chicago: University of Chicago Press, 1982). Also, Jacques Derrida, "Three Questions to Hans-Georg Gadamer"; Manfred Frank, "Limits of the Human Control of Language: Dialogue as the Place of Difference between Neostructuralism and Hermeneutics"; and Donald G. Marshall, "Dialogue and Écriture," in *Dialogue and Deconstruction: The Gadamer-Derrida Encounter*, ed. Diane P. Michelfelder and Richard E. Palmer (Albany: State University of New York Press, 1989), 52–54, 150–61, 206–14; Jacques Derrida, *Limited Inc*, trans. Samuel Weber, Jeffrey Mehlman, and Alan Bass (Evanston, IL: Northwestern University Press, 1988).

only among philosophers but also across the humanities, including theology. The various hermeneutical options were, however, increasingly challenged by various critical theories that raised questions about the very ability and reliability of identifying the aims of authors in complex social and cultural fields; about the stability and coherence of the text and the literary forms being employed with various voices, characters, and arguments being negotiated; and about readers and their shifting horizons and complex social and political dynamics as these factor into the historical of interpretation and reception of literary forms. These doubts about the possibilities of dialogue were not only instigated in the academy. They reflected the critique of dialogue caused by the frustration and anger at the failures of dialogue in situations of social upheaval in society associated with genocide, the cold war, colonialism, and global patterns of poverty, oppression, slavery and racism, sexism, and sexual identity. Laments, grief, and agonistic struggle eventually became categories that were employed by philosophers and more broadly in the humanities to address the failure of dialogue in human relations and society.[20]

Scriptural Testimonies of Laments

By the time of the 1985 Extraordinary Synod of Bishops marking the twentieth anniversary of Vatican II, increasing laments across a spectrum of viewpoints were being voiced in the church, from those who resisted dialogue to those who thought dialogical approaches were not being implemented fast enough and effectively. It has become increasingly evident over the last fifty years that investigating the frustrations and failures of the church implementing practices of dialogue is at least as important for ecclesiology as determining the intentions behind and achievements of these endeavors. It has thus become clear that lamentations provide a particularly rich theological justification for reflecting on the frustrated intentions and thwarted aspirations of

---

[20] See Judith Butler, *Precarious Life: The Powers of Mourning and Violence* (New York: Verso, 2004); Butler, *Frames of War: When Is Life Grievable?* (New York: Verso, 2010); Bonnie Honig, *Political Theory and the Displacement of Politics* (Ithaca, NY: Cornell University Press, 1993); Honig, *Antigone Interrupted* (Cambridge: Cambridge University Press, 2013); Chantal Mouffe, *The Democratic Paradox* (London: Verso, 2000); Mouffe, *Agonistics: Thinking the World Politically* (London: Verso, 2013).

the church and a rationale for incorporating the lessons learned from laments in the study of ecclesiology. A phenomenology and hermeneutics of the church's dialogical identity and mission finds its necessary counterpart in the study of laments in the church and the world.[21]

To advance the study of laments in ecclesiology, I explore one trajectory among others that provides its own theological rationale for the role of lamentations in providing a response to the limits of dialogue in the church and society. Specifically, here I wish to consider how the testimonies of lamentation in the Hebrew and Christian Scriptures provide the most prevalent biblical idiom refracted in numerous genres and reflective of various kinds of social dynamics and conflicts that can enable individuals and groups to negotiate and respond to the limits and struggles of dialogue.[22]

The speech act and genre of lamentation in the Hebrew and Christian Scriptures offer rich resources for individuals and groups seeking to respond to situations of conflict, frustration, and failure in the dialogical dynamics of personal and communal life. The particular literary form of lamentation finds expression in the full range of literary settings in the Hebrew Scriptures, in the complaints of the Hebraic peoples and Israelites embedded in the grand narrative settings in the Torah, in the historical books, and in prophetic literature. The largest repository of laments is found in the Psalms where they are combined with prayers of petition, repentance and rededication, professions of

---

[21] Theologians who draw special attention to laments or comparable genres, experiences, or memories invariably employ critical *background theories* (using Francis Schüssler Fiorenza's formulation) and *explanatory methods* (as described by Paul Ricoeur) in their investigations to augment and offset commonplace phenomenological and hermeneutical assumptions. So, for example, Edward Schillebeeckx's *negative contrast experiences* and Johann Baptist Metz's attention to *interruptions, anamnestic solidarity,* and *Leiden an Gott* (suffering unto God) reflect the influence of the critical theories of the Early Frankfurt School of Max Horkheimer, Theodor Adorno, Walter Benjamin, and Ernst Bloch. See Francis Schüssler Fiorenza, *Foundational Theology: Jesus and the Church* (New York: Crossroad, 1984); Paul Ricoeur, "What Is a Text? Explanation and Understanding," in *Hermeneutics and the Human Sciences,* ed. and trans. John B. Thompson (Cambridge: Cambridge University Press, 1981), 145–64; Edward Schillebeeckx, *Church: The Human Story of God,* trans. John Bowden (New York: Crossroad, 1991), 1–45; Johann Baptist Metz, *A Passion for God: The Mystical-Political Dimension of Christianity,* trans. J. Matthew Ashley (Mahwah, NJ: Paulist Press, 1998).

[22] This argument is proposed in my *Prophetic Obedience,* 76–80.

trust, and expressions of gratitude and praise. In the aftermath of the Babylonian conquest and subsequent ascendance of the Hellenistic Empire, laments were reformulated into shriller forms in later wisdom and apocalyptic traditions.

One frequent feature of lament psalms that distinguishes it is *the cry for God to listen and respond*. Roughly a third of the lament psalms use this formula: "Give ear to my words, O Lord; give heed to my groaning. Listen to the sound of my cry, my King and my God, for to you I pray" (Ps 5:1).

At its most basic level, a lament offers testimony to personal and collective suffering in the form of complaint, grief, frustration, and despair. The motivation of the speech act that gives rise to this genre is not in its barest form to plead for help, which is a reflex step that is not always taken. At their core, laments express the pain of unfulfilled aspirations or intentions. The reasons for pain may be limitations or failings, personal or collective, singular or compounded, episodic or chronic. Whatever the cause, however, whether named or nameless, whether known or hidden to consciousness, the result is an ache, tension, rage, dissipation of energy, a numbness, all of which contribute to the state that Walter Brueggemann has aptly described as "disorientation."[23]

The driving forces behind the literary form of lament are, as Claus Westermann demonstrated over sixty years ago, two basic questions: why and how long?[24] The most important distinguishing structure of the lament is the complaint formula that involves a *triadic relationship*. First, there is the I or the we who laments; second, there is God as the one addressed; and third, there is the other, often identified explicitly or by implication as an enemy, accused of contributing to the reason for the lament.[25] The lament provides the occasion to struggle with the harsh reality of these relationships and with the limited and

---

[23] Walter Brueggemann, *The Message of the Psalms: A Theological Commentary* (Minneapolis: Augsburg, 1984), 51–58, at 54; Brueggemann, *Theology of the Old Testament: Testimony, Dispute, Advocacy* (Minneapolis: Fortress Press, 1997), 317–406.

[24] Claus Westermann, "The Structure and History of the Lament" [1954], in *Praise and Lament in the Psalms*, trans. K. R. Crim and R. N. Soulen (Atlanta: John Knox Press, 1981), 165–213.

[25] Westermann argues that the lament is only complete when it has three dimensions pertaining to God, the one who laments, and the enemy (ibid., 169). Westermann

distorted views of self, community, others, and even God revealed in situations of suffering.

Through the labor of lament, energy is activated in the lamenter in ways that can go undetected or be distorted in consciousness. At one level, the person or community confronts the experience of brokenness in situations of suffering, darkness, and disorientation. At another level, there is an attempt to negotiate the power differentials between the lamenter and God, and between the lamenter and the others—often identified as enemies, false witnesses, or accusers. The work of lamentation aims to reconceive and redistribute power between the one who laments and God, and between the one who laments and the others. The lamenter stands up to God not out of hubris, or to call into question God's transcendence, but to dare to pose liminal questions and to respond to the invitation to become a partner and collaborator with God in the midst of a suffering world. Simultaneously, the lamenter stands up to the others and calls into question destructive power dynamics by offering resistance and working to renegotiate the relations with authorities and along borders.[26] Ultimately, in all laments, there is taking place, above or below the surface, a trial where everyone is called to accountability, and no one escapes interrogation: God, the self, the community, and the others. The scrutiny of the exercise of power and the dissection of pain in the laments of the Hebrew Scriptures can lead to blame of the self, and of one's enemies, and even of God.

The lament provides a space and time in contemplation, in cult, and in community to be receptive to God's answers to the questions of why and how long in the face of impasse. The limitations and failings of persons and communities are exposed; questions of God's purposes, wrath, and mercy are raised; deeper fears and projections about the perceived enemy are allowed to surface.[27] And it is precisely here that

---

speaks of the structure in terms of an address (or introductory petition), lament, turning toward God (or confession of trust), petition, vow of praise (170).

[26] See Walter Brueggemann, "The Costly Loss of Lament," in *The Poetical Books: A Sheffield Reader*, ed. David J. A. Clines (Sheffield, UK: Sheffield Academic Press, 1997), 84–97, at 87–88; originally in *Journal for the Study of the Old Testament* 36 (1986): 57–71.

[27] One of the interesting features of laments is that they provide a space to accuse the other of being perverse, sacrilegious, and godless, while at the same time recognizing that the enemy acts friendly toward the lamenter (Ps 55:21), greets (Ps 144:8), and

the mystery of God, the hiddenness of God, and the eschatological character of the human person, the church, and the world are confronted. Laments serve as a furnace that releases base ingredients of pity and anger, retribution and remorse. This caldron need not produce deadly toxins but can provide a crucible for compassion, where baser forms of pain yield purer forms of love-in-action and a truer, more purified understanding of the identities of self, others, and God.[28]

Are there instances of lamentations in the Christian Scriptures stitched into the narrative fabrics of the stories of Jesus, his disciples, and the nascent church? One might be inclined to answer that "the New Testament is characterized by the absence of lament."[29] But closer examination suggests otherwise. Such an investigation consistently takes its bearings from the focal invocation of the lament psalm voiced by Jesus's cry on the cross in Mark and Matthew: "My God, my God, why have you abandoned me?" (echoing Ps 22:1-2).[30] No less pertinent is Paul's conviction that where there are the groans of human bodies, as of creation itself, with "sighs too deep for words," we discover the breath and voice of the Spirit at work, "searching everything, even the depths of God," and attesting to grief in the midst of precarious life alongside of pangs of new life emerging.[31] The new life issued forth in the resurrection of Jesus Christ and in the Pentecostal descent of the Spirit cancels neither the lament of the crucified Jesus nor the future of all lamentations.

---

spends time (Ps 41:5–6) with the lamenter. See Westermann, "Structure and History of the Lament," 180–81, 188–94.

[28] For Kathleen O'Connor and Diane Bergant, the barest literary form of lament offers difficult medicine with no prognosis in sight. See Diane Bergant, *Lamentations* (Nashville: Abingdon Press, 2003); Kathleen M. O'Connor, *Lamentations & The Tears of the World* (Maryknoll, NY: Orbis Books, 2002). A wider range of issues is raised in the collection *Lamentations in Ancient and Contemporary Cultural Contexts*, ed. Nancy C. Lee and Carleen Mandolfo (Atlanta: Society for Biblical Literature, 2008).

[29] Markus Öhler, "To Mourn, Weep, Lament and Groan: On the Heterogeneity of the New Testament Statements on Lament," in *Evoking Lament: A Theological Discussion*, ed. Eva Harasta and Brian Brock (New York: T&T Clark, 2009), 150–65, at 150.

[30] Stephen P. Ahearne-Kroll, *The Psalms of Lament in Mark's Passion* (Cambridge: Cambridge University Press, 2007).

[31] The contention that the expression of human laments and the groaning of creation comes from the Spirit is based on Paul's claims in Rom 8:22-26 and 1 Cor 2:10. See Joseph A. Fitzmyer, *Romans*, Anchor Bible Commentary (New York: Doubleday, 1992), 504–21.

In Luke's and Matthew's gospels, we also find Jesus expressing laments about people who have lost their way: "O Jerusalem, Jerusalem, killing the prophets and stoning those who are sent to you! How often would I have gathered your children as a hen gathers her brood under her wings, and you would not?" (Luke 13:34; Matt 23:37). And in Mark's gospel one can detect a lament in Jesus's reaction to the multitude longing to hear him teach: "he had compassion on them, because they were like sheep without a shepherd" (Mark 6:34; cf. Nm 27:17; 1 Kgs 22:17; Ezek 34:5).

These two laments by Jesus insinuate the underlying and often implicit source of his own sense of mission: the laments of the people of God inspired him to teach in order to reveal a new vision of life, to touch so as to heal, to cast out demonic powers in order to free captives, and to share table fellowship with outcasts and sinners and by so doing to reveal God's compassion. Jesus' mission as herald of God's reign was his response to the laments of those overwhelmed by destructive powers. Those who exercise political, religious, economic, or social power often damage the poor, the marginalized, and the disrespected. Jesus establishes his mission to reach out to those who suffer. The one who laments on the cross is suffering the consequences of responding to the laments of the people of God. The configuration of Jesus' identity and mission finds in his encounter with those who lament its deepest plot.

This narrative structure in the gospels establishes a framework for a series of specific laments voiced by the disciples of Jesus both during his lifetime and after his death and resurrection that bear on the identity and mission of the nascent church. Two in particular came to define nascent Christianity as it emerged from the midst of Jewish and Hellenistic populations and cultures. On the one hand, the resistance by Jews to the message of the gospel of Jesus Christ was the source of Paul's lament "that I have great sorrow and unceasing anguish in my heart" (Rom 9:2), but it was also the occasion for him to learn that "the gifts and the call of God" to the Jews "are irrevocable."[32] The frequent and long-standing failure of Christians to learn

---

[32] See Krister Stendahl, "The Apostle Paul and the Introspective Conscience of the West," in *Paul among the Jews and the Gentiles* (Minneapolis: Augsburg Fortress Press, 1976), 78–96.

from Paul has yielded the history of laments of Jews persecuted by Christians. On the other hand, Paul lamented Peter's betrayal of the truth of the gospel by yielding to the pressure of the Judaizers who insisted that Hellenists should follow the eating practices of Jews (Gal 2:13-16; cf. Acts 10:10-35). These laments disclose how Christians negotiated their own identity as aliens and sojourners amid members of diverse cultures and religious traditions and they also witness to the sinfulness of the church.

Other laments in the early church reflect concerns about who is to exercise authority and how it is to be exercised. One lament concerns privilege and jealousy among leaders in their desire for glory and power, as featured in the request of James and John to share in the heavenly glory of Christ and the reactions among the apostles (Mark 10:35-45). A second set of laments concerns the role of women in the community. The story of Martha grumbling to Jesus about Mary sitting at Jesus' feet and listening to him (Luke 10:38-42) has frequently been interpreted as the complaint of the activist against the contemplative, but it likewise implicates complaints about the roles of women as disciples and apostles and not just as hospitable hosts. This latter interpretation coincides with the grumbling about women speaking in church (see 1 Cor 14:34), daring to teach and claim authority among men, rather than remaining silent (1 Tim 2:12-15), and about women uncovering their heads as if they were created in the image and glory of God and not in the image and glory of man, her head (1 Cor 11:17; see Eph 5:22-24).

The lessons learned from these biblical laments often concern the Jewish and Christian dynamics of repentance and renewal. *Why do people lament?* The causes of pain are manifold. Laments frequently are traced back to the vestiges of idolatry and disordered loves. Laments are also often caused by frustration at human limitations; grief at the loss of life, human flourishing, and loving relationships; anger caused by experiences of conflict and the failures of leadership, religious and social; failures in communication and in deliberation; or anguish at seemingly insurmountable situations of injustice. Here the modern limits of dialogue in church and society find expression in this classic idiom. Biblical laments address the problems of human limitations and sin. *How long will this season of lament continue?* One view is that it continues until the individual or the group accepts their limitations, as well as repents of sinfulness, and rededicates themselves to God's covenant.[33] But laments are not only about personal conversion and reform. Lamenters are also challenged to reexamine their most basic convictions about who God is and how God works in the world, and about the need to confront situations of crisis and conflict, frustration and failure. Can we be receptive to new ways of reforming the community of faith and envisioning a more just world? These biblical witnesses attest that laments provide a process of purification on the way to a deeper wisdom about God, self, community, and others.

Laments and Prophecy

The inescapabilty of lamentations in the Hebrew and Christian Scriptures invites in a special way a consideration of its relation to prophecy. It has been customary in the study of prophetic discourse in the Hebrew and Christian Scriptures to characterize the nature of prophecy as a word or message given by God that is received by a prophet, which is then communicated by proclamation (word) or witness (in word or action). This kind of approach to prophecy is in evidence in the documents of the Second Vatican Council and is a significant part of its renewed approach to the Scriptures. This approach to the character of prophecy, as word received and witness given, enables theologically focused and flexible analysis of diverse biblical literary forms and of the history of Christian prophecy since the apostolic period.

John J. Collins provides the simple rationale for why this framework has been so influential: "The word prophecy comes from the Greek *prophētēs*, 'proclaimer,' and refers to one who speaks on behalf of a god or goddess. The roles of such spokesmen or spokeswomen vary from one culture to another, and various terms are used to describe them. Prophets typically receive their revelations in a state of ecstasy,

---

[33] The logic of lament that leads to conversion and rededication, gratitude and praise is expressed in the literary structure of individual lament psalms and in the dynamic of the entire psalter, characterized by Brueggemann in terms of psalms of orientation, disorientation, and new orientation, and in the larger canonical polyphony where laments are imbedded in redemptive and consoling narratives and prophecies, sage wisdom or apocalyptic visions. See Brueggemann, *Theology of the Old Testament*.

either by seeing visions or by direct inspiration."[34] Walter Brueggemann urges the acknowledgment of diverse manifestations of the phenomenon of prophecy in Israel and the inevitability of missing details in any general formulation. Yet his own working description of the nature of prophecy confirms the primacy of this framework: "Prophecy as a mode of mediation begins in the inexplicable appearance of individual persons who claim to speak Yahweh's revelatory word, and who are accepted by some as being indeed carriers of such a revelatory word."[35]

This prophetic message is described in terms of receiving a word, a vision, a thought, some special perception or awareness. The prophetic call to witness in word and deed is correlative to the message received. The message is often specified in terms of prophetic denunciation or consolation: destabilizing or validating political or religious leadership, cultic practices, or scribal traditions; challenging audiences to rededicate themselves to singular devotion to God (as in the *Shema*), the Torah, or some specific tradition. This particular formula is largely indebted to patterns found in the classical period of prophecy associated with the major prophets (Amos, Hosea, Micah, Isaiah, Jeremiah, Ezekiel, Jonah), and less so with the earlier, sometimes called primitive, tradition associated with the Deuteronomistic history, traditionally known as the Former Prophets, as found in the books of Joshua, Judges, Samuel, and Kings. This schema provided the operative frame for major mid-twentieth-century Catholic theologians.[36]

There is, however, an alternative framework for considering prophetic discourse, one that can be detected within prophetic literature in the Scriptures and that corresponds to my earlier argument concerning lamentations. This alternative framework intersects and is intertwined with the primary framework. Yet it illumines an equally

---

[34] John J. Collins, *Introduction to the Hebrew Bible*, 2nd ed. (Minneapolis: Fortress Press, 2014), 299.

[35] Brueggemann, *Theology of the Old Testament*, 622.

[36] See Karl Rahner, "Prophetism," in *Encyclopedia of Theology: The Concise Sacramentum Mundi*, ed. Karl Rahner (New York: Seabury, 1975), 1286–89; Joseph Ratzinger, *The Theology of History in St. Bonaventure*, trans. Zachary Hayes (Chicago: Franciscan Herald Press, 1971); Yves Congar, *True and False Reform in the Church*, trans. Paul Philibert (Collegeville, MN: Liturgical Press, 2011); Hans Urs von Balthasar, *The Glory of the Lord: A Theological Aesthetics*; vol. 4: *Theology: The Old Covenant*, trans. Brian McNeil and Erasmo Leiva-Merikakis, ed. John Riches (San Francisco: Ignatius, 1991), 215–300.

basic, interdependent, and at times prior summons received by the prophet. The prophet is called upon to face reality, bear the burdens of this reality, and engage this reality.[37]

In this schema, communication is not initially by means of a word or message received, but through the wailing of the Spirit heard in vulnerable and grieving people suffering from the ravages of personal and social sin and difficult contingencies of life, and the clamoring of the Spirit in the created world abused by the negative consequences of sin and affected by the calamities of cosmic history. Without denying the periodic use of pneumatic themes in classic prophetic literature in the Hebrew Bible beginning in the eighth century BCE, this alternative framework likewise acknowledges the stress on the agency of the spirit of Yahweh associated with individual and group experiences of trances, mental dissociation, charismatic powers, and wonder working as found in older prophetic materials in the historical books.[38] As Joseph Blenkinsopp insists, the older and newer prophetic traditions in the Hebrew Bible should not be dichotomized or separated.[39] Acknowledging this alternative framework decenters the typical paradigm of prophetic discourse, and expands the semantic field and narrative configurations for construing the ways the Spirit of God and the Word of God are depicted in the Scriptures and in theology, beyond a divine word given and message received. Most important, the two frameworks can work in tandem as laments and aspirations are engaged in relation to a message received and witness given. For Christian theology, this new framework places the identity and mission of the Spirit at the heart of the identity and mission of Jesus, prophet, Word made flesh, in relation to God, the source, the one addressed as Father, Abba.

What commands our attention in this dual orientation is that the prophet is beckoned to perceive, listen, and empathize from God's point of view, to participate in God's solidarity with a people and the created world in complex religious, social, and political situations, and

---

[37] This formulation echoes the motif of Ignacio Ellacuría as quoted and discussed by Michael E. Lee, *Bearing the Weight of Salvation: The Soteriology of Ignacio Ellacuría* (New York: Crossroad, 2009), 42–50, at 48–49, and Hinze, *Prophetic Obedience*, 145–47.

[38] Joseph Blenkinsopp, *A History of Prophecy in Israel*, rev. 2nd enl. ed. (Louisville, KY: Westminster John Knox Press, 1996), 37–37, 53, 63, 73.

[39] Ibid., 36, 49, 66, 73.

from this vantage point to speak out in God's name to and for these people and the damaged world, and against destructive powers, in the interest of fuller life. The sources of laments are myriad, but laments are always sites of conflict between powers intent on destruction and desires and aspirations striving for flourishing, and for the fullness of life and relationships that yield love and reconciliation in truth. Biblical scholars such as David Aune give a great deal of attention to the literary forms of prophetic utterance—judgment, salvation, assurance, admonition, and trial[40]—but this equally basic struggle for life over death is always a focal point for the divine calling of the prophet and derivatively of all God's prophetic people.

Conclusion

Lamentations lay bare the limitations of dialogue in ecclesiology and in hermeneutics. They challenge the quest for dialogue motivated by a naive hope for mutual enrichment, common understanding, and collective action. They incite the candor (*parrhesia*) associated with conflict, protest, and public contestation especially expressed by the marginalized and the excluded without the promise of resolutions and consensus.[41] The repression and rejection of laments in communities inevitably foster dissent and withdrawal and threaten the vital of community. The question is whether the critical insights generated by the interruption of lamentation can contribute to a purification and differentiation of the aims and objectives of dialogue in hermeneutics, in the church, and in civil society. Any real benefits to be gained by a dialogical approach to hermeneutics or ecclesiology will only be realized if there is room for the work of lamentations to take effect.

---

[40] See, for example, the emphasis given to the forms and functions of prophetic discourse in David E. Aune, *Prophecy in Early Christianity and the Ancient Mediterranean World* (Grand Rapids, MI: Eerdmans, 1983), 18–19, 49–80, 88–100, 114–20, 163–70, 247–338.

[41] On *parrhesia*, see Pope Francis, "Greeting to the Synod Fathers During the First General Congregation of the Third Extraordinary General Assembly of the Synod of Bishops," October 6, 2014, https://w2.vatican.va/content/francesco/en/speeches/2014/october/documents/papa-francesco_20141006_padri-sinodali.html; Michel Foucault, "Discourse and Truth: The Problematization of *Parrhesia*," six lectures at the University of California at Berkeley, October–November 1983, http://foucault.info/documents/parrhesia/; Torben Bech Dyrberg, *Foucault on the Politics of Parrhesia* (New York: Palgrave MacMillan, 2014).

Contributors

Susan Abraham is Associate Professor of Theological Studies at Loyola Marymount University in Los Angeles, California.

Dominic Doyle is Associate Professor of Systematic Theology at Boston College, School of Theology and Ministry, in Chestnut Hill, Massachusetts.

Anthony J. Godzieba is Professor of Theology and Religious Studies at Villanova University in Villanova, Pennsylvania.

Judith Gruber is Assistant Professor of Systematic Theology at Loyola University in New Orleans, Louisiana.

Bradford E. Hinze is the Karl Rahner, SJ, Professor of Theology at Fordham University in Bronx, New York.

Andrew Prevot is Assistant Professor of Theology at Boston College in Chestnut Hill, Massachusetts.

Ormond Rush is an Associate Professor and Reader lecturing in theology at Australian Catholic University, Brisbane campus, Australia.

Sandra M. Schneiders, IHM, is Professor Emerita of New Testament Studies and Christian Spirituality at Graduate Theological Union, Jesuit School of Theology, Santa Clara University in Berkeley, California.

Robert J. Schreiter, CPPS, is the Vatican Council II Professor of Theology, Catholic Theological Union in Chicago, Illinois.

Francis Schüssler Fiorenza is the Charles Chauncey Stillman Professor of Roman Catholic Theological Studies at Harvard Divinity School in Cambridge, Massachusetts.

Fernando F. Segovia is the Oberlin Graduate Professor of New Testament and Early Christianity at Vanderbilt University Divinity School in Nashville, Tennessee.

John E. Thiel is Professor of Religious Studies at Fairfield University in Fairfield, Connecticut.

www.ingramcontent.com/pod-product-compliance
Lightning Source LLC
Chambersburg PA
CBHW051936290426
44110CB00015B/2002